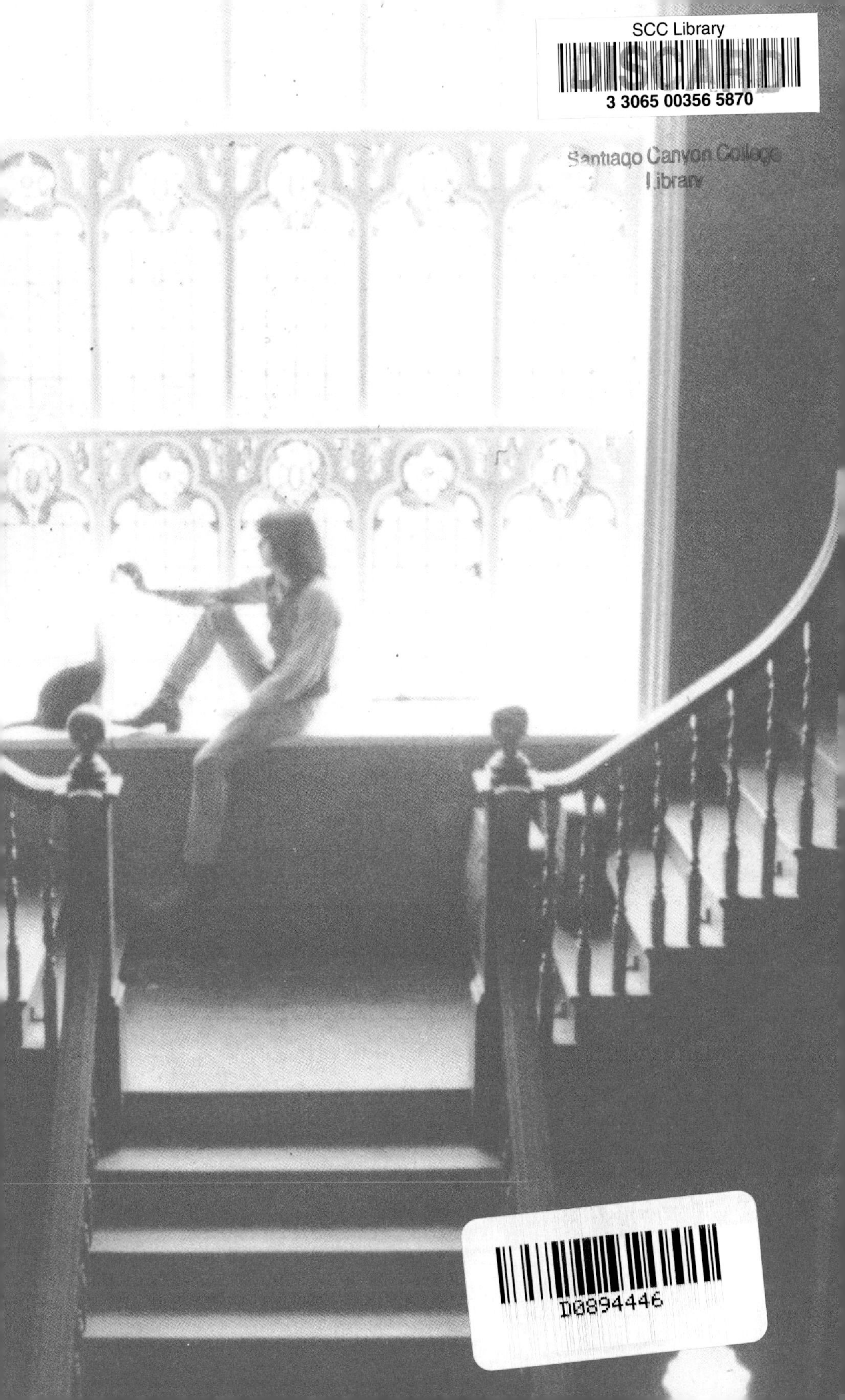

tony visconti

Bowie, Bolan and the Brooklyn Boy

tony visconti

Bowie, Bolan and the Brooklyn Boy

the autobiography

foreword by morrissey

📖 HarperCollins*Publishers*

picture credits

HarperCollins*Publishers* would like to thank the following for providing photographs and for permission to reproduce copyright material.

While every effort has been made to trace the owners of copyright material reproduced herein, the publishers would like to apologise for any omissions and will be pleased to incorporate missing acknowledgements in any future editions

The Speedy Garfin quartet © James J. Kriegsmann
Tai Chi and Kung Fu magazine image © Mark Mahaney

HarperCollins*Publishers*
77–85 Fulham Palace Road,
Hammersmith, London W6 8JB

Published by HarperCollins*Publishers* 2007
2

A catalogue record for this book
is available from the British Library

ISBN-10 0 00 722944 5
ISBN-13 978 00 722944 4

Printed and bound in Great Britain by
Clays Ltd, St Ives plc

To Mom, Dad, Morgan, Jessica, Sebastian and Lara

contents page

foreword, by morrissey

Many of the early records bearing Tony Visconti's name made me eager to get out into the world – if only to agitate. In 1971–72 the mighty blaze of T.Rex singles were beyond price to me. They had all the immediate eager motion of pop records, but were also strangely reflective – a mad stew of Englishness and worldliness with Tony's name on each side of the label. If you enjoyed the music of T.Rex it seemed to prove that you were someone. Here, it seemed, was Art in motion: guitar savagery chopping up the soundstage; pop with intellectual distinction, using full orchestra – if only for a mere twenty haughty seconds.

Making the T.Rex soundscape both fantastic and naturalistic was an abrasive clash of non-traditional routes to the pop conclusion. The wealth and detail and contrast of layered orchestration wrapped around the unravelled riddle of Marc Bolan's poetry (well, let's call it that) worked so well that Bolan stayed beside Tony almost until Bolan's life ended with death. At its highest artistic peak, with the strange flood of 'Telegram Sam' and 'Metal Guru' we are assaulted by the musical equivalent of secret stairways and false walls, and something enters into me which I can barely fathom. I wanted pop music to be true, and it was with David Bowie's LP *The Man Who Sold the World*, which enlivened 1972 as a forgotten reissue, edging up to #26 in the British charts. It is a soft sound, with luxuriant confidence from Bowie, whose imagination was served by the Visconti methodology. Still, today, it stands as David Bowie's best work. The first side, especially, is musical literacy delivered.

With Bowie, the tone and cadence are all there: no sentimentalism. The instrumental textures are wispy and often child-like; acoustic and recorder sounds of turn-of-the-'70s dropout London. The Bowie-Visconti vision is concentrated. A good producer gets at something in a singer (or musician) and Tony was there to nail the gift of Bowie just perfectly – making suffering sound like a superior condition – live this life or don't live any. Listen to the album even now and you are right back there. The mavericks are those who liberate themselves, and Bowie and Visconti did so with *The Man Who Sold the World* . . . and we played our part by listening.

The Mael machinery of Sparks utilized Tony for their 1975 surgical offering, *Indiscreet*. The versifying of Ron Mael introduced a new style of pop poetry, and the scattershot pace of Russell Mael's vocals sounded like someone running out of a burning house. Russell had been a T.Rex fan, and by 1975 it was Sparks themselves who were shaking public tastes. *Indiscreet* was their fifth album of great resonance, lunging to #18 in the chart. The sound of this album is so chaotic that it often seems to play for laughs. Either the Maels, or Tony Visconti, were asking: *What can we show them that is new?* From a tipsy teatime waltz to unstoppable violins, the pace pulverized the listener, and Russell's mouth seemed unable to close. There are so many latitude and longitude instrumental textures that the masterstroke was just *almost* overcooked. Since Ron and Russell Mael were obviously insane, Tony could only have walked into this session armed with a swirl of guesswork. The disorder lay in the electronic savagery of the Maels, who had spent their early lives strapped to an iron bed. Pulling them back from the edge, *Indiscreet* (somehow a commercial venture) produced two riotously diverse hit singles.

The most important feature of recorded noise is the pleasure it can bring to the listener. Tony has always – *somehow* – been a part of my life, but I didn't ever imagine that his success-ridden career would lead him to me, nor I to him, yet in 2005 we recorded *Ringleader of the Tormentors* in Rome. As a non-musician/ skimmer-scholar, I've always known what I wanted without always knowing how to get it. Many years on from the escapist spirits of Bolan and Bowie . . . it is still there . . . in the Visconti walk. An actor would be thrilled to discover a new expression for the camera, as Tony Visconti is delighted to ambush the end of a song with a new musical twist. He has astounding recall of whatever it is he's just heard, and he can talk and listen at the same time. The point of a good recording is to make us more aware of ourselves – as singers or musicians, and *Ringleader of the Tormentors* stands as a joy greater than pleasure for me. In several countries across Europe . . . it zaps to #1.

Tony understands the code of music brilliantly, and he is not authoritarian in the patronizing way that so many producers who have left their fingerprints on the 1960s and 1970s are. He is persuasive without ever making you need to disembarrass yourself; his role is complicity. There are many respected bores of Tony's generation, nursing memories and resentments and never letting the trapped listener forget – but Tony isn't like that. He doesn't pick over the Saxon remains of T.Rex; the time is always now. He is a noble example of the self-flogger who knows that the song doesn't end just because it's over. Musical notations are images, and the Visconti style is timeless and lionized and is therefore forevermore.

MORRISSEY
October 2006

introduction
what is a record producer?

A group of musicians and a lead singer pour their hearts out into a handful of microphones. When the song finishes a cheerful voice from the control room booms over the speaker, 'That's it boys, it's a take!' and the band members slap each other on the back and run into the control room to their awaiting girlfriends who are, of course, all models and starlets. It's a notion and an image that has Hollywood's fingerprints all over it – reality is a little different.

On my first recording session, I was the bass player; I too heard that booming voice, only he said, 'That wasn't very good. You guys will have to keep going until you get it right. Bass player: your E string is flat!' We were desperately bashing out this song for an hour or so under the audio equivalent of a microscope. The booming voice was right. The playback of our last take was sloppy and my bass was out of tune. Left to our own devices we would've given up and said that was the best we could do. But the booming voice was persistent, and the next few takes steadily got better, all the more so for checking the tuning of my bass before each take. The booming voice saved the day.

When I grew up I became a booming voice, well, actually a booming voice with the nasal Brooklyn accent. I wanted to be the lead singer or at the very least just one of the boys in the band, but circumstances put me in the director's chair instead. The circumstances uprooted me from Manhattan and planted me firmly on British soil at the height of Swinging London. I took root and stayed there for nearly 23 years. In the end, I think it was a better deal.

The role of a record producer hasn't changed much since Fred Gaisberg cut the performances of opera singers to wax cylinders in the 1890s. He instructed them to move closer or further from a horn; he was the voice of experience, helping the artists to get their performances to a high standard onto the recording medium.

The first time I heard the term 'Producer' was in the '60s when a mad looking man on the Jack Paar TV show (one of the very first talk shows) audaciously proclaimed that he dictated the musical taste of teenagers in America. He was introduced as a record producer and his name was Phil Spector. I already loved his productions without really knowing that someone other than the artists and musicians were involved (I still melt when I hear 'Walking In The Rain' by the Ronettes). It was Spector who brought this role to the public's attention, but most records of that time were still produced anonymously. It was many years later that the great Quincy Jones admitted to arranging and producing 'It's My Party' for Lesley Gore in 1963.

When I heard a Beatles record produced by George Martin I began to understand that record production was an art form, not just an aural mirror of a live performance. Before those intricate Beatles recordings it was just that, a live performance captured on cylinder, disk or tape. It is said that once Bing Crosby, the legendary crooner, discovered that two performances could be edited together by cutting audio tape with a razor blade, he gave birth to the 'art' of record production.

There was one pioneering genius who stood the recording world on its head and changed everything forever – Les Paul.

His name is on millions of the solid body electric guitars that he designed. But his greatest contribution was his concept of the multi-track tape recorder. With his wife, Mary Ford, he produced supernatural recordings of complex arrangements (supernatural in the sense that two people sounded like twenty). His guitar was used over and over again on a single song as he created a guitar orchestra. For very fast passages he slowed the tape down, played a phrase and then returned the machine back to normal speed. The result was impossible tinkling runs of demisemiquavers. Wife Mary was transformed into a very precise female jazz vocal quartet. At first his one-off 8-track tape recorder was considered a novelty, but when multi-track machines were mass-produced the world of making records changed forever. Since the '60s most recordings have been made in assembly line fashion, not all the sounds recorded at once, but in layered overdubbed sessions. Even in the sacrosanct world of classical music Maria Callas broke the rules by overdubbing a missed high 'C' in an otherwise perfect performance. There was a critical furore but since then classical record producers have been doing virtually what a pop record producer does.

A record producer is responsible for every aspect of a recording. In the early days the word 'producer' was more descriptive because the record producer put up the money for the recording and hired a team of experts to execute the various creative jobs. Eventually the role of a producer became more creative and resembled that of a 'music director'. George Martin crossed the line and wasn't shy about giving the Beatles positive feedback and suggesting changes in their musical arrangements. A straight up producer would not be qualified and certainly not welcomed to give such dramatic direction, but George Martin was a very accomplished orchestrator, pianist and oboist. I think his most glorious moment in the Beatles' recorded repertoire was his stunning string octet arrangement for 'Eleanor

Rigby'. Equally stunning is the sheer wizardry of 'Strawberry Fields Forever'. Of course the Beatles contributed greatly and John Lennon refused to take 'no' for an answer when he wanted two disparate takes, recorded on different days, in two different tempi and keys to be joined together. George Martin and their extraordinary engineer Geoff Emerick stayed up all night and made it work! There might have been four Beatles, but there were two more Beatles working in the shadows. Record production, as we know it today, started with George Martin and the Beatles. I make it no secret that I fashioned my style of production after Martin's.

To be responsible for every aspect of a recording a record producer should have a working knowledge of recording techniques and music. Many modern record producers are experts at one or the other or both. I have read that we also have to be psychologists, but that's a bit far fetched. I see us more as coaches, a job where some psychology might be necessary. My mentor, Denny Cordell, instinctively knew how to get the best out of an artist and the best sound out of a sound engineer. My policy is to interfere as little as possible, but to draw out the best in the artists I work with, especially the singers. Sometimes I offer advice for the substitution of a word or a melody (for which I don't take a royalty); I've also sung backing vocals and played various instruments too. The best part is towards the end, when I sit at a mixing console and put it all together.

All in all it's a very nice occupation.

prologue
touchdown

BOAC Flight 506, April 1967

It's been a long day.

I'm a night person, but I had to get up very early for my daytime flight and now it's nearly 11 p.m., London time. The flight is about seven hours long; adding the extra five hours of time zones makes this day surreal. I had hardly slept at all the previous night, nor did I sleep on the plane, and with sleep deprivation comes a dream-like state. As the BOAC jet is landing at London's Heathrow Airport I keep saying to myself, 'Is this really happening to me?' Some realities are evident, but this reality is yet unformed. I've been out of my country of birth only three times, once to play three weeks in a Toronto nightclub, a Far East tour with a '50s revival group and to Paris for a week, with a side trip to Monaco, in a show featuring Liza Minnelli. But this was the trip to the Mecca of modern pop music. No one did it better than the Brits and no Brits did it better than the Beatles. I also had an eerie feeling that I was returning home. A week earlier I had turned twenty-three years old. This was some birthday present.

In a short time I would be going through British Customs and Immigration with four guitars and a lot of explaining to do. I didn't have a visa that allowed me to work in Britain.

Looking like a nervous zombie I approach the long row of immigration desks. I'd been told to stick to my story, no matter how much I'm drilled: 'I'm here on vacation.' If I said I was going to do even one hour's work in England I'd be sent back to New York on the next plane. Even in my zombie state, I'm repeating my mantra – vacation, vacation, I'm here on vacation. Oh God! I want to work in this country so bad. I want to learn how they do it. How did the Beatles make a record so clever, so profound as Revolver? *And I'd recently heard that they're finishing a new album, which took nearly a year to make. Tony, don't blow it. Remember it's a vacation.*

As I stand in line at Immigration, I'm wondering if I made the right choice. What a pair of balls, the audacity. What right did I have coming here? As an arranger I'm not that good, I'm unproven I tell myself. I'm just an all-round type of guy, maybe clever but not great at anything, with just enough wits about me to survive in the music business. There are hundreds of arrangers Denny could've picked. I feel the sudden need to go to the toilet.

Customs! Immigration! . . . What the fuck do they think this is, the Garden of Eden? I couldn't believe the 'Gestapo' waiting for me on this little island in the North Sea. Immigration wasn't so bad, I asked for a six-month visitor's visa. Then I was asked what I would live on and I had to show them all the money I had – four hundred dollars in cash (I wouldn't have my first credit card for a few years). 'I'll give you a month,' said Basil Fawlty (or his brother), 'and don't you even think of doing even a minute's work whilst you're here!' File me under 'apprehensive'. I was in trouble immediately. I thought I had failed Denny. I was going to be booted out in a month. Denny swore he would get me working papers, which takes a long time, but he needed my services immediately. I just barely made it through Immigration, but I still had Her Majesty's Customs ahead of me.

Back then Customs and Immigration were a lot tougher. It's a relative breeze through now; strangely so in these times of global terrorism. It wasn't only me; every time I returned to Britain there would be a queue of woeful people sitting it out, waiting to be interrogated further. The Customs tables would be groaning under the weight of mountains of underwear and dirty laundry. Their cousins in Scotland Yard had busted Mick Jagger, Keith Richard and Marianne Faithful for having too much fun, with a Mars Bar so it was said. Swinging Londoners seemed to be in short supply at Heathrow. With my long hair down to my shoulders I was very much in the minority. I also had four suitcases and four guitars with me, and I expected Customs to believe I was coming for just a vacation. Luckily I was prepared for the worst.

H.M. Customs:	Why so many guitars, if you're on holiday?
Me, the scruffy one:	Oh that's easy. I'm a professional musician and all of these guitars are different types – electric, acoustic, a bass; I have to practice each one daily!
H.M. Customs:	You will not sell one of these instruments whilst you are in the United Kingdom. Is that understood? When you leave here you must be in possession of all of these instruments!
Me:	Yes, sir.
H.M. Customs:	Open this suitcase. *(He eyes my black kimono, my bathrobe.)* Do you intend to perform in this country?
Me:	No, sir.
H.M. Customs:	Ah ha! Got you! This is your stage gear. *(He waves my kimono over his head.)* Why did

> you bring this with you if you say you're not performing *(he was so '66, kimonos were out, military clothes were in)*?
>
> **Me:** It's my bathrobe! I'm not performing.
>
> **H.M. Customs:** Your bathrobe? You mean your dressing gown?
>
> **Me:** What's a dressing gown? It's my bathrobe!
>
> **H.M. Customs:** Yes, that's a dressing gown. But you wear it on stage, right?
>
> **Me:** No, only in my house, after I take a shower *(it really was my bathrobe)*.

This conversation preceded a complete search of my four suitcases. All my fellow passengers were long gone as I was grilled over and over again. I told them that Denny was waiting for me and he would verify my story (about coming for a vacation). So they found him in the Arrivals lounge and grilled him too.

At around 1:30 a.m. we pulled up to the door of Denny's basement flat in the Fulham Road, his family (a wife and two small boys) asleep. He showed me to a couch, which I quickly learned was a settee. 'That's where you'll sleep tonight. Would you like me to draw a bath for you?' I declined, since I hadn't had a bath since my mother last gave me one. I needed a shower, which Denny's and most English homes didn't have. But he had the biggest bathtub I had ever seen. This was awful. Even though I eventually succumbed to bathing in my body's dirty water and rinsing myself with water from a cooking pot, I wouldn't have an American-style high-pressure shower until I had one installed in my English home five years later. Nevertheless, despite my Heathrow ordeal, the alienation of alternative words, and the unfamiliar English customs, both at the airport and in Denny's home, I still felt that I belonged.

* * *

Like many American guys my age, I grew my hair long, and learned the chords and lyrics to every Beatles record as well as many other cool British pop songs that were invading our airwaves. I even managed a *wannabe* Liverpool accent (only to amuse myself) as a result of going to see *A Hard Day's Night* ten or twelve times during its first month of release. The Dave Clark Five, Freddie and The Dreamers, The Animals, The Zombies, The Who, and The Kinks were household names across America. But while British pop was similar, it was enigmatically different to anything that was being made in America.

To my ears, British pop seemed to hark back to the Elizabethan age, when major and minor keys weren't as formalized as they are today. As a young wide-eyed musician this thrilled me to no end. I had forsaken the simplistic American pop styles of Chubby Checker, Bobby Rydell, Fabian and their ilk for the luscious harmonic unpredictability of jazz. My generation had been brought up on the likes of Elvis, Chuck Berry, Little Richard and Buddy Holly, but they had all slipped out of fashion for one reason or another by the early to mid '60s – of course poor Buddy had no choice. American pop had become bland and predictable. Nasty, cigar-chomping guys controlled the music industry, which proves that very little changes, except that I'm not sure they chew so many cigars these days.

I had read about British pop stars like Tommy Steele, Lonnie Donegan and The Shadows, but only heard snippets of their music; British Pop of the late '50s and early '60s was even blander than ours. After the Beatles told America that they wanted to hold our hand I intuitively knew that something was happening to me. My mind and body were responding to this first real wave of great British pop. Liverpool, London and Manchester were more important to me than the city of my birth. It seemed like nothing was happening in New York City while everything was happening over in England. By mid '65 there was first The Lovin' Spoonful, and then The Young Rascals, but as talented as they were they lacked that British mystique. No matter how hard we tried in New York, somehow the Brits always did it better; they seemed to possess 'the knowledge'. Some inner voice was telling me that I needed to get myself over there to see how it was done, I needed to learn the arcane studio secrets that only the British knew.

In the months prior to my flight to London my life had taken such a strange turn. For about a year my wife, Siegrid, and I had been taking weekly acid trips. We were freethinking hippies that espoused the teachings of pop culture gurus – Tim Leary and Richard Alpert (now Ram Das). Our acid wasn't bathtub street acid; it came directly from Sandoz, the drug manufacturer based in Switzerland, and at this time it wasn't technically illegal. I don't remember exactly how this came into our hands, but we were in possession of a jar labelled D-Lysergic Acid-25, with Sandoz printed in bold letters above that; we kept it in our refrigerator. While there was no recommended dosage on the label we managed to apportion out an entire year's worth of trips from this bottle, about fifty each. One drop in a glass of orange juice (or placed on the tongue) was all it took to have a twelve-hour excursion into the psychedelic unknown. We stuck close to the advice of Leary and Alpert who had deduced that a trip had a shape very similar to the description of the Bardo, the after-death experience described in *The Tibetan Book of The Dead*.

After a year seeking enlightenment through chemistry, Siegrid and I hit a psychic barrier. For the uninitiated an acid trip is in a league of its own, it's not a social drug or an addictive drug. There is an enzyme in our brain called serotonin. This keeps your sensory sections discreet. Acid is a catalyst that dilutes the serotonin, making all the sections of the brain merge together. LSD doesn't create the experience, your brain does.

This is why trippers used to say that they could 'hear' colours and 'see' music. Insight and confusion fluctuate rapidly on acid. Everything seems so awesome, so beautiful; it's incredible (Man!). But there's a dark downside. Sometimes a feeling of sheer terror came over me when I listened to what normally seemed harmless songs. I sometimes heard nefarious messages in the lyrics that conjured Bosch-like images of hell. I became very aware that certain types of music were not for my listening pleasure while on an acid trip. As acid became more widespread it was not surprising that a darker acid cult evolved – who hasn't heard of Charles Manson?

Siegrid and I decided that we could no longer keep taking this particular path to enlightenment; it was too unpredictable, too dangerous. One of our favourite acid activities would be to read the great religious books of the ages, and not only the then-popular Eastern variety – the *Bhagavad Gita*, the *Upanishads*, and the *Tibetan Book of The Dead*. We also read aloud both testaments of the Bible – from cover to cover. Reading them was one thing, getting to understand them was quite another. What we really needed was a teacher. An artist friend of ours, Barbara Nessim, commissioned a spiritualist to make 'soul charts' for our birthdays, which were exactly one month apart. These were beautiful abstract compositions drawn with pastel chalks on coloured felt, in which the background colour of the felt was supposed to represent our essence. Red was earthy and passionate, blue was spiritual, and so on. These representations of where we were at spiritually almost needed no explanation, we immediately recognized our inner selves in those drawings. What was amazing to us was the fact that they had been done without the artist ever meeting us. It was her clairvoyance that enabled her to produce these first charts, and when we eventually met the artist she explained the symbolism in her drawings. We knew at once that Ellen Resch was the teacher we had been searching for. We never dropped acid again.

We began studying with Ellen, allowing her to take us through guided meditations. As part of her small group of followers we would try to make direct contact with our spiritual guides, mine was Rama. We were told to test our guides and ask them for evidence that they were there. I swear that on the rainiest, most blustery bleak nights in New York, every time I asked Rama for a cab one would turn the corner in seconds. Ellen would also give us direct messages from our guides whom only she could hear clearly. I remember so well the warmth of that group, which included others of our own age as well as people up to forty years older, all sharing this wonderful psychic experience together. Ellen, a short, dark, German woman, took on an aura of another person during these sessions: that of a solemn Indian guru from ancient times. Reincarnation was, of course, a strong tenet of our group. Siegrid and I were told that we were once brother and sister, temple dancers, in ancient India.

One day I told Ellen that it was my dream to go to London to work in the music industry there. Ellen predicted that I would, very soon, meet an Englishman who would change my life. As far as I was concerned if she could teach me how to get cabs to come by positive thought there was no reason why the Englishman wouldn't. Two weeks later Ellen's prediction came true.

I was working at The Richmond Organization (TRO) as a signed songwriter and was in the early stages of becoming a record producer. One day I was standing by the water cooler in Richmond's offices when a tall, striking, grey-haired man walked up and poured himself some water. He certainly didn't look like an American; he dressed differently – he looked like an outsider's concept of a hippie. I introduced myself and he replied in a most beautiful accented voice, 'Hello, I'm Denny.'

Bingo, an Englishman! He asked me what I did there and I told him I was the 'house' record producer. His face beamed as he exclaimed, 'Ah, my American cousin.' This was my introduction to Denny Cordell.

'I'm a producer too. I'm working with Georgie Fame, and I've produced The Moody Blues and The Move,' said Denny.

I was already a fan of Georgie Fame, and knew of The Moody Blues from their top ten US hit with 'Go Now', but I hadn't heard of the Move. I was instantly captivated by that accent, so quintessentially posh English (not the monotone Scouse of the Beatles), his grey curls, the regal eyes. I later learned that he was in fact Denny Cordell-Laverack and had been born in Buenos Aires in 1944, but educated at a British public school. Nevertheless to this boy from Brooklyn he was like King Arthur. This man was a class act.

I'm not sure if Denny knew he had an 'American cousin', but Howard Richmond had certainly never told me that I had a 'British one'. Denny talked about his work in London; he was in a far more advanced stage of his career than I was.

'I've got something with me that you might like to hear,' said Denny.

I took him into an empty office and from his briefcase he pulled out an acetate that he placed on the turntable. As he lowered the tone arm onto the grooves I had no idea what to expect. Instantly I was hit by the sound of a haunting organ played over a steady medium-slow rock beat. It was a sad, almost gothic composition, worthy of Bach, and I had heard it before. It was a variation of 'Air On a G String' (I had paid attention during music appreciation classes in high school). At first I was under the impression that this was an instrumental as the intro was so long. After almost thirty seconds my illusions were shattered when a voice, which I took to be a black soul singer – but was really Gary Brooker – began singing those surreal, but now immortal, lyrics: 'We skipped the light fandango, turned cart-wheels 'cross the floor.' What the hell did that mean? Who cares? These disparate elements blended so incredibly well together.

'It's a new group I've discovered and I took them into the studio for a few hours in order to make this demo. They're called Procol Harum.'

The name was as strange as the music. Of course the song is now so famous, so a part of our collective consciousness, that it seems impossible to recall a time when it didn't exist. But there was I, probably the first American to hear 'A Whiter Shade of Pale'. For many it's one of rock's most seminal songs, and for me, it literally changed my life.

Denny was not in New York just to play me 'A Whiter Shade of Pale'.

'I'm working on a track called "Because I Love You" that I've already recorded with Georgie Fame,' explained Denny.

'I adore "Yeah, Yeah" by Georgie Fame. It always reminds me of my favourite jazz vocal group, Lambert, Hendricks and Ross,' said I, hoping to impress Denny with my knowledge and sophistication.

'I have already produced a British version of the song with Georgie but I want to cut it again with some of New York's finest jazz players. I've booked what I'm told are some of the top session musicians,' said Denny. He told me that he booked Clark Terry, a trumpet jazz icon, and booked A&R studios (owned by a young Phil Ramone) for three hours.

'Wow! Can I have a look at the charts, Denny?' (A chart is jargon for a musical arrangement.)

'Charts!' said Denny. 'There are no charts. I'm going to ask them to "busk it".'

For the first time in our conversation I looked a little bewildered. It turned out that this meant that they would 'fake it' – it was the first of many lessons in British English.

'You'll be crucified financially if you expect an eight-piece session band to make up an arrangement. This is New York, and obviously things are different in London but here everything is "union this, union that". Clark Terry will charge you a fortune to sit down and sketch out a trumpet part while the studio clock is ticking. Before you know it you'll be paying overtime. Do you normally "busk it" in London?'

'Well, I suppose you could say that. I'll book the studio for a whole day and we'll record an A-side and then do a quick B-side. Everyone will hang out, smoke a few spliffs, and then we'll record it after each musician has kind of worked out what they'll do. By midnight we'll have our take.'

Oh, I loved this. It explained how, and why, the Beatles took nine weeks to record their album *Revolver*. In America albums were almost always recorded in less than a week, sometimes in one day. After this brief introduction to British recording techniques Denny became pensive. As he slowly turned a whiter shade of pale he said, 'The session is taking place in an hour. What am I going to do?'

I felt responsible for delivering such bleak news so I asked to hear the demo of Georgie's song. He put the acetate on the deck and I heard the British version of 'Because I Love You'. It was good but Denny was correct in his hunch that a group of New York musicians could give it a more authentic feel. What irony, he wanted to record in New York and I wanted to record in London – for that 'feel' thing.

'I think I can probably write a decent sketch of the arrangement in an hour.' Denny looked very relieved.

All my years of paying attention in my high school music dictation classes paid off in that hour. I am fortunate that once I know the key of a song I can write out the notes without reference to a piano. I first transcribed the chord changes to the song and then added a guide bass part, a simpler version than the one on the record. I added a few indications for the drummer of where to play fills, and when to stop and start. Then I wrote the two trumpet parts on top of the same staff. With minutes to spare I had all the important ingredients of the arrangement written out on several pieces of manuscript paper. The same pages would suffice for all the different instruments. I rushed around to the Xerox copier – a cool new gadget in the '60s – seconds later we were running down 48th Street, demo and charts in our hands.

When we got to the studio everyone was set up and waiting for us. Denny had asked Harvey Brooks, a member of the group Electric Flag, to help with the production. Harvey had the band playing some 12-bar blues to warm up, while at the same time giving the engineer a chance to adjust the individual microphone settings.

'Can I have the charts?' asked Harvey of Denny.

'Well, Tony here wrote some parts out, I hope they'll be okay.'

I knew they would be fine but I couldn't help feeling very nervous – I had just crashed a party of musicians I had only dreamed about working with. I mean – Clark Terry. Come on.

Denny's acetate played as the band scanned my instant all-in-one arrangement. No one questioned anything; they just silently imagined how they'd interpret the music as they listened to the British version. Leaving the control room they took their places in front of the microphones. The drummer counted in and I immediately heard the efforts of my dictation pulsing through the air. (God bless you Dr Silberman, head of the New Utrecht High School Music Department, your protégé is finally having his moment of glory.) It sounded okay, a little stiff maybe, but Harvey and Denny immediately began to refine the band's interpretation. I was so impressed by their ideas and clarity. This was the first big time, class-A recording session

I was really a part of. I had also saved Denny at least two hours of studio time and extra musicians' fees and he was going to get a killer backing track in the three hours he had booked.

After an hour it became clear that things were not quite going to plan. It wasn't in the total groove it needed to be. Turning to King Arthur I asked, 'How do you feel?' 'Apprehensive,' he pensively answered in a Shakespearian voice that would've impressed Sir Larry. While this kid from Brooklyn had seen that word in print, he'd never heard it uttered aloud. 'Apprehensive' was never in my spoken vocabulary and I had to think about its meaning in this context. Quickly I surmised that he wasn't happy.

A break was called during which Denny and Harvey talked about what to do.

'It's the bass player,' said Harvey, 'I've not worked with the guy and to me he's out of his league.' Brooks suggested that he should play the bass instead. Denny and I (having written the 'chart' I now included myself in the production 'team') thought this would hurt the bass player's feelings. Harvey ruthlessly waived our considerations aside. 'Fuck that! I'll play the fucking bass!'

Denny was getting the full-on New York City experience . . . all in one day. Brooks diplomatically told the bass player to sit it out, and asked if he could borrow the bass. The improved bass groove seemed to be what was missing after all! This was a big lesson for us, and even for the rejected bass player who sat in the control room as we were all caught up in the infectious groove. What was also so cool about this session was that everyone played at the same time. Shortly this ensemble method of recording would come to an end, the dawn of the 'piecemeal' approach was just around the corner; a method that continues to this day, for the most part. I was witness to the end of an era.

* * *

Denny was to take the backing track to London for Georgie Fame to record his vocal. This was like science fiction at the time – the music recorded on one continent and the vocal recorded on another.

'Tony, you've done a great job. I'm impressed with your expertise. I'm looking for an American arranger to be my production assistant back in London. I'm very much in demand and don't want to lose out on any opportunities because of the restraints of only being able to be in one place at a time.'

Denny went on to explain what the role of his deputized assistant would entail, which as far as I could gather was to do the basics when he was elsewhere. 'I need someone who is an accomplished musician who can interpret my thoughts. I only know a few chords on the guitar,' said Denny.

In the flush of today's minor glory I told him to look no further, I was his man. But Denny had other plans. He wanted to lure a really big name to England, and then said the most preposterous thing I'd heard all day, or any day for that matter.

'I'm flying to Los Angeles tomorrow to meet Phil Spector, to ask him to be my assistant.' Given Phil's track record of hits this put a whole new spin on *chutzpah*. I gave Denny my phone number just in case Phil Spector declined the job. Afterwards as I made my way home I tried to imagine the conversation between the two producers:

'Phil, I'm a little *apprehensive* about asking you this, old boy, but would you mind coming back to London with me to work as my assistant?'

'Denny, what are you smoking, man?'

My experience with Denny seemed like a dream; Siegrid could scarcely believe what I told her. Later I told Ellen about my Englishman and what had happened. 'It was probably a false alarm because he was looking for someone with more experience than me.'

'No!' said Ellen very adamantly. 'He's the one! He's the Englishman who will change your life. He will ask you to work with him in England.'

As much as I wanted to believe it, I felt that my psychic energy was only good enough to make cabs appear at three in the morning. What happened with Denny was a false start, a one-off experience at best, a good barstool story.

'Stay hopeful,' was all that Ellen would say.

A few days later our phone ringing at 11 a.m. interrupted our morning idyll, which was far from ideal as we had only got to bed at 6 or 7 a.m., as was our habit. Not just any call, it was a call from overseas, the first I'd ever received. The voice on the other end sounded like it was coming out of a short-wave radio, with whistles and pops as the backing track. 'Phil Spector didn't work out' were Denny's opening words, 'I've also tried to get Artie Butler but he's also said no.'

Artie was an old buddy of mine who had worked with the legendary producer Shadow Morton as well as playing the piano on 'Remember (Walking In The Sand)' and 'Leader of The Pack' by the Shangri-Las. 'Who does this fucking Limey think he is?' is how I imagine Artie with his Flatbush arrogance would have put it.

'Tony, I was wondering if you're still interested in the job?' This woke me up completely, but I still had to ask Denny several times if he was serious. He kept repeating, 'Yes'.

'How will we do it?' I asked.

'I've spoken with Howard (Richmond) and he'll arrange the airfare,' said Denny.

'When do you want me over there?' was all I could think of to say.

He explained how very overworked he was and that he needed me there as soon as possible. Somehow I came up with the arbitrary answer, 'How about in two weeks?' Quite honestly, if I didn't have some explaining to do to Siegrid, I would've left immediately. I stared at my beautiful wife as she slept, seemingly oblivious to the phone call. With blinding insight it dawned on me that things would never be the same. This is the lucky break everyone dreams of, but it didn't necessarily include her. For starters Denny didn't even know I had a wife.

I gently woke her up. She asked who had been on the phone and I said, 'It was the Englishman, the ENGLISHMAN. And we're moving to London.'

'Oh no,' she groaned, and went back to sleep.

Later I went to see a sceptical Howard Richmond about my plans and to further convince him it was a good idea to let me go to London, 'to learn how the Brits do it.' His plan had been for me to develop local New York talent for his forthcoming label, but to be honest I really didn't know how to do that. I explained that I needed to learn how the Brits did it and bring that secret knowledge back to TRO. Howard finally agreed that I could have two months of a recording education in London. Little did he know that I intended to stay longer; my fingers were crossed behind my back. The next day I called Denny and said I'd be there by the end of April, which pleased him greatly. I told him that I had just collected some car accident insurance money and I was going to buy some cool clothes for London. Unphased by that non sequitur, Denny just said to make sure I got there, and to bring my guitars. He'd supply me with an office and a demo studio.

In the two years Siegrid and I had been together we'd hardly spent any time apart. She understood how much I wanted to go to London, because as a little girl in Germany all she'd wanted to do was to live in America. We agreed that I should go to

London first because it would take a month for Siegrid to get rid of our apartment, during which time I would find us a place to live in London. I couldn't bear it if she didn't agree to go to London. So I said goodbye to my longhaired beauty, my lover, my ancient Indian temple dancer, and my partner in virtually everything. Both excitement and gloom accompanied me on my flight to London.

In the morning after my ordeal with Customs and Immigration I met the rest of the Cordells: Mia, Denny's wife, and his children Tarka and Barney. Wow, even the little kids had English accents. Like Denny, Mia was prematurely grey, but an English Rose, and Tarka and Barney were two of the cutest kids I'd ever seen. For breakfast, only toast with marmalade and tea was offered. That was fine by me, as I was not yet a coffee snob, but the marmalade was strangely bitter for a jam.

Soon we were motoring to 68 Oxford Street, to Dumbarton House, the office of Essex Music. It was also home to Denny's boldly named company, New Breed Productions. The language confusion persisted when I tried to fathom why the suite of offices was on the first floor, when we'd clearly gone up one flight of stairs to get there. In New York, we'd be on the second floor. It was explained to me that the floor I took to be the first floor was called the ground floor in England. Fine! I'm getting it – the first floor is the ground floor, the couch is a settee and a bathrobe is a dressing gown. I expected to be told later in the day that a vest was an undershirt. It is: I was.

Denny introduced me to the girls at the reception desk – all 'dolly birds' in miniskirts – exactly what I expected from pictures in magazines, a pleasant surprise on my first day. Then I was ushered into an office, that of David Platz, the President of Essex Music International (Howard Richmond's equivalent in London). He was also Denny's equal partner in New Breed

Productions Ltd and couldn't have been any more different in appearance and demeanour. Denny Cordell might look and speak like King Arthur but he wore ripped jeans, moccasins and an Afghan waistcoat. David Platz was bespectacled, dressed in classic British tweeds, had a short conventional hairstyle and puffed on a briar pipe – a Basil Rathbone look-a-like. He spoke through his nose, or rather down his nose at me, and had a disarming way of invading one's comfort zone as he spoke a few inches from my face. I had not encountered this nose-to-nose, smooth-talking, passive-aggressive style before but soon learned that, unlike a brash American big shot CEO, David Platz had developed subtle means to keep you in your place.

I immediately got the distinct impression that bringing me here was all Denny's idea and that, perhaps, David had a 'thing' about Americans: a negative 'thing'. This was confirmed later when I had one-to-one meetings with Platz. Ironically, as I was to learn, he wasn't English at all, but came to England as a young Jewish refugee during the Second World War. He had tragically lost his parents in Germany, but his aunt, Mrs Harvey, the chief accountant at Essex Music, fostered him. Mrs Harvey was soon to become my 'aunt' too. But in every other way, David Platz was quite the upper-crust Englishman.

Our initial meeting was brief, just an exchange of pleasantries really, but it had an ominous feeling. He was a proud man, and it is no accident that the initials of Essex Music International are EMI, and that David Platz's idol was Sir Joseph Lockwood, president of the other, iconic British record company EMI. To the young hippie I was, David Platz represented The Man, everything that was bad about the corporate world. It wasn't an auspicious beginning.

Afterwards Denny took me to his small office, which was in stark contrast to the grandeur of the oak panelled walls of Platz's huge office. Denny's office was about 8 by 11 feet with walls that were a yellowish colour, which I assumed had once been white; it contained one, by necessity small, functional desk. Into this space of less than a hundred square feet were crammed Denny, his assistant and budding songwriter Richard Kerr, and a publisher who worked there part time called Jon Fenton. In a few months a record plugger and a team of African-American songwriters, including Richard Henry, joined us and somehow or another we all shared this space. As the day went by some of the other Essex Music employees poked their heads in the doorway to meet the new Yank on the block. Graham Churchill, David Barnes and Don Paul all greeted me warmly. They were all song pluggers (they pitched songs to singers and producers to record) and all three eventually went on to greater things in the British music biz. Don discovered the street busker Don Partridge, who had a big hit with 'Rosie'. Richard Kerr went on to have a solo singing career and wrote many hit songs, included 'Mandy', a huge hit for Barry Manilow. Graham and David became big executives in the music business. They all made me feel very welcome, in contrast to my cool reception from Mr Platz.

Essex Music was described as the 'sister' organization of The Richmond Organization, but in actual fact I learned that Howard Richmond outranked David Platz; each company administered the other's catalogue in their own country. Platz had some early success in the UK with songwriters that included Lionel Bart (he wrote the musical *Oliver!*) and Anthony Newley ('What Kind Of Fool Am I?'). He also had the King of British Skiffle, Lonnie Donegan, who signed a young writer called Justin Hayward to his own publishing company. Justin, as a member of The Moody Blues, wrote 'Nights In White Satin' at the age of 19; we would later become firm friends. A year or so later Gus Dudgeon, a recording engineer, who after doing some satisfactory production work for Platz, was rewarded with a production company of his own, with Platz, again, the equal partner. Unfortunately for Platz, Gus moved on prior to producing all the early Elton John albums. Platz seemed incapable of holding onto his discoveries for more than brief periods in their careers. His excuse would usually be, 'I'm only a publisher, and I don't understand the record business.'

With barely enough time to acquaint myself with my new surroundings Denny announced that we had a recording session with Manfred Mann at 2 p.m. My first day. And I was about to meet my first famous British group. Denny had agreed to produce their next single and that's why I had to be there. He was fully occupied working on Procol Harum's debut album in order to satisfy the demand created by 'A Whiter Shade Of Pale', which was on its way to becoming a smash hit. Interestingly, the demo that Denny played for me in New York could not be bettered by re-recording, so they released it as it was. He also had to start work on the Move's album, as their single 'I Can Hear The Grass Grow' was heading towards the top ten. While Manfred Mann was almost a burden on his workload he didn't want to turn them down.

Denny drove to the Phillips recording studio, just off Marble Arch, like he was in a Grand Prix – we were travelling at dangerous speeds in this ridiculously small car, a 'Mini'. To make matters worse, the steering wheel was on the wrong side AND we were driving on the wrong side of the road. The Mini's tiny dashboard could, at any moment, have been the recipient of my head because there were no seat belts in this toy car – nor were there any seat belt laws. Instinctively my foot stamped down on a nonexistent brake pedal as Denny weaved in and out of traffic along Oxford Street. Finally we arrived, and to my disbelief Denny parked the car in a space the size of a yoga mat. My stomach was like a butterfly cage. I was not sure whether it was in anticipation of what was to come or what had just happened.

On the way there Denny announced, 'I shall need to leave you in charge for a few hours after we get started.'

So, after just three hours in a New York studio with Denny, and with my limited experience, I was to be a 'producer'. As a musician I had never been allowed inside the control room, as oddly it was forbidden in those days. I barely knew what to say let alone do. Walking from the car to the studio I began to feel queasier, like I imagined I'd feel if I were being led to my execution. I assumed that I was just going to watch and learn during the first few days.

The studio turned out to be clean and pretty, unlike the squalid ones I had worked in back home, and by the standards of 1967 the console was huge. The Manfreds were warmed up and had been waiting somewhat impatiently for Denny; I sensed an unmistakable hostility in the air. I was introduced but instantly ignored, probably regarded by them as 'something the cat dragged in'. As a keen student of British bands the first thing I noticed was a change in personnel: Mike D'Abo had replaced Paul Jones (actually Mike was the kindest to me, maybe because we were the two new kids on the block). They had been rehearsing 'So Long Dad', a darkly humorous and cynical song by the American writer Randy Newman. Denny quickly changed the mood in the studio and started making suggestions. I quickly saw why this man was so respected as the group hung on his every word. King Arthur was in full swing; it was something that I'd only glimpsed in New York.

After a couple of hours of recording Denny was satisfied with a great take by the drummer and bassist. I must emphasize that it was Denny who'd decided what the best take was, after the group wanted to call an earlier attempt a great take. I could see that Denny's standards were incredibly high. He was relentless

as he made them play the song again and again until it had all
the elements and subtleties he deemed perfect. He was super
critical with the engineer, making him tweak the console controls and adjust the microphones until the sound was as perfect
as possible. In fact the sound was amazing, even better than
what I had heard on Beatles' albums, my personal criteria of
great sound. It was the confirmation I had been seeking – Brits
did do it better. I was overwhelmed by this crash course as I
watched Denny make his engineer jump through hoops; it was
something you'd never have got an American engineer to do
back then.

During a break Denny turned to me and said, within earshot
of the band, 'I have to go to Olympic Studios in Barnes for a
Procol Harum session. I'm not sure about that take; I think I
would like you to try for an even better one. When you've done
that guide the group through the overdubs', the 'fiddly bits' of
guitar parts, keyboard parts and vocals.

'No problem,' said I. As scary as this all seemed I decided to
'do or die'. If Denny thought I was up to it then I was determined not to let him down. This desire to live up to the belief
people have in me has been running my life since.

With Denny gone the hostility returned – the Manfreds obviously felt that Denny was fobbing me off on them. In their
minds they were paying for Denny Cordell but were getting
Tony 'Nobody'. However, they begrudgingly got behind their
instruments and played six lacklustre takes; I could see I was
in trouble. Having little experience with this kind of situation
I drew upon that of one of my few recording sessions. As a
15-year-old bass player, when things had been going badly the
mysterious voice coming from the control room would say
things to cheer us up and put us at ease. I had to be cheerful in
the face of adversity. Leaning into the talkback mic I announced,
'Hey, this is take seven, lucky take seven. We'll get it now.'

My 'jolly hockey sticks' tactic was received with audible groans and we never did get that 'better take'; the magic created by Denny had left with him.

Undaunted we proceeded to use what Denny had considered the best take. We were using a 4-track tape and had used up two tracks for the backing. The entire drum kit and bass guitar were recorded on track one and a rudimentary keyboard part was on track two, which we replaced with a carefully played one. On the two remaining tracks we had to record the guitar solo, vocals and some special effects noises. Since the tracks had to be shared, the additional parts had to be carefully dropped into the same tracks. The guitar solo was recorded on the vocal track with fractions of a second to spare. Dropping in too early would erase part of the vocal, as would dropping out too late. In America, the same procedures are called 'punch-ins' and 'punch-outs'; no doubt a psychiatrist would find this mildly amusing.

Slowly the band dropped their hostility towards me, or maybe I had taken their comments too seriously. This was my introduction to 'taking the piss', or 'taking the Mickey'. What I assumed to be very hurtful insults were just good-natured British sarcasm. We managed to get everything on tape: a guitar solo, coins jingling, hand claps, backing vocals, lead vocal, a second keyboard part – all on the remaining two tracks. Denny returned later in the evening and was thrilled with what he heard. The band was visibly relieved and I had a little invisible halo over my head. First blood. A few days later, after Denny mixed the track to mono, he said I'd done an amazing job with the overdubs, but left him with a very difficult mix because there were so many different elements on the two busy tracks. I think this was a compliment.

That was my first day under my belt. If this wasn't exciting enough Denny told me I was going to meet, and work with, Procol Harum the next day. What I didn't know was that I would bump into Brian Jones of the Rolling Stones in a corridor at Olympic Studios, and I would also see Jimi Hendrix jam later that evening at the Speakeasy in Margaret Street – a club that was the epicentre of the music industry during the early summer of '67. God knows what would happen on my third day.

chapter 1
birth, bananas, heroin and marriage

Three men made the greatest difference to my career: Milton Anderson (also known as Drake), Dr Israel Silverman and Leon Block were my mentors, to whom I owe an enormous debt. But they came along a little later. First I had to survive early childhood.

From the area where I was born you can look across the Narrows to Staten Island where the Statue of Liberty is sited – you don't come more New York than me. The area of Brooklyn where I was born is called Dykers Heights. I arrived on 24 April 1944 at Victory Memorial Hospital, I was a war baby. None of my family was involved in the fighting; my father was drafted too late. Avoiding war would be a tradition I would carry on when I avoided the dubious Vietnam War draft in my own unique way. My mother says that she named me for the British Foreign Minister Anthony Eden – the fact that Anthony was also my father's name was irrelevant according to her.

In the early years of their marriage my parents were living in various homes with relatives, in Red Hook, Flatbush and, ultimately, Bay Ridge – all located in Brooklyn. My mother's name is Josephine, her maiden name was Ciampo and she was born in America. My grandparents Gennaro and Rachela arrived from Italy in separate years, and came through Ellis Island in the early 1900s. Emigration from Italy was not the result of any one single event. Overpopulation, high taxation, unemployment and a wish for property of their own were all factors in driving the migration to 'the land of the free'. From 1870-90 an estimated 355,000 Italians went to the United States. Many quickly sent word back home of the prospects that existed in America. Initially it was mostly people from Northern Italy who made the journey. In the spring of 1898 there were food riots in many regions of Italy after a smaller than expected wheat harvest the previous summer. Faced with increasing economic problems at home the steady stream of émigrés became a flood. Between 1890 and 1914 nearly four million Italians went to L'America.

When my grandparents arrived the Irish-American immigration officer couldn't spell Ciampo so he shortened it to Campo; it's something that happened to lots of immigrants. My grandparents bought a house in Red Hook (now called Boerum Hill), although when I was growing up it was simply known as 'Downtown' Brooklyn. My Dad, Anthony Ferdinand Visconti, was born in 1917 in Jersey City, New Jersey, very much a contemporary of Frank Sinatra. At some point in his early years his family moved to Warren Street in Brooklyn, which is where he met my mother. They became childhood sweethearts and stayed together all their lives until my dad passed away in 2005.

Like most people my recollections of my early years are patchy, although I do remember riding a tricycle when I was about two or three. One afternoon I rode my little tricycle around the corner and I got lost; I started crying. Someone came up to me and asked me my name. 'I'm Simon Ackerman,' I replied. A strange answer, but not so strange because at the time there was a radio commercial for an insurance company; the sign-off line for the advert was. 'What's my name? – Simon Ackerman.' I had heard this so often that it seemed the obvious answer.

birth, bananas, heroin and marriage

My idyllic life in sunny Ocean Parkway came to an end when my parents decided to move briefly to my grandfather's house. He lived alone because my grandmother had been in hospital for about ten years having fallen out of a window. She was paralysed from the waist down and over the years dementia had taken hold to the point where she didn't really recognize anyone and was kept alive by basic feeding and care.

Grandfather Campo could speak almost no English; he never bothered or needed to learn, living as he did amongst the Italian community in New York. He spoke in a strong Neapolitan accent and made a great living as a fruit salesman. He walked around Brooklyn all day with a big wooden cart full of fruit, mainly bananas, and used the few words of English that he knew. He would yell out at the top of his lungs, in a very raspy voice 'BANANA', he also knew the words for American money ('ten-a cents-a'; 'a quarter-a'). He was a feisty guy, full of spirit. He was fun to live with except that the neighbourhood where he lived was terrible; it was little more than a slum.

The house was rat-infested. We had this incredible cat called Tommy, a huge tabby with a scarred face from having been in too many fights. Best of all he was a champion ratter. He would regularly drop a big plump rat at the feet of my grandfather to show what a great job he was doing. I was very wary of rats as a little kid; I instinctively knew I was an easy target. When I was about five my mother went to the corner shop and for the first time left me at home alone for a few minutes. As soon as she was gone the rats intuitively knew I was alone. They could hear me or smell me and all of a sudden there was much scurrying in the wall cavities, and it wasn't just a little bit of scurrying; I could hear what sounded like twenty to thirty rats. I thought they were coming to get me. I started to scream at the top of my lungs. Fortunately, a tenant of my grandfather's, on the top floor of our three-storey building, came running down to see what was the matter. He wrote a note to my Mum. 'The rats scared me I am upstairs in Dominic's apartment', signed Anthony. My mother never left me alone again. Shortly afterwards my father was asleep with his arm hanging over the side of the bed and was bitten by a rat; his finger became so swollen it looked like a small salami.

Many Italians lived on our street. Next door was a family of Sicilians and above us was also a Sicilian immigrant, a tenant. The older people only spoke Italian and really didn't speak too much about the old country, one that held bitter memories. If anything they talked about America and making money. Italian music would pour from windows, either from 78-rpm gramophone records or from the non-stop Italian broadcasting on AM Radio; the DJs only spoke Italian. The smell of red sauce pervaded the air and more often than not Italian food was the main fare on our table every night. My mother's mother was an excellent cook by all accounts and she taught my mother well. I remember that the Italians kept to themselves, yet there was an undermining class distinction amongst them. The Neapolitans (us) thought that we were better than the Sicilians; I was brought up to believe this too. But it wasn't an issue because I played with the Sicilian kids next door, who were every bit as American as I am. In fact, I felt rebellious about the amount of peasant Italian culture that was forced on me and I held my ears shut when my mother or grandfather tried to speak Italian to me. It was different for my father as his mother never taught him Italian because she wanted her children to grow up as 100 per cent Americans.

Our neighbourhood was predominantly Italian but there were also Puerto Ricans living at the other end of the street, and a couple of Arab families. Back then it was a broken down working-class neighbourhood, today apartments there go for about half a million dollars and up.

birth, bananas, heroin and marriage

My mother sang all day long when she was cooking and doing her housework; she would sing in both Italian and English. My Dad, a carpenter by trade, was an amateur accordion and harmonica player; he also sang bass in a barbershop quartet. The quartet sometimes rehearsed in our kitchen and the strains of 'Sweet Adeline' became ingrained in my young brain – all four parts.

When I was five years old my parents bought me a plastic ukulele. I had seen it in the window of a toy store and I wanted it. It was not just any old ukulele, but a Popeye ukulele, with transfers of the great man, Olive Oil, Wimpy and Swee'Pea on it. Each nylon string was a different colour – the A string was blue, the D string was red, the F sharp string was yellow and B string was green; with it was a book on how to play a dozen or so songs. Songs like 'Ain't She Sweet', 'Side by Side', 'Goodnight Ladies' – really old songs from the 1920s and 30s. Although I couldn't read music the chord symbols were easy to read since the ukulele has four strings; the first chords you learn are all done within the first three frets, because most use open strings and require only one or two fingers to press the frets of the rest. The coloured strings corresponded to the coloured strings in the book. I taught myself every chord in the book; it only took an hour. I realize now that even as a five-year-old I had good powers of concentration.

Next I learned how to sing the songs, many of which I already knew. Before long I was strumming my ukulele and singing at the top of my lungs. My parents, and everyone who heard me, were impressed and for quite a few years afterwards I was a 'party piece'. My repertoire of chords had increased to at least fifty, and by the time I was seven I was looking for a much bigger instrument. My ambition was to graduate to the guitar, but my father's guitar was way too big for me and the strings were steel and too high from the frets. It was a better cheese cutter than a musical instrument. I just needed to become bigger, but in the interim I played the larger baritone ukulele.

Around the corner from our house in Warren Street was Wyckoff Street and the families that lived there were predominantly African-American; I didn't grow up feeling a victim of racial hatred, but occasionally the young kids there felt bored or feisty and they would come around the corner and beat up the Italian or Hispanic kids. It wasn't so much a racial thing as their street against our street. Conversely our back yard, about 20 by 10 feet, where my grandfather grew tomatoes, bordered on the back yard of an African-American family and my mum and the mother of that family were on great speaking terms.

We lived near the Gowanus Canal and on more than one occasion, when gang warfare broke out, we'd hear of a body found floating in the canal. My parents decided that the neighbourhood was getting a little too rough and so my grandfather sold the house and we all went to live at my other grandparents' house; we moved in with the Viscontis.

My father's father was Nicholas Viciconti. My father grew tired of kids making fun of his surname in school (Anthony Visit-The-Country). My grandfather told him that a long time ago the family name was Visconti, so my father changed our family name to Visconti when he was old enough. Nicholas, who was connected with the early Italian mobs, was a very talented violinist. He knew loads of songs and my father and I – I was about seven years old – would play with him at least once a week. Nicholas claimed that he played in bars with Jimmy Durante, a famous singer/comedian whose career stretched from the '30s to the '60s. Durante played piano and he had a sidekick called Eddie Jackson who did most of the singing and soft shoe dancing. It sounded like my grandfather did this on a regular basis and I had no reason not to believe him. But he never became a professional musician whereas Durante went on to form a vaudeville trio called Clayton, Jackson and Durante. He pursued a solo career and was enormously successful as a comedy actor and host of his own television show.

Nicholas was a sharp dresser; he made a lot of money in the wholesale vegetable and fruit business in what is now Tribeca in Manhattan – he operated from a large warehouse on Vesey Street close to the site of the World Trade Center. I have seen photos of him wearing a three-piece suit with a very thick gold watch fob and wearing white spats over his shoes, topped off with a white fedora on his head. That business was controlled by the Italian mob; Nicholas casually admitted to me one day that he had counted Al Capone as a friend.

He made enough money to keep a love nest in Manhattan with a beautiful, ginger-haired Irish mistress. He went home to Brooklyn at the weekend and gave my grandmother a weekly allowance to feed herself and the three small children; he would often beat my father and yell abusively at my grandmother. The stock market crash of 1929 ruined him. He took my uncle Eddie (as moral support, I guess) to his love nest and paid off the mistress to get rid of her; my uncle Eddie was only a small boy, but when he came back he told the rest of the family that she was a beautiful woman. Thereafter my grandfather moved back in with Elizabeth, his wife, and she nagged him every single day of the rest of his life. Nicholas was actually a very kind man by the time I was a little kid. He slept in his own room to escape the rants of my grandmother. His lucrative business was now reduced to just selling brown paper bags to the fruit merchants; he could never afford to build up his inventory of farm produce after the crash.

My grandmother, Elizabeth, came from a well-educated family in Rome, where her father was a judge and others in the family were lawyers; her maiden name was Cantasano. She became betrothed to my grandfather without ever meeting him. All she knew before setting out for New York was that her husband-to-be came from a wealthy New York Italian family. She was sent to New York. She arrived in America, with a big trunk, in which was a dowry. My grandfather was told by his parents to go and meet his future bride and bring her home. Off he went to the port, or so he pretended, before returning home without her, lying that she'd missed the boat. Having been born and raised in New York he did not want to marry an immigrant girl from the old country.

Ironically my grandmother was a very cultured woman. My great-grandfather was a very forward thinking man and had sent all his children to some form of higher education, and so she spent a year at university in Rome, which was very unusual for any woman in the early twentieth century. She spoke about three languages fluently, Italian, Greek and Albanian, and later on she picked up Yiddish and Spanish in New York working in a sweatshop – she was a very smart lady. Alone in New York, she went to an address she had been given of some relatives where she stayed for a few months. Eventually my grand-parents met and they married, but it was no fairytale ending and proved to be a very stormy marriage.

Although my earliest memories of my grandparents were that they would fight all the time, constantly bickering and yelling, the sixty- to seventy-year-old grandfather I came to know was a lovely man, a real cool guy by then. He taught me how to play the mandolin and I have fond memories of my father, my grandfather and I sitting around the kitchen table playing old songs.

I was around six when we went to live with the Visconti family on 74th Street between 11th and 12th Avenue. It's the area of New York that I think of as home, a very safe neighbourhood that I later learned was mob controlled. Most people who lived in this neighbourhood were simple Italian folk, just like back in the old country, and the traditional Italian hierarchy controlled everything. Many years later I asked my mother why there were hardly any other ethnic groups living in our neighbourhood. Most everyone was Italian, Irish and Catholic, with just a few Norwegian Lutherans; there was a conspicuous absence of other ethnicities.

'Well, you know who lives down the hill don't you?'

'No, who does?'

She mentioned the name of a very prominent Italian family who have been known to indulge in many *Soprano*-like activities.

'They ran the neighbourhood, even the real estate agents. If a Black family came to our neighbourhood and asked to see homes the estate agents would say that all the homes were taken and they had nothing even coming up on their books.'

This general neighbourhood is the one made famous in *Saturday Night Fever*. The opening scene in which John Travolta walks beneath the elevated train is 86th Street. The place where he bought a pizza is one where I bought pizza slices many times as a kid.

I wanted to be a pop star since before I was a teenager. I've got photos of me posing as Elvis and also – even though I didn't need them – with horn-rimmed glasses posing as Buddy Holly. By the age of eleven my parents realized two things: I definitely had musical talent, and my hands were big enough for me to have a guitar. Being a precocious kid I used to play my ukulele at the drop of a hat, I had no shame. I remember one exasperated relative asking, 'Do you always bring that ukulele with you?' Getting a guitar coincided with Elvis Presley's arrival on the scene, not that my parents were keen on my learning to play that kind of music, so they sent me to a very good guitar teacher in Ocean Parkway, Flatbush, called Leon Block. I would take the bus from Fort Hamilton Parkway carrying my new guitar in its cloth case for my weekly half hour lessons; from day one he began to teach me to read music. Within a few months my repertoire was hundreds of songs, having quickly relearned everything I knew on the uke. I learned from books that Leon Block had published which had simplified guitar arrangements of popular songs, like 'Que Sera Sera', 'The Shrimp Boats are a Coming', and 'All Shook Up'. He wrote them in keys that were easier for a beginner guitarist to play.

After a few months Leon Block said, 'I want you to try this out, you're a good reader now.' He opened a *piano* book called *Two Part Inventions by J. S. Bach*; this was a whole new level for me. They are quite difficult pieces for above average inter-mediate piano students. They have independent melodies for the left hand and right hand; each 'invention' was in a different key. The fifteen pieces teach independence for each hand, which is tricky on the piano, and even more difficult on the guitar, even though Segovia had adapted some. Leon Block would tell me to learn the treble clef part for the right hand and then he'd play the left hand bass clef part, so that we played a duet.

The first time I played one of these pieces my mind made a quantum leap – this was real music, I thought. During lessons I forgot about Elvis, Chuck Berry, Little Richard and Buddy Holly. I had been quite unaware of the guitar's versatility until Leon Block pointed out that it was capable of being a mini orchestra with almost the same potential as a piano. After we went right through *Two Part Inventions* I began learning the bass clef and we reversed our roles. During the two years I studied with Leon Block I got into classical music, flamenco and jazz – his musical influence, the first major one I'd had, has stayed with me always.

* * *

birth, bananas, heroin and marriage

I worked away at home practising every day to improve my playing. My ear-training made it easy for me to learn the cute little solo on 'Party Doll' by Buddy Knox in a couple of minutes. The same was true of Buddy Holly's songs, although the intro to 'That'll Be the Day' took a little longer as it was quite tricky. At 13, I began playing in a couple of different bands, one of which was called Mike D and the Dukes, and played my first paying job with them, an Italian wedding for which I was paid five whole dollars.

Like most other kids growing up in this golden era of rock and roll I was riveted to the radio by the great music that was being played. I worshipped DJs Alan Freed and Jocko. I couldn't wait to hear the next single from Little Richard, Fats Domino, groups like Frankie Lymon and the Teenagers and The Cleftones. I was thrilled by a song called 'Little Darlin'' because Freed would play the 'white' version by The Crewcuts and Jocko would play the 'black' version by The Gladiolas. Rock and roll was an alternate universe where I wanted to live.

As a singer I joined a doo-wop group on my street called The White Bucks, named after the shoes that Pat Boone made popular. Our best song was also called 'White Bucks'. Besides singing doo-wop I loved dancing to it, especially the slow songs, and particularly with a girl named Rosemary. We were part of a little neighbourhood gang of kids, not a real gang, but just a bunch of friends; there were about a dozen of us. On Friday nights we would go down to my friend's basement and unscrew the white light bulb in the ceiling and screw in a red one. We'd play 45 rpm records and dance. Two songs I particularly remember dancing to were 'In the Still of the Nite' by the Five Satins and 'Pledging My Love' by Johnny Ace, probably due to the fact that they aided my erotic stimulation. They were played over and over again and we would dance 'The Fish' which evolved to 'The Grind', which leaves nothing to the imagination.

You would just hold your girl as close as possible and grind your hips together while pressing your chest against her chest; it was as close as I got to real sex at twelve.

Best of all was the chance to dance with Rosemary. She had very rounded hips, an Italian beauty with dark curly hair, a sweet face and very ample breasts (us guys would debate whether they were a C or D cup – a favourite pastime). It was always a fight to get to dance with her and she knew it – we all knew it. One or two dances with Rosemary in an evening were the closest thing to heaven. I once casually, and totally accidentally, brushed my hand on the side of her breast while we were dancing and she slapped me in the face so hard, I heard bells and saw stars. It was okay to grind erotically but not to touch. It was at an early age I started learning the rules of sexual etiquette on the dance floor. It was at this time in my life that I learned what 'blue balls' were. I will always associate slow do-wop with teenage sex – or lack of.

Alan Freed would host rock 'n' roll shows at the Brooklyn Paramount Theatre. I went as often as I could, as soon as I could take the subway by myself. I usually went in a mixed group and we had to queue from about 6 a.m. to get into the first show, which started at 9 a.m. We would be kicked out after the show because there was a new group queuing for the second show. On one occasion I managed to hide in the men's room and saw the show all over again. I saw Fats Domino, Buddy Holly and Chuck Berry all in the same show. With hindsight I find it totally amazing that these guys performed show after show all day long. Usually it was six shows a day with each of them performing a couple of numbers. Sam the Man Taylor led the house band, which was more like a Count Basie-type band playing Be Bop, big band and jazz. They would back artists like Frankie Lymon and the Teenagers, The Cleftones, Mickey and Sylvia and The Cadillacs. Many of the 'cats' were top session players who played on the original recordings made in New York.

Most of these records were 12-bar blues or the famous 'Heart And Soul' chord changes. C-A minor-D minor-G7 – no one played them better than these guys. Of course not everyone was backed by Sam the Man's house band. If in the darkness you heard a buzz from an amp on the stage you knew it was either Buddy Holly, Chuck Berry or Bo Diddley because someone was plugging in their guitar; kids would scream because they knew that one of your three guitar heroes was about to come out. If it was Buddy Holly he would come running on stage followed by Jerry Allison and the other Crickets and launch into 'That'll be the Day', or 'Oh Boy'. Afterwards we would go around to the backstage door to try and get autographs: I got Little Richard's and Mickey 'Guitar' Baker's; Mickey and Sylvia had a big hit in 1957 with 'Love is Strange'. Later these shows moved to the New York Paramount and so it was a longer subway ride. Alan Freed stopped doing the shows and Murray the K, another DJ, took over. Both venues have since been torn down, but I'm left with vivid memories of an exciting and magical time in our musical history.

In High School I auditioned for the orchestra and was assigned the double bass. I picked it up immediately because the top four strings of the guitar are the same tuning, it was a no-brainer. We played Gershwin's *Porgy and Bess* suite in an arrangement for a high school orchestra. Besides the orchestra I played in the marching band but instead of plucking I was blowing, I played the tuba. During the lunch period in my senior year I took a string class and I would sometimes play the cello, which I taught myself. However, most of the time there were too many cello players and I would be the only bass player, which meant I played the cello part of a string quartet, but an octave lower.

In my second year I took music appreciation classes with Dr Israel Silberman who would play us classical music and tell us why we should like these pieces. He really was a great guy who also gave the string classes during the lunch break. In Music Theory class he would play us a string quartet and then say, 'Now listen to the next sixteen measures carefully. I want you to write out the second violin part. Ignore all the other parts, the first violin, the viola, the cello part, write the second violin part.' This was fantastic training for my ears. I had three glorious years of this, while everything else about school was horrible – I hated it. If it had not been for Dr Silberman I'm not sure I'd be in the music business today. He was the second greatest musical influence in my life.

We did an annual show called *Sing*. I was the leader of the pit band in my sophomore and Junior years and then in my final year I was President of the senior *Sing* – I was in charge of the whole thing. A friend of mine, David Geffen, who later formed Geffen Records, Geffen Music and Geffen Films and generally became an all around music industry legend, took the role of treasurer. One of the main guys in *Sing* was Gary Lambert, a talented trumpet player. He was so handsome; girls adored him. Tragically, like a lot of my friends, Gary died in the Vietnam War. His father was a top New York session violinist and I'm sure Gary would have become one of the world's greatest trumpet players. (He died of a heroin overdose in Vietnam; ironic, really, as he never used heroin before being drafted.)

In my senior year I met my teenage sweetheart, Bunny Galuskin. She came from a Jewish family and for the next four years we lived our version of *West Side Story*. Although my family loved her, our relationship had to be kept a secret from her parents. Ironically her aunt ran off with an Italian boy and the family held a funeral for her, sat *Shiva*. Her grandfather eventually lost his mind over losing his daughter.

birth, bananas, heroin and marriage

With all my music interests I had little time for English, maths or history and I failed these subjects miserably. I barely graduated by the skin of my teeth. When I was fifteen I spent the summer working as a musician in the Catskill Mountains, and I assumed I was done with school. When I got back to New York City in September they sent round a truant officer to the house who said I had to be in school as I was still under 16 and not of legal age to leave. So very reluctantly I went to night school and completed two history classes that I had failed. Finally I passed the Regents exam and got my High School diploma, which made my mother very happy. For me it made no difference; I just couldn't wait to get out into the world and be a full time musician.

Before all that happened and while I was still at school I had made my first real foray into the world of recording with a neighbourhood guy called Carl Pace. A songwriter and entrepreneur called Jay Fishman wanted to cash in on the duo thing; we were supposed to be the new fourteen-year-old Everly Brothers. Carl, who was being tutored by Jay, found me through the neighbourhood grapevine. Jay named us the Taylor Kids and took us to a small record company, Dorset Records, to cut a song called 'The Kite'. Bob Lissauer, whose claim to fame had been discovering the Kaylan Twins, who had a massive hit with 'When', ran the label. While this was not quite the Brill Building it was the next best thing; it was located in another music biz building around the corner on 55th Street between Broadway and 7th Avenue. The orchestrator who wrote the arrangement for the Kaylan Twins arranged our record, which had the opening lines, 'Upon my brand new kite right there in plainest sight, I went and painted your name in letters two-feet high.' How could anyone forget a lyric like that?

Looking back it seems like a dream, so much so that I can

remember very little of the recording session – which is a shame as it should have been something I'd always treasure. I do remember the guitarist in the band was Everett Barksdale, a prodigious session player who recorded with Art Tatum, Sarah Vaughan, Lena Horne, Dinah Washington and Sammy Davis Jr.

This was not our first session for Jay Fishman, we'd done one about a year earlier – it was a disaster. Jay wanted us to do six songs in one day and quite honestly I had never worked so hard in my life. On top of which I was due to take my girlfriend, who was a year older than me, to her prom that night. After the session I took my hired tuxedo to her house to change, but before I could I was violently ill in her bathroom – there was some blood involved. A doctor came and put me to bed and I was diagnosed with a very mild case of tuberculosis, which was not helped by the fact that I was already smoking cigarettes. As an asthmatic with a history of bronchial troubles I shouldn't have been smoking, nor should I have been working so hard. It forced me to slow down, temporarily.

This enforced break allowed me to spend time with my other passion, photography. I was around eight years old when I really got keen; my father had a great folding roll film camera that used what is now an obsolete size, 616. He showed me how to frame a picture in the viewfinder and to guess the exposure (a guide was on the box the film came in). I would take a few pictures on a roll and then wait maybe weeks for my Dad to finish the roll and get it developed at the drug store. As a treat I was given my own roll of film occasionally and I took some decent photos. He showed me how to take long exposures at night by setting the shutter to 'bulb' and resting the camera on a sturdy surface. When I was around nine or ten I was taking experimental photos by moonlight and streetlight.

When I was in my early teens I started to see 'available light' photos in magazines, mainly of jazz musicians. I could tell that no flash was used (I hated photos with flash). I started to buy photography magazines that had articles on the new, faster Tri-X film and that the speed could be 'pushed' during development. As luck would have it the flat underneath us was vacated by my uncle Eddie and a family moved in by the name of Rizzo. Frank Rizzo was a professional photographer and he took a keen interest in me. I told him I was so unsatisfied with the way pictures came back from the drug store and didn't look anywhere near as good as pictures in *Life* magazine; he showed me to his darkroom and I was hooked. He showed me how to develop black and white negative film, how to load the film onto a developing reel in complete darkness, how to mix the chemicals from powder, how to heat them and maintain temperature throughout development – and how to 'push' the speed. As an old-timer he was completely against grainy black and white photos but it didn't stop him from showing me how. Then he taught me how to 'crop' a negative, to enlarge only parts of it to make a better composition, and how to choose the right contrast paper to make the best print – all sorts of techniques. I saved my money and bought the cheapest enlarger I could get, but Frank said that the most important part was the lens and I didn't chintz on that. I got the money from gifts from relatives and from my weekend work as a musician; by the time I was 14 I had a fully functional darkroom in my bedroom and I would fall asleep to the stench of chemicals after a heavy printing session.

When I went off to the Catskill Mountains it was a little like my own version of *Dirty Dancing*, only I wasn't dancing. If you don't live in New York, or even if you do and you're under 40 years old, the lore of the Catskills will be a mystery to you. It was a great summer retreat, predominantly for Jewish families; there were literally hundreds of hotels up there. I say up there because it's about a hundred and ten miles north of New York City. The first summer I was there, when I was 15, I played at the Granite Hotel in the odd-sounding town called Kerhonkson. The owner of the hotel was Irwin Gewurtz, a great guy. I was in a band called Ricardo and the Latineers. Ricardo, whose real name was Richard Ritz, was not Latin American, nor was Artie Butler or Bruce Karp, the other players in the band; they were all Jewish kids from Flatbush, Brooklyn. They loved Latin-American music, which was very popular in the late '50s and early '60s. They asked me to play guitar for the summer – it was a no-brainer. It got me away from my parents' house for two and a half months and they paid me $50 a week, which was pretty good money back then. We got room and board and we had tax taken out so at the end my weekly salary was $39 and change. We worked six nights a week and on our night off we would drive back to Brooklyn.

Artie Butler went on to become a very famous arranger, producer, conductor and composer working with Frank Sinatra, Louis Armstrong, Neil Diamond, Dionne Warwick, Barry Manilow, Barbra Streisand and even Joe Cocker, whom I also worked with but at a different time. He was a phenomenal piano and vibraphone player. Ritchie Ritz was the drummer, a very tall, lanky guy. Bruce Karp was my best friend in the band, a fine flute and sax player. He was a student at Brooklyn College and like me he was taking the summer off to make some money. He and I had great philosophical discussions, lying beneath the stars outside the cottage we all slept in. We used to take our cots outside to see the brilliant starry night before we fell asleep, without the impediment of city lights. One night Bruce said, 'Do you realize that this entire universe and all these stars in the sky, and us, you and me and everybody in the band and everybody in the world and everyone in the universe, we could be only one atom inside a dingle berry hanging off a dog's arse in another universe, a bigger universe, and that universe could be an atom in a dingle berry hanging off another dog's arse and on and on and on.' This is actually an Ayurvedic concept from the Vedas of Hinduism. Bruce had heard of this concept before, but it was new to me and I started to sob.

Granite owner Irwin Gewurtz had a great idea to hire two female impersonators to bring in more bar business. He thought people would come into the bar and stare at them and end up buying drinks; unfortunately they just came to stare at Rick Carlson and Kim August. Kim went on to be an 'actress', even though he was a guy, playing female roles in some films including *No Way To Treat A Lady* with Rod Steiger. He turned out to be a good friend who spoke candidly about his sordid life. He was a handsome man when he wasn't in drag, but he had to draw on masculine eyebrows as they were shaved. On a few occasions he'd let us watch him get dragged up for the evening. As more feminine makeup would be put on the higher the pitch of his voice became, until he put on the wig, turned around and there he was – a woman. At 15 years old this was all rather eye-opening. With Kim there was no sex involved and although Rick had a crush on me, nothing ever came of it. This overexposure to the drag queen world made me question my sexuality but I didn't want to go down that route; there were too many sweet female Jewish young things to keep me on the straight, and not so narrow.

In the middle of that summer I got a call from a guy I knew who was in a band called The Crystals. A guy named Jimmy Nebb managed them and was going to finance a recording of a single. I was the only bass player in Brooklyn they knew and despite my insistence that I would not join them on a permanent basis I agreed to the session. There was only one problem; it was a Tuesday night, which wasn't my night off at the Granite. The other Latineers had no problem with me having a night off but I had to go to Mr Gerwurtz and ask permission – it was not something I relished, as he had a very stern side to him.

'Mr Gewurtz I have this opportunity to go down to New York and do something really big time.' Looking back I can't believe I actually said 'big time'. 'I have been asked to play bass at a recording session next Tuesday night.'

'You have Tony? That's great, what kind of music is it?'

'It's rock 'n' roll Mr Gewurtz.'

'Hmmm, well, if it is the chance of a lifetime I can't be heartless, so I'll give you the day off.' Then he added, 'I'll have to dock you one day's pay.'

The upside of having my pay docked was a promised session fee of $25. The name of that song was 'Malegeuna Rock', based on the Spanish classic Malageuna. The bass part followed the main melody of the song, which is why they desperately needed a bass player. It was very exciting to record in a really nice recording studio in Manhattan, although I can't remember its name (and it's probably not there anymore). This was my first encounter with a record producer. We weren't allowed in the control room, but a man's voice kept coming over the talkback speaker giving us feedback like, 'Hey, bass player. Your E string's flat!' I didn't like his tone and found his interjections very annoying.

After the session Jimmy Nebb said, 'You were really great kid, we love the way you play bass. Would you like to join the group?'

Maybe it was the euphoria of playing on a session, maybe it was the idea that we might have a hit on our hands, whatever it was I agreed to join The Crystals after the summer.

'Right,' said Jimmy, 'as you're now a member we'll not be paying you a session fee.'

birth, bananas, heroin and marriage

There was no point in arguing; it was simply a case of welcome to the music biz.

After returning to the Catskills for the rest of the summer I was soon back in the city playing with The Crystals. In October 1960 Jimmy Nebb secured a gig for us on a TV show called *The Saturday Prom* on NBC television; the host was Merv Griffin who was just beginning to be noticed on TV. He was in competition with Dick Clark's *American Band Stand* and the show went on the air on a Saturday evening. A weekly feature of the show was to run a contest to form *The Saturday Prom* band made up of New York teenagers. The first week they discovered a trumpet player, whom they found legitimately from somewhere, but then they also added Johnny Syvertsen, the sax player in The Crystals. The first week house musicians from the show's orchestra augmented Johnny and the trumpet player.

'Well, we've found our first two band members,' said Merv. 'Next week we'll add another.'

That was none other than our drummer Frank Steo. In the following weeks Jim Petricionne, our piano player, and Joey Strobel our guitar player were added. In the final week it was my turn.

'Ladies and gentlemen, here's our bass player Tony Visconti.' In my week we played 'Lullaby Of Birdland' in a Latin/Jazz style.

The week I joined the star of the show was one of my idols – Fats Domino; his 'When My Dreamboat Comes Home' was the first record that I ever bought. There was another bonus from being on the television. The studio audience were often friends of NBC employees, and many were wealthy teenage WASPy girls that came from uptown New York City – 5th Avenue, Park Avenue, Madison Avenue. Through them I got invited to a couple of teenage society parties; I was out of my social depth, but flirtation knows no boundaries. Several firsts happened as a result of joining The Crystals. We got a gig on a TV show in Detroit and we flew there in an eight-seater aircraft – it was my first flight. We got another gig in Washington DC and that was my first road trip. I had only ever been as far as Indiana and Florida on family holidays. I was not quite 16, but I'd met the Fat Man, flown in a plane, been 'on the road', and met some rich girls – life was good.

I had been listening to jazz records since I was 12 years old and from these I learned how to imitate bass lines from the likes of Milt Hinton and Charlie Mingus. I got to sound pretty convincing when I played with a drummer like Frank Steo – one of the best drummers I've ever worked with. We became good friends and I would lug my bass over to his parents' apartment and we would play for hours and hours on end. We would discuss the merits of playing in front of the beat, in the middle of the beat, or behind the beat. I was really fine-tuning my jazz chops and at the same time developing big thick calluses on my right hand; my little party trick was stubbing out a cigarette on my callus. The Crystals were also jazz players; pianist Jimmy Petricionne also played alto sax and we would jam in his parents' basement in Brooklyn. I still have tapes of Frank Steo, myself, and Danny Kalb, a guitarist – he went on to form the Blue Project with Al Kooper – and we sound great; almost like a Blue Note recording as it was done so well. I had a three-channel mixer into which I would stick three microphones, balance it and send the signal to my Dad's mono tape recorder; I got a really good sound. It was the beginning of my interest in the recording process. Jazz was my calling at this point, rock 'n' roll and what ever else I did, I did for the money. It wasn't until I heard the clarion call of the Beatles that I knew rock was *the* place to be. If people were going to write songs with chord changes like that, I wanted back in.

birth, bananas, heroin and marriage

My best friend, Bruce Tergesen, whose family was one of the few Norwegian families in our neighbourhood, made the mixer for me. Bruce was two years older than me and we had become friends when I was about ten years old. Bruce was also the first person I knew who had a transistor radio. He went to Brooklyn Technical High School and he was an electronics genius. He modified and improved the sound of a couple of vacuum tube radios for me, and also my Fender guitar amp and the tape recorder on which I made my early demos. Bruce had a brother called George who was ten years older than us; he and his wife Ruth introduced us to jazz.

My enthusiastic musical endeavours earned me a devastating ultimatum from my father. In the words of the do-wop classic by the Silhouettes – 'Getta job.'

'But Dad, I have a job.' I had a standing arrangement with a society band organizer, Lester Lanin, *the* big name in the world of society events bands. Each weekend I'd play weddings and bar mitzvahs; at 16 I looked pretty cool in a tuxedo. I'd play the standards on my conventional bass and then come out to the front and play and sing rock songs with my guitar. My father, who was working as a carpenter, couldn't get to grips with me lying on the couch during the week watching TV while he went out to work – it infuriated him, despite the fact that I was earning $100 a weekend – about the same as he was earning from working all week.

'Junior, you either get a job or you get out of this house. You can't rely on music, it's not steady work, what are you going to fall back on?'

I was offended, because I felt I was a professional musician with a union card, but no argument from me would convince my Dad, it all fell on deaf ears.

With this ultimatum hanging over me I got a phone call from

one of my society musician friends. 'There's a job going at Ben Maksik's Town and Country Club,' he told me.

This famous Brooklyn nightclub was run by Ben Maksik, who had worked in Las Vegas before deciding to bring Vegas to New York, and while he couldn't bring the gambling he could bring the opulent shows with high-kicking dancing girls, and singers such as Tony Bennett and comedians that included Buddy Hackett. The bass player in the house band had left and my friend, who didn't know how old I was, suggested me. But there was a problem, you had to be 18 to work in a nightclub and have a clean criminal record. Of course the latter was no problem and despite the age issue I still went for the audition with the leader of the house band, Ned Harvey. He had worked with just about everyone, and liked my playing very much. From my school experience I learned to sight-read Schubert's Symphony No 1 and *Finlandia* by Sibelius, so reading some simple band arrangements for bass was a breeze. As soon as I had auditioned I came clean.

'There's a bit of a problem here because I'm under eighteen.' I admitted.

'Just borrow somebody's card and then you can work here', was Ned's simple solution. As luck would have it a friend of my father's had a cabaret card but didn't use it any more, and so for a year and a half I was this guy. My money increased to $150 a week, and it was enough to convince my father that I had a proper job. I also got to play for a vast range of performers. There was Sophie Tucker, Robert Goulet, Jackie Mason, The Ritz Brothers, and even Milton Berle.

Uncle Miltie and I became great backstage friends – and yes, his penis is a foot long, and he willingly showed it to all and sundry. I had taken up karate and had lessons for a couple of years and one day he saw me practising backstage on a break and asked if I could teach it to him. I said, 'Sure, can you teach me some one-liners?' He was trained in burlesque and was a master of the one-liner. ('You've got some great material, too bad it's all in your suit.' 'You've got some great lines, too bad they're all in your face.') My parents and their friends came to see the cabaret show one night. I told 'Uncle Miltie' (his nick-name) that they would be sitting next to the stage. He spotted them instantly because, I guess, my dad and I resembled each other. He asked them to take a bow and pointed to me saying, 'These are the parents of the Karate Kid.'

Because he could never remember my name he always called me 'the karate kid'. This was 1960, years before the film was even written, or probably even thought of. He made my parents take a bow – it certainly convinced my Dad that I was now, at last, a real professional.

Tony Bennett came to the Town & Country club to play for several weeks. He brought his own rhythm section, piano, bass and drums, so I never played for him. Instead I'd wander around the club with my camera, armed with the fastest colour film available and a 135mm telephoto lens. One picture of Bennett came out really good and I showed it to him. He loved it. He invited me to meet him at Columbia Records the next day. He was releasing a new LP, and he wanted this photo for his cover. For an 18-year-old amateur photographer this was tantamount to winning the lottery. Next day I met him and the company's art director, a very smug, overtly gay man. He took a quick look at the transparency and said, 'Can't use it, we have so many like this already', and he walked off. The meeting lasted 15 seconds. Bennett turned to me, slightly embarrassed and said, 'Gee kid, I'm sorry. That's how it goes.' I was crushed but managed to hold back the tears. A few minutes later I was back on 7th Avenue in Manhattan and walked aimlessly downtown. I found a movie house playing *Mondo Cane*, a gross film about gross things, and sat in the darkness fuming and aching.

In the summer when the nightclub closed down Ned Harvey's band would play the Catskill Mountains. With Ned I played the Hotel Brickman, a glorified *Kochalain*, a Yiddish word for a collection of sprawling bungalows that seemed to have been thrown together – far from fancy. The Brickman was more than that; it was a proper hotel with a lobby, outdoor swimming pool and tennis courts. The band lived in a drafty wooden building with two bathrooms that were shared by about thirty of us. The Brickman is now an ashram run by Siddha Yoga Dham of America Foundation; the hotel closed down in the 1970s when New York's Jewish community found other places to vacation. Back then when people would enquire at what age the Brickman took children their proud boast was, 'If the kid breathes we'll take it.'

For three summers I would migrate the 110 miles north to what was popularly called the Borscht Belt, or the Jewish Alps, in upstate New York. Only nine of us made up the Ned Harvey Band during the summer, in New York the band numbered fourteen players. This was another fantastic period for my musical education during which I learned to write arrangements. Milton Anderson, a.k.a. Milton Drake, a baritone sax player was the band's arranger as well as a composer (he co-wrote, 'Mairzy Doats And Dozy Doats And Liddle Lamzy Divey'). He not only taught me how to write arrangements, he also showed me how to hold the italic pen correctly, and how to copy music from a pencilled page to a very professional-looking inked page and how to mix the ink. He had a very secret formula for mixing India ink with another ink so that the notes were embossed on the page. I owe this other Uncle Miltie a lot, and when he died he left me his darkroom equipment.

birth, bananas, heroin and marriage

In the Catskills I met many great players. Most Tuesday nights there was a jam happening somewhere. I got to play with jazz pianist Mike Abbeny and Eddie Gomez, a bass player with whom I felt great rivalry (I'll bet he never noticed me). There was also a great alto sax player called Artie Lawrence and all these guys went on to have stellar success in the jazz world. Eddie played with Bill Evans, and even turned down a job with Miles Davis. During my third summer in the Borscht Belt another band was working the hotel. The Del Capos, a five-piece band led by Speedy Garfin, an amazing sax player, which included a girl singer. They were so hip and cool and they did a lot of Louis Prima and Keeley Smith material, because it was Speedy's goal to head a Las Vegas lounge band.

"Sam" (not his real name), the Del Capos' piano player, was a heroin addict and this was the first time I came face to face with hard drugs, something of an occupational hazard. An affable pot-head called Freddie Klein had exposed me to marijuana during my first Brickman summer; he worked the hotel diner flipping burgers. Larry Rosen, the drummer from Ned's band and I would hang out with Freddie. Larry would later become the R in GRP Records, the highly successful jazz label he co-founded with Dave Grusin. The first time I smoked a joint we went back to the diner and watched Freddie at work. In the middle of eating our burgers and drinking our cokes through straws, disaster struck – the 'high' kicked in. For some unaccountable reason we looked at Freddie and began to laugh. We laughed so hard into the straws that it caused all the coke to be displaced and fly all over our clothes and all over the place. Freddie started laughing from behind the counter. Larry and I were laughing so uncontrollably we had to go outside and roll around on the forest floor, because we couldn't stand up.

Sam was a different proposition altogether. He had spent three years in London, which was where he became addicted to heroin. He got heroin on the National Health Service, which you could do very easily in those days, but was arrested in London for possessing marijuana. He spent about six months in prison before being unceremoniously deported back to New York. Sam became one of my music idols; he could play piano like Oscar Peterson, he was so cool – even down to his cool haircut. He was laconically cool, not at a real loss for words, but stoned on heroin. I didn't know that at first. There was another guy I befriended at this point called Frank and later I discovered he too was a heroin addict. This was the beginning of a very dark period in my life. I was 19 and heroin and I gradually became acquainted.

When I first took the ugly drug I had a very bad experience. The buzz lasted all of five minutes and then I spent the next few hours just vomiting uncontrollably. I vomited because I wasn't yet an addict. I was encouraged to take it again by Sam and Frank, to give it a chance. From then on I didn't vomit, which meant I was getting what was called a 'Jones'. I would say that I flirted with heroin for a while, and was addicted for about a three-month period. There was a doctor in New York who would prescribe methadone but only enough to use through withdrawal (a seven-day supply). It was expensive. I managed to keep it a secret from my parents for most of the time, although eventually my mother did find my hypodermic needle (you can't hide anything from Mum); she discovered my 'works' in a hollowed out book and she was wise enough not to tell my father, who would've beat me to a pulp – he was very old-school and behaved exactly as his father had done when it came to discipline. She saw me through one methadone pro-gramme and I managed to stay off the drug for a long time.

There was another risk about being an addict in New York City. It meant that to acquire heroin you needed to go to some very bad neighbourhoods. Sometimes I used to go up to Harlem, but only when things were really desperate. For a young white guy it was a very dangerous place to go. I was nearly mugged on several occasions and came close to being arrested once. My main procurer was a waiter, who exacted a high price for his services and would slowly and cruelly fix in front of me before I was able to use his works. A typical hazard of addiction is to overdose, it happened to me twice; luckily both times I was with friends who knew exactly what to do. They injected a saline solution into my veins to nullify the effects of the heroin and walked me around the room so I didn't die. Many people in a similar predicament were not so lucky, either their friends would panic or wouldn't know what to do. I heard stories of overdosed users who were dragged up stairs onto an apartment roof and left to die.

Despite the horrors of heroin there was, bizarrely, in my case a positive that came out of all this. Many of my friends from high school had already gone to fight in Vietnam, and a number of them had been killed in combat. When I was twenty I got the letter I had been dreading from Uncle Sam. It said 'Greetings you have been selected to fight in the armed forces of America.' 'Great, now they're going to make a man out of you,' was how my Father greeted the news.

I went to the appointed place, at the appointed time, and sat in a room full of men all about my age. In came this US Army sergeant who began yelling at us.

'Everybody, listen up! You're in the army right now. You're about to take an IQ test. If you fuck up this test you're in the army anyway, but you're going to spend the next four years of your life doing KP, that's kitchen patrol, so you better not fuck up on this test, you better do your best. If you do your best you are going to get promoted quickly, you might even apply for private, you might be a private first class in six months.'

People pay thousands for motivational speakers like this these days! He was on a roll. 'You're going to have a blood test first and while it's being analysed you're going to take the IQ test, which is about two hours long.'

This confirmed what I had already decided to do the night before. I didn't want to join the army and die in Vietnam. Like millions of Americans I saw this war as unnecessary and immoral. If we were under attack as a nation I would volunteer to defend my country, but I wasn't having any of this. I wasn't prepared to leave anything to chance. By this point in my life I was, strictly speaking, off heroin. However, I shot up with a friend the night before, I had heard that the army was rejecting addicts yet this was a big risk. I thought I could be reported to the police if things went wrong. After I had the blood test I took the IQ test and answered the questionnaire. I admitted to using drugs. I was standing in line in my underpants with about 500 other inductees, waiting for our physical examination when I heard, 'Visconti, get dressed and follow me.'

I was ushered into an office where a man in a suit, sporting wire-rimmed glasses and a goatee, an aspiring Sigmund Freud who turned out to be a psychiatrist, turned to me and said in a thick German accent, 'You have passed your IQ test.'

That was lucky I thought; maybe the blood test wasn't foolproof? What was I doing here talking to Dr Freud?

'You seem to have scored high, but on the questionnaire you indicated here that you have frequent and terrifying nightmares and you take drugs. Which drugs do you take?'

'All of them.' I said.

'What?' he said. 'What, drugs?'

'Well, everything, barbiturates, amphetamines, marijuana, heroin.'

'Are you an addict?'

I hesitated; maybe it was a trick question. 'Yes,' I carefully admitted.

'Would you like to not be an addict? Would you like to quit?' he asked.

This was the $64,000 question. If I say yes, what is he going to do to me? Am I going to be arrested, or sent to some kind of institution? If I say no I might be arrested anyway, would he tell the police, because I didn't cooperate? My brain was short-circuiting. But I thought I might as well play out this drama as planned.

'Yes.'

'Yes, to what?' he asked me.

'Yes I'm an addict and yes I'd like to quit.'

The truth was, this was the truth. I had already tried using methadone, which I had to acquire illegally, but I continued to use heroin occasionally. The German psychiatrist started writing some stuff down and said, 'Well since you are being so candid with me and you want to quit I will put down that you are rejected from the army because of neurological reasons.'

Even though there was a box for drug addiction he ticked the box that said 'neurological' and showed it to me. 'It will go on your permanent army record that you are a 4F classification, which means you are unable to serve. You will never be allowed in the army!' With this he concluded my session and sent me downstairs to meet a colleague.

'There, they'll make arrangements for your rehabilitation.'

This sent me into a flat spin, I had a gig that night, and there was no time for rehabilitation. Feeling trapped by my own actions, I trooped downstairs to see a very nice woman who had the demeanour of a loving mother. She was thin, with her hair piled on top of her head in a big bun and wore overlarge horn-rimmed glasses. She looked at me kindly and compassionately and said, 'President Kennedy is appalled that fifty per cent of the men called up to serve are ineligible. The two main reasons for this are drug addiction and homosexuality and the United States government now had a programme that will cure young men of both, and then try to rehabilitate them.' I understood being rehabilitated for drugs, but was baffled by curing homosexuality. The US Government still thought of it as a disease. She went on to ask me lots of questions about why I used drugs.

'It's an occupational hazard. Everywhere I turn in the music business I see drugs. If it's not marijuana it's amphetamines or heroin – I just got unlucky,' I explained.

'Do you think drugs make you play better?' she asked.

'Well, they made Charlie Parker play really good,' was my quick retort.

'Yes? But imagine how Charlie Parker would have sounded if he didn't use drugs,' she countered. She had a point. I still felt cautious about what I should or shouldn't say. I wanted to debate further but I thought it best to get out of there unscathed. I was told I had automatically volunteered to attend group therapy sessions and I agreed. That was it; I walked through the door and out into the street.

These sessions were on Saturday mornings, in downtown Brooklyn, close to where I had grown up. The first thing they did was to give me a prescription for methadone. For the first time in my life I had a legal prescription, and I didn't really need it; I was totally committed to not taking heroin anymore. The army induction episode scared me. More than that, I started to scare me. If I hadn't made up my mind to quit, the experience I had to face up to would have done it for me. Everyone in the group were still hard-core addicts, most of the guys were thieves. They would interlace their stories of shooting up heroin with how they had broken into a car the night before or how they stole anything they could; I just sat there wide-eyed. The most appalling thing were the girls, who were my age and younger; they all entered the world of prostitution. I was sitting in the company of girls describing painful anal rape and guys bragging about stealing hubcaps – it was surreal.

When it came time for me to speak I repeated what I had told the psychoanalyst.

'It's an occupational hazard. I'm a musician. I don't steal. I earn money by playing music, I just like to take drugs, that's all.'

Without exception they looked at me with utter disgust, including the group leader. I hardly ever spoke again in the group. After six months in the programme I told the group leader that I truly felt I had been cured. During that time I never once touched heroin. He gave me a deep look and simply said, 'OK.' Three per cent of addicts never go back on heroin. I was one of the lucky – and determined – ones.

That's the happy ending to a very dark and horrible period. I had been spending all my money, my entire salary, on the drug. I had even borrowed money from my grandmother on occasions. I never stole, but I had some very, very desperate, dark moments when I was a millimetre away from the bottom of the barrel. Using heroin is not clever, it's not creative and rock 'n' roll has mythologized its use. Those therapy sessions exposed the reality of 'heroin chic' for me.

I would only tell this story to confidants over the years; I was very embarrassed about this period of my life, about using heroin and loads of other drugs. I was off heroin when I had to go up in front of the Draft board, but I was determined not go to Vietnam, so this was a very drastic measure for a 20-year-old. Believe me, I was scared shitless on that day.

The group therapy was so God-awful it sorted me out. My heroin-using friends hated me for stopping, as I was one of the few amongst us that worked steadily and I could always be relied on for a fix. But when I quit I had the wisdom to never tempt myself again so I stopped seeing those friends completely. I told my parents that I was not drafted for 'neurological reasons', the same excuse the psychiatrist used on my military record for volunteering for therapy. My father turned to me in disgust and said, 'That's a shame. The army could've made a man out of you.' My mother, though, was overjoyed; this was a time of conscription, so lots of young men my age were drafted for that war, and I lost a couple of friends.

My friendship with Speedy Garfin and the rest of his band continued when we returned to New York. I ended up joining the band, replacing both the girl singer and Sam the piano player. To me Speedy was a kind of rock star and being the fourth member in a group with him was far more rewarding artistically. I sang the girl's part, in a high falsetto, but instead of playing bass I played the guitar. We played a nightclub on the East Side of Manhattan run by one of the ladies referred to in the song, 'Lullaby Of Broadway': 'she's a classy broad,' as Sinatra would have said. She was brassy, sassy and on the wrong side of fifty, but she commanded respect. The club boasted a varied clientele, including the local priest who came in once a week to drink at the bar, only leaving after he got a donation for his church. There were people that worked in the neighbourhood, actors and actresses, members from other bands; we also had the Mob drop in fairly regularly.

'The Don' would always arrive with eleven or so of his closest friends – mostly guys but also a few women as well. I only knew him as 'The Don' and he always brought with him a handsome young guy of about eighteen or nineteen. Speedy had a party piece – 'Come Back To Sorrento' – during which he would drop down on one knee and play his soprano saxophone with great intensity. The very first time we played it 'The Don' sent one of his 'friends' to us who said, 'He wants you guys to have this.'

He handed us a $100 bill, which was a lot of money in 1963, even when it was split four ways. The next time 'The Don' was in we played 'Come Back To Sorrento' and we all got down on one knee, threw our heads back and looked as passionate as we could. We got another $100. This ritual was played out many times.

One such evening 'The Don' himself got up from the table and came up to me. This was most disarming because he was a very large man with unquestionable dubious credentials.

'Hey kid can I talk to you.'

I gulped and said, 'Sure.'

'You know that kid I always bring with me,' said 'The Don', pointing to the young boy at the table. 'He's an actor. He's my protégé. He likes guys, and he likes you, and he wants you to come home with him tonight, is that OK with you?'

'Well, I – I – I don't know,' I stammered. 'I'm really not that way, I've never done anything like that before.'

'Hey, come on, how old are you kid?'

At this point 'The Don' moved even closer to me and I was eclipsed by his height and girth. I told him I was nineteen and this caused him to become somewhat exasperated.

'You're nineteen, you know when I was nineteen I didn't know if I liked boys or girls. I mean, you know, what's the difference, what's the big deal? Come on kid are you going to go with him or not?' He was practically shouting in my ear.

I was getting to the point I could barely speak; I couldn't believe that this was happening to me.

'I – I – I – I don't know.' But he was not taking no for an answer.

'Hey listen, he was just with Tony Curtis the other night' (this couldn't be true, he was just trying to impress me) '. . . this kid is a good looking guy he can have anybody he wants.'

I was terrified and confused. I'd be damned if I do and I'd be damned if I don't. They'll throw me in a car and I'll end up with a pair of cement boots. I had no idea what to do; my brain simply froze with 'The Don' hovering over me waiting for a decision. In the middle of this sleazy Zen dilemma, Buddy Monticelli, our bass player, appeared from behind the curtain where he'd been listening to the conversation.

'Can I have a word with you?' says Buddy to 'The Don', in Italian.

He nodded his head and casts me a dirty look. Buddy took him aside talking to him all the while in Italian. Within a minute 'The Don' came back over to me and said, 'It's okay kid, I didn't know you were married.'

Buddy, thinking on his feet, fabricated a story that I married a nice Italian girl very young and we had kids. As I was in that most sanctimonious of Catholic Italian institutions I was excused from 'The Don's' plans of debauchery with his protégé. As beautiful as the song is, 'Come Back To Sorrento' will always remind me of that frightening evening.

We did gigs in other parts of America, including six weeks at a Holiday Inn in Scottsdale Arizona – it was fantastic. The band was no longer called the Del Capos, instead we were The Speedy Garfin Quartet and, given our leader's ambition, our repertoire was Las Vegas lounge-style that included songs like 'Jeepers Creepers' and '(Your Kisses Take Me To) Shangri-La' – all in four part harmony. We played instrumentals and lots of Sinatra's songs because the drummer, Tony De Mar, could really nail Frank. Buddy Monticelli also had his own version of a Sinatra voice; we were a very versatile group.

While I was in Arizona I would often take the bus to downtown Phoenix, a world apart from Brooklyn or anywhere on the East Coast. I even went 'native' and bought myself a cowboy shirt and a belt with a silver buckle. I slept out under the stars at Camel Back Mountain one night and was dwarfed by 14-foot saguaro cacti in the daytime. I shared a room on this trip with Speedy who would often go off to stay at the home of a girl he had met. One day while he was away Tony and Buddy were with me in my room when Tony noticed Speedy's wallet on top of the TV. Tony cheekily opened it and inside the wallet there was a note saying 'Tony you are not worth the paper this note is written on. You stole the money from my wallet and may you and the other two guys in the band go to hell.' The three of us froze; we were innocent. I had no idea that there had been a theft in our room, but from here on the morale of the band went downhill. When Speedy came back I told him it wasn't me, and even to me the explanation of how we discovered the theft seemed dishonestly shallow. He just said, 'Don't talk to me.' He was totally contemptuous of me.

On that sour note we went back to New York to play a month's residency at a nightclub in Queens, New York. Two weeks before the run ended Speedy said, 'That's it, I'm breaking up the band at the end of the run, and this is your two weeks' notice.' With that he slammed our week's salary on the table and walked out.

After our dismissal from Speedy's band Tony, Buddy and I became the Crew Cuts. That's to say we joined original member Rudi Maugeri on the road. They had had a No 1 record in 1954 with a cover of the Chords hit 'Sh-Boom', and a year later went top three with 'Earth Angel', a song originally recorded by the Penguins. There are some people prepared to argue that 'Sh-Boom' is the first rock 'n' roll record, but that would definitely be stretching a point. Rudi kept the group going after the others had drifted away. We played a seaside concert hall in Atlantic City, New Jersey. Our last gigs were played in the Far East –

The Philippines, Japan, Korea and Okinawa, mainly at US armed forces bases. I turned 21 during this period. Our first gig as the Crew Cuts was playing a five-day residency at a club in Tulsa, Oklahoma.

Tulsa was a strange place. There were no public bars then, you had to buy a bottle from an off licence or a state liquor store and then you gave it to the bartender and he would write your name on it. Every time he poured you a drink he would make a mark; this was the law. On our first night in Tulsa the owner poured us a round or two from his bottle, but we had to buy our own bottle of tipple the next day. When we had our first drink with him he said we would have no problem finding 'poontang' in his club. We didn't know what he meant by the word, but we soon worked it out.

The crowd was middle aged, the Crew Cut generation, but two beautiful, younger women were sitting by themselves and making eyes at us. Two of us in the band introduced ourselves and were invited to sit with them. One of the women was about my own age, her name was Siegrid and I found out that she was recently separated from her husband. She was blonde, elegantly dressed, had pronounced Nordic cheek bones, cat's eyes and a beautiful figure. She told me she had married very young, and she too had just turned 21. The other woman turned out to be her sister-in-law, who was also estranged from her husband.

I discovered later that Siegrid had married a wealthy uranium prospector who was twenty years her senior. Despite having everything money could buy, their marriage was not working out. They lived alone in a building he owned made up of nine apartments, all of which were empty except the one they lived in and another where Siegrid's cats lived.

For Siegrid and me it really was love at first sight. The following night she and her sister-in-law were there again and afterwards I took her back to the hotel where I was staying. We talked all night, we felt like we had so much to say to each other. This was the woman I had been waiting for, an intelligent, beautiful soul mate.

We talked much about philosophy and spirituality and I confessed to having had some remarkable spiritual experiences with LSD. I had taken two acid trips to date. She listened wide-eyed. 'I have two doses with me,' I told her. 'Oh goody, let's take it right now,' was her immediate reaction.

Within an hour the drug had taken effect and we were surfing the cosmos together, my first time with another person. We were having the same symbolic experience, a total appreciation for each other as the female and male principles, the Yin and the Yang, transforming visually into Hindu gods and goddesses. We could both hear the music of the cosmos and see colours beyond the range of human experience. We were melting into each other.

It was one of those great acid trips – no down moments, no bummers, and no bad heads, nothing negative. When the sun came up we were so happy we got in the car and drove to the roof of a supermarket, a car park as large as the supermarket beneath it. We were the only people there. We got out and spontaneously sang songs from *West Side Story* and danced around the roof. We were inseparable after that and consummated our relationship on the third night.

On the last night that Siegrid and I spent together she said she was going to leave her husband. I told her I was going to break up with my girlfriend Bunny immediately by telephone and I did. We phoned each other everyday for three weeks and Siegrid announced that she wanted to come to NYC to live with me. My parents didn't know what to think, but they agreed to have Siegrid live with us. We spent a year of bliss in the converted loft atop my parents' apartment, which I helped my father and uncle to build for me when I was 16.

Unfortunately life wasn't pure bliss. We needed money because I quit working with the Crew Cuts. There was no question of getting a normal job, this was the '60s; it was unthinkable. A partial solution was Siegrid's valuable jewellery, which she sold without telling me. We were able to live off that for a while. One morning, after what was probably our twentieth acid trip, we were listening to the radio and said almost simultaneously, 'We can do better than that!' We were so disgusted with the current songs on Pop radio. We started writing songs together that day. I taught her how to sing harmony, and sometimes she would take the lead and I would do the more difficult harmonies. We wrote for two voices almost always, for us to perform. Soon we were doing gigs around New York as Tony & Siegrid.

After surviving a couple of abortive attempts at securing a manager and a dreadful audition with songsmiths Jerry Lieber and Mike Stoller, we somehow ended up at The Richmond Organization (TRO). Company boss, Howard Richmond, had started in the business as a publisher; his first published song, 'Put Another Nickel In The Nickelodeon', became a huge hit. He later signed many successful American songwriters including one of my favourites, Pete Seeger. We were assigned to a publisher/manager called Marvin Caine who had an A&R friend, Danny Davis at RCA Records, and that's how we ended up with a recording deal. We wrote what we thought were some really good songs, and till this day I still wonder if we had had a more sympathetic A&R man and producer then maybe we could have achieved something much greater. Unfortunately, out of the whole batch of songs that we had written Danny picked a quasi hillbilly song called 'Long Hair'. We wrote this song as a novelty/comedy song for our live shows. It was kind of our 'fuck you' song to rednecks, albeit the Brooklyn variety. Back in '65 it wasn't easy having long hair. 'Are you a boy or a girl? Are you a boy or a girl?' I have heard many men of my generation brag that the proper retort was, 'Suck my cock and find out!' I am dubious that you would escape without a severe beating if you said that in a diner in Kansas. I'd hear this question over and over again every day and when we travelled anywhere out of New York City it would be even worse. We seemed threatening and we were threatened, sometimes with implied violence.

As a debut single I detested 'Long Hair'; it's an awful song.

Long hair, long hair so you think I'm queer,
Well hush up your mouth and chugalug your beer,
Because I don't really care what you think of my long hair.

It was a wordy song with intentional 'r's in them so we could sound like real hillbillies. 'Long hairrr, long hairrr' – we'd stretch out those 'r's for as long as possible. Ironically it started to get airplay on New York radio. One guy who loved it was a DJ called Zacherly. As a 'VJ' in the 1950s he would dress up as a ghoul on late night television and introduce horror films from the 1930s and '40s. He would cut in scenes of himself into these films where he would do things like chop a slimy cauliflower in half, pretending it was a human brain. But he loved 'Long Hair' and played it so much it became a minor local hit. I think it reached the 30s in a local singles chart for a week before it dropped out.

Having saved a little money, Siegrid and I left my parents' house and moved to 50 West 88th Street, which was only half a block from Central Park. Here we continued to drop acid and some-times communed with nature in the park. At New York's first 'Be-In' (the precursor to 'Love-Ins'), about 10,000 of us descended on the park where we openly smoked pot and formed a long human daisy chain. We held hands and ran through the park screaming and laughing. We wore beads and had flowers in our hair and our trousers were flared. We witnessed in awe Alan Ginsburg and his lover Peter Orlof sitting on a big boulder openly smoking a joint. The New York police were powerless; it wasn't that they didn't dare do anything, they were just bemused by it all – one or two cops even had flowers stuck in their caps.

Being signed to TRO meant I was spending more time there than writing songs and I was getting into some production work. I used to make demos in a little studio that was in the same building as Atlantic Records, which is where my childhood friend Bruce Tergesen had gone to work. Bruce came to my 9th floor studio one day and said, 'Yeah, that sounds really cool. Let me have your tape and I will go down and play it to Tom Dowd.' Dowd was the electrical genius that put Atlantic Studios together and also became a legendary producer. Now and then Bruce would sneak me into Atlantic Records, so I could sit at the back of the room to witness a few recording sessions. One such session, not long before I met Denny Cordell, was when Arif Mardin was adding the orchestra to Aretha Franklin's 'You Make Me feel Like A Natural Women'; it was fantastic to see an orchestral overdub session, my first. At some point Mardin came into the control room for a playback and was not pleased. He seemed to address everyone in the room in his Turkish accent, 'Something's not sounding right, what's not sounding right?'

I tapped Bruce on the shoulder and whispered to him that the French horns were out of tune.

'My friend Tony here said the French horns are out of tune,' said Bruce. I thought I was going to die and be evicted for being so bold, in that order. Instead Arif had it played again and said, 'Your friend is right.'

By the way, through Bruce I got a pithy answer from Tom Dowd regarding my own demo: 'Tom says, "More bass".'

chapter 2
london makes its marc

Now that I was doing what I'd dreamed of for so long, I started to settle in London. For a while I stayed at Denny Cordell's flat on the Fulham Road but I needed to find somewhere a little more permanent as life there was crowded; there's only so long that anyone could be expected to sleep on a sofa. Besides which I also had to get to grips with washing my hair in the bath – why don't they have showers in this country, was all I kept thinking? My plans were somewhat fluid, as I only anticipated being in London for six months, which certainly made me determined to enjoy every minute of my stay and not miss out on a single experience. Professionally my goal was to learn how they made records with alchemy rather than with equipment. On the cover of the *Magical Mystery Tour* EP were some words about four wizards and a grand wizard, alluding to the Beatles and George Martin – I took this literally. I knew, as I walked down Fulham Road to the tube station, that I loved London – the people, the funny money. I was in a movie, my own *A Hard Day's Night*. I knew I was in way over my head but something inside me kept saying, you could get ahead in this city; with hindsight I suspect that everyone else was too. I kept telling myself, I will learn the arcane arts of British recording and someday I'll be a mover and a shaker here. I was what would later be called 'driven' – back then I was just a crazy Yank.

It was confusing to me that most London streets only went on for a few blocks before they ceased to exist. New York is a grid city, mostly. I grew up on 74th and 11th; I went to school on 79th and 16th; the subway was on 69th and 11th. In New York I always knew where I was and where I was going. It took me *months* to get familiar with my London surroundings; in the first few weeks I walked a lot.

London accents were probably the hardest to fathom. I saw *A Hard Day's Night* and *Help!* a total of 30 times or so, and I knew the Scouse accent of course; I just wasn't prepared for the Cockney accent. Even a thick Glaswegian accent was easier to understand. I would tilt my head sideways like a dog and try to understand this new, twisted English.

I noticed that there weren't many young kids that were dressed like the Beatles or the Stones. Most people just had ordinary jobs and dressed rather dowdy. But I was totally impressed when I saw a long-haired guy wearing a military jacket from Portobello Road – that's what I expected to see – but the ratio of hipster-to-square person was about the same as New York at the time. I wore my hair long in London and I was stared at and sometimes sneered at by the older generation. Girls in miniskirts drove me crazy. Skirts were short in New York but in London girls were wearing their skirts unbelievably short, maybe just an inch or two below their most delicate parts. I'm sure I strained my neck many times – before I was joined by my wife.

The food was awful. The Wimpy burger tasted like dog meat. Coffee was as bland as dishwater. Fortunately I liked tea, as my mother used to make it with milk and sugar although most New Yorkers took it with just lemon. I realized very quickly that I had to learn words for food, like chips for French Fries, etc. I wasn't used to eggs fried in oil either. They tasted disgusting. But I did like British sweets and cookies, known as biscuits. I discovered digestive biscuits with and without chocolate covering and often made a meal of a packet. I loved English milk, it was far tastier and richer than American milk.

The British money system just didn't make sense at all. I'm sure I was taken advantage of in the first few weeks. Not only were there 240 pennies in the pound but each coin also had a few different names to memorize. There was a half crown, but there was no crown. There was a ten shilling note that was referred to as a ten bob note, and a sixpence piece, that many called a tanner. None of this made sense. Just when I became familiar with the system Britain went decimal.

Of course I couldn't take a shower wherever I lived. Washing my hair was an ordeal; I don't think I ever satisfactorily rinsed it out with a saucepan or two of water.

Television and radio were very disappointing. Radio hardly played rock or pop. I had to tune into Radio Luxembourg for the hour or so that they played music in the evening. Radio Caroline was okay although the signal was weak. But the DJs were awful; they sounded old and had a patter like vaudevillian comedians. The television was all of three channels then and they flickered off between 11 p.m. and midnight. That's it, all of Britain was meant to go to bed like well-behaved children. If I wasn't working in the studio everyday with Denny Cordell I would've gone back, there was nothing else exciting to do in those first few months.

One thing that was very obvious was English reserve. In the '60s in New York you could make a good friend within 15 minutes of meeting the person. Americans were always more informal than the British and the heady Flower Power made us 'all one'. This was not so in London during the same period. My wife was told at a Sunday tea party that we were not of their 'set'. I think it took a year to make a good English friend, although it was easier to be more casual with musicians.

Denny Cordell became a good friend the first day we met, and during those early days in London I went everywhere with Denny and learned his routine, although there was little routine about it – it was insane. Denny was a guy who couldn't say no. He was also at the top of his game, which made everything possible; he couldn't turn down anything, especially if it was cool and lucrative. He was recording Manfred Mann, the Move, Procol Harum and Denny Laine simultaneously at sessions catered with tea, digestive biscuits and spliffs. These Jamaican-styled hashish joints were a revelation to me and despite their strength Denny could still recite the table of elements while he smoked. My tolerance was far less and cocaine was not yet in fashion. Being at Denny's beck and call twenty-four hours a day was very definitely worth it for the experience. It allowed me to infiltrate the sanctity of British recording studios and I was a quick learner. During my first month in London I heard a white label of *Sgt. Pepper's Lonely Hearts Club Band* and that alone was worth the price of admission.

Records like *Sgt. Pepper* were the result of all night sessions and so there was a downside to all this. As budgets grew larger, tempers grew shorter. To this day I am still dealing with the anxiety of recording artists who want to sound great, and better than their competition. It was ever thus, but as a novice in 1967 I had to learn about this. Recording in New York was still a superficial process compared to the depth and attention to detail that was going on in London. But I said to myself, 'if this is the way the Brits do it I have to learn.'

Denny had recently become an Associate Producer at Deram, a division of Decca Records, which is how I met Tony Hall. He was in charge of Deram's PR Department and for a while he put me up in his flat; I moved up from a sofa to my own bedroom. Tony had been a radio DJ in the early '60s and he was working hard at promoting the careers of the Move, Denny Laine and

Procol Harum. The contrast between Tony's two-floor flat in Mayfair's Green Street and Denny's basement flat could not have been greater. I was only just getting to grips with London's geography and had no idea about the demographics of London neighbourhoods, but I quickly realized that Mayfair was 'posh' (another new word for me). Tony was a lot more conventionally British than Denny. He wore cardigans and suits as an executive for Deram, but most amazing of all – he had short hair. Then again he must have been in his forties, which to me, aged 23 (just), was ancient. But he said something that made it all right with me to live at his place: 'I went to George Harrison's home in Henley-On-Thames. When I arrived along with some other people George opened a little Indian pill case he was wearing around his neck. He pulled out an acid tab and popped it into each of our mouths. I had no idea what I was taking, but soon found myself on a ten-hour acid trip. I had the most awful time, people's faces became grotesque; it was my first and last acid trip.'

Maybe so, but dropping acid with a Beatle made you instantly cool in my mind.

It was through Denny's deal with Deram that I began working with Denny Laine, who was so easy to get along with by comparison to the Manfreds. Twenty-three-year-old Denny had been the lead singer with the Moody Blues who had a No 1 in the UK with a cover of Bessie Banks's, 'Go Now'. The band had split up in late summer 1966 and while they had reunited with new members, Justin Hayward and John Lodge, almost immediately, Denny pursued a solo career.

There must be something in the name Denny because DL was as adept at making spliffs as DC. I became close to Denny L early on, especially as Siegrid did not arrive in London until the latter half of May. I would go to his flat over a Greek diner in

Moscow Street, Bayswater and work out things with him; I wrote the string arrangements for his Electric String Band. He had a guitar stringing ritual that always amazed me. It started with rolling a giant spliff. Then he'd put the first string on, wind it up to the correct pitch and improvise a long, usually Eastern-flavored melody on the one string. Then, after several pulls on the spliff he would wind on the next string and improvise a two-string melody, which was usually a rock riff oriented thing on the low E and A strings. This would continue with each string, wind–play–smoke, wind–play–smoke. An hour later the guitar would be strung up, in tune and we'd be stoned out of our minds. Our subsequent recording sessions were fairly unfocused, and no wonder. Denny Cordell would be in charge, we'd have a room full of great musicians, the string players came from the Royal Academy of Music, but Denny Laine would just run out of steam after a few hours. He'd say that he had great ideas for this section or that section, but nothing was ever finished, save for one song – 'Say You Don't Mind'. This was a small hit on British radio and a promise of great things to come, but Denny had a habit of leaving things unfinished.

One of the greatest experiences I had in the short time since arriving in London was to write five string arrangements for Denny Laine and then have them played on the stage of the Shaftsbury Theatre at a rock show. Jimi Hendrix was also on that bill and Denny Cordell grabbed me backstage saying, 'Visconti, come, you must see this.' Hendrix poured lighter fluid on his Stratocaster and threw a lighted match on it – so that's why two members of the Fire Brigade were standing in the wings, one with an axe in his hands and the other with a fire extinguisher. The audience went berserk and I was just horrified. It would take me years to save up for a Stratocaster.

After Denny's set, which was very well received, Tony Hall came on stage and asked me to come out from the wings to take a bow as the arranger. I wasn't expecting this at all. I was introduced as a young, up-and-coming record producer from New York City and he told them that they'd be hearing lots of good things about me very soon. It's a good thing I was only told *afterwards* that the Beatles and the Stones were in the audience as I might have embarrassed myself.

I had already seen Hendrix at the Speakeasy a few nights after landing at Heathrow. I sat next to Kit Lambert, the producer of The Who's *Happy Jack*, one of my favourite records. I was anxious to ask him how he got the sound on the record. It reminded me of *Not Fade Away* on which you can hear the reverb of a small room, like there must have been just a few mics picking up the slap back coming off the walls. This was typical of me back then, I used to imagine how records were made because there were no books or college courses teaching the art of production. I would try to mentally picture how things were done, which served me well when I started producing myself. Kit had no recollection of recording *Happy Jack*; in fact I was looking into the eyes of a very vacant man that night. He was already into advanced stages of whatever. He died after a coke dealer pushed him downstairs but he was on other things too, like Mandrax, a hypnotic drug; he was certainly zonked out that night. Hendrix got up to jam about 1 a.m. They never even put a spotlight on him; he literally played in the dark. I don't know who played drums or bass but it wasn't the Experience. Hendrix was really great. After two long jams Denny said, 'We've got a 10 a.m. start tomorrow, we need to get going.'

Denny Laine was another who was caught up with the whole business of how records were made. He had ideas about how the Beatles did it and urged Paul McCartney to give him some insights. According to Laine, Paul would say in a session, 'I want you to set up this kinda loop thing where I keep taping guitar solos and then I could go back and take guitar solo number 7 and mix it with guitar solo 9.' It was sort of multi-tracking meets electronics, but nothing like that had been invented yet. McCartney misled him, as a prank, making up fantasy techniques. As a believer in recording alchemy I almost believed it. But it got ridiculous: if some big star, especially a Beatle, had said, 'I plunged the microphone into a bucket of water', some people would rush off and do it and destroy perfectly good microphones. It was a strange, strange period – but really exciting.

Being a guest at Tony Hall's flat had one particular downside; I had to help with feeding his two cats, a valuable Abyssinian and a common fat, black cat. This was a nice arrangement for a couple of weeks, but I felt a growing familiarity with Tony, which made me feel uncomfortable. We would often chat late into the night over a few drinks, as I didn't know anybody and had no place to go. I began to feel a little trapped in this luxurious apartment with this well-spoken man in his 40s. I imagined that he had other interests in me than just friendship. I was wary of such attention because I was hit on by gay men throughout my teens. Tony never hit on me, I'm sure it was all in my imagination, but in this first month in London I didn't know how to read a social situation yet. Things were very different here. I felt more secure once Siegrid arrived from New York and came to live at the Hall residence.

When I had gone to the airport to meet Siegrid I was unprepared for what she'd done. She had cut off all her beautiful long blonde hair and had a very short boyish cut; it didn't really suit her. She had an Indian prayer shawl draped around her shoulders and carried a spiritualist book in her hand. She topped it all off by wearing wire-rimmed glasses, which she had never worn before. She had changed dramatically; especially with a holier-than-thou attitude she'd adapted in the month we were apart. The first casualty of this situation was our sex life – it stopped. Tony Hall did not like Siegrid and our nightly chats had come to an abrupt end. Siegrid and I kept his flat immaculately clean and tended to the cats' needs which included cleaning out the stinky litter tray. As a couple our stay was very brief. Soon after Siegrid arrived we left in search of a place of our own.

Besides working with Denny Laine during the few weeks that I stayed in Mayfair I also worked with Denny C on Procol Harum. He was frantically trying to finish their first album at his favourite studio, Olympic in Barnes, a state-of-the-art studio across the river from Hammersmith. A Whiter Shade Of Pale came out at the end of May and was a huge hit. One evening Denny and I were walking in the hallway that separated Studios A and B and bumped into Brian Jones; he was there working on tracks for an album that would become Their Satanic Majesties Request. Brian was dressed in what looked like a French noble-man's jacket in a shade of blue and made of crushed velvet, with frilly, laced cuffs sticking out; he was also wearing makeup. If I'd approached him from a distance, and had seen him coming towards me, I might have taken this in my stride, but we liter-ally bumped into him as we turned a corner. I was shocked.

'Hey man, I love the Procol Harum single. I heard it on Radio Caroline, and I've just sent my chauffeur out to buy it for me.' I was struck by how well spoken he was.

Denny introduced me to Brian though I was still reeling to see such a (well, there is no other word for it) fop in a record-ing studio; it wasn't the 'uniform'. Of course, Brian was at the forefront of creating that hippy chic look. I was still a scruffy guy with jeans and a pale blue workman's shirt, which was what everyone was wearing in New York; I even had a pocket flap with a hole for a pencil to go through.

The Rolling Stones were in Studio A, which was a lot bigger than B; the latter was adequate enough to record a rock group or a small string section. In Studio B I was assisting Denny with the Procol Harum album, but it was far from smooth sailing. Denny was having a problem with the band's drummer and Denny's solution was simple: he fired him in the middle of a session. Cordell had very high expectations for drummers and this one was not the first to feel his displeasure. In contrast Gary Brooker and Matthew Fisher were a joy to work with, and Keith Reid was always lurking in the background overseeing the entire affair. He made me feel like he knew more than anyone about what was really going on in the studio – only he wouldn't tell us because that would be cheating.

Studio A was an enormous cine stage studio with a screen and a projector; it was used for film scores. After the Stones left, Dudley Moore was in doing a score for some film, while we were in B with Procol Harum. We had to be very quiet for about 30 minutes while he recorded a little piano motif with three flutes.

One aspect of that first Procol Harum album that I couldn't get my head around was the fact that it was in mono; stereo was still regarded as inconceivable for rock music or pop in Britain. In New York groups like the Lovin' Spoonful and others were experimenting with stereo and I found it weird that in England, where they were making superior sounding records, stereo was mostly a no-go. It certainly answered my question as to why there were no stereograms in the homes of British people I visited; David Platz had supplied me with one for my flat.

The fact that Siegrid and I had to do some flat hunting tempered the joys of working. We eventually found a two-storey flat in Elgin Avenue. Our flat led out to the garden from the basement; the bedroom and rear living room was down there. Upstairs was another living room and a second bedroom where we kept instruments and a writing table for Siegrid. It may sound quite nice but the walls were damp and there was plenty of mould. It was a furnished flat with furniture that would have been old around the start of the War. There was a small bathtub, a larder but no fridge, and the electricity worked only when we put a shilling in the meter; we had never seen anything so primitive. The bath water was never hot enough and we often ran out of shillings to keep the electricity running. An electric fire in every room, which ate about three shillings an hour, emitted the heat. Luckily it was summer and there were many beautiful days when the windows stayed open and the fires stayed off.

One day, not long after we moved in, Tony Hall called and asked if we wouldn't mind taking his cats for a few weeks while he went on holiday. He said he was impressed by how we took to the cats and how much they liked us. In the States we had three cats so we welcomed these furry guests. The cats were never out of their flat and were totally freaked out during their first few days with us. One gorgeous day we left the top floor living-room window open and the cats sat on the window ledge watching the birds in the trees. There was a ten-foot jump from the window to the garden; a leap we assumed the cats would never attempt. The fat, black cat didn't, but the Abyssinian was a mean, lean cat machine; after she made her leap we scoured the area for her but never did find her. Tony Hall was so pissed at us when he came back, he told us we might as well keep the fat cat, Shoshone, named after a Native American tribe. She stayed with me until 1971.

London continued to cast a weird spell on me. Once I was walking with Viv Prince, the drummer in a group called The Pink Fairies. This was the first time I witnessed the chasm between the young and the old. Viv was a wild man who partied to the hilt, and he was dressed in a flowery shirt, very tight trousers, Cuban heeled boots and a kind of Edwardian velvet jacket. His hair was dyed yellow (not blond) and he wore pink-tinted glasses. Of course he was stared at. He would get back at the gawking passers-by by shouting and hooting at them, which I found embarrassing. We turned into Fulham Road underground station and Viv stomped down the escalator, causing everyone to turn to see the commotion. As we were passing a fragile OAP, Viv pulled a rubber spider out of his pocket and waved it in front of the old man. He retorted quickly in his London accent to Viv, 'They don't frighten me, I've seen 'em before you git!' This was my version of a Beatles movie – the old man resembled Wilfred Bramble. It was hysterical – Viv had no come back.

Denny's bread-and-butter band was the Move, although I don't think he ever took them as seriously as Procol Harum. In Denny's mind they were just a pop band, but with both Carl Wayne and Roy Wood as lead singers, and Roy's incredible melodies and hook-laden songs I think they were much more. I was called upon to write string parts for them.

My first string session was for a song called 'Cherry Blossom Clinic'; it was about an insane asylum. The string writing was the easy part; the hard part was conducting the twelve string players. Having loved the fabulous strings on 'Eleanor Rigby', it was clear to me that none of the players I had were from that group; mine were a tough lot. They refused to wear headphones so we had to play the track quietly on the studio speakers; we couldn't allow the drums and other instruments to 'bleed' into the microphones for the strings. They seemed to be old school players who were used to classical conductors. In that world it is customary to conduct ahead of the beat because they play with a delayed reaction. Pop musicians respond to the throb of the beat and I was conducting in that fashion, with the result they lagged behind. It wasn't going well until the lead violinist came up with the suggestion: 'Perhaps you should hold a pencil in your right hand and tap the beat on the palm of your left hand, that way we can follow easier.'

This reduced me to a human metronome stick but it got the job done. It wasn't so much that I was a bad conductor, although I probably was; their refusal to wear headphones had made it come to this.

My next session with the Move was my biggest accomplishment in those first months. I wrote a score for a small wind quartet for 'Flowers In The Rain'. Denny was unhappy with the track and felt that his production and performance didn't nail it; especially the bridge that lagged behind, almost imperceptibly. Denny's solution was to trash the track – with no plan of re-recording it. But I loved the song; I said I thought it was a hit single and my wind quartet arrangement would smooth over the rough edges. I persuaded Denny to indulge me. I convinced him that we could one-up the Beatles and George Martin (who changed the sound of pop with classic instrumentation on songs like 'Yesterday') and choose an instrumental combination that they hadn't yet thought of. Instead of the usual string section I chose a quartet of flute, oboe, clarinet and French horn. My logic was simple – the song had a pastoral theme (albeit through the context of magic mushrooms). I used instruments that Mendelssohn would have used, paying homage to him by quoting the *Spring Song* in the outro. I asked Denny to record the quartet at half speed during the dodgy bridge to create a very special effect; the instruments sounded like they were played by pixies sitting on mushrooms in an enchanted forest. The Move and Denny, and even the very staid session musicians, thought the experiment was a success.

The crowning glory was when 'Flowers In The Rain' reached No 2 on the charts and all for the relatively small expense of hiring four classical musicians at £12 each. It was kept from the top by Engelbert's 'Last Waltz' but had the distinction of being the first ever single played on the BBC's new 'pop' station, Radio One by Tony Blackburn shortly after 7 a.m. on Saturday 30 September 1967. 'Flowers In The Rain' became the first release on the resurrected Regal Zonophone label, which EMI used exclusively for Denny's Straight Ahead Productions. The label originally dated back to the 1930s but had been used in the early '60s to release records by the Joy Strings, the Salvation Army's very own pop group.

That Engelbert Humperdinck kept the Move from the top of the charts was a stark reminder that 1967 was a year of very contrasting musical styles. There we were, stuck in the middle of 'the summer of love' with a man wearing a dinner jacket and bow tie topping the chart. Britain not quite as I thought it was going to be from 3,000 miles away.

One of the guys that worked for Essex Music told me, 'I've got the arrangement for the new Tom Jones single.'

'Can I take a peak?' I was amazed. It was in three-four time and I could see the chorus was absolutely crass cabaret mush. The song was 'Delilah', which would become a No 2 hit for Tom early in 1968. Two years earlier he had blown us all away with 'It's Not Unusual'. It all seemed very strange.

There was an interesting, and costly, postscript for both the Move and Roy Wood in particular as well as Regal Zonophone. The group's manager, Tony Secunda, decided to send out a flyer with a caricature of the Prime Minister performing a sexual act to promote 'Flowers In The Rain'. Unfortunately Harold Wilson took the offending promotional postcard somewhat to heart and sued Regal Zonophone. The judge found in favour of the P.M. and he decreed that all royalties from the sale of the record were to be paid to charity, a situation that is still in existence. All rather unfortunate for the song's writer, Roy Wood, who, like the rest of the band, was

Above Me at 18 months.

Above left Aged 4, wearing my favourite beanie cap on Warren Street, Brooklyn, New York.

Above right At Lake Ronkonkoma, Long Island, New York.

Above Aged 17, singing a rock 'n' roll speciality number with the Ned Harvey Band, at Hotel Brickman, Catskill Mountains, New York.

Above With comedian Milton Berle, backstage at Ben Maksik's Town & Country Club, Brooklyn, New York.

Above 1962, Abby Lane, Xavier Cugat and me, aged 18. Cugat was a famous Spanish-Cuban bandleader who appeared in many film musicals of the '40s and sold millions of records. Abby Lane was his singing wife (they divorced and he married Charo). I played bass for their cabaret show at the Town & Country Club, Brooklyn.

Above Aged 18, playing valve trombone at an outdoor event, with the Ned Harvey Band, Hotel Brickman, Catskill Mountains, New York.

Above The Ned Harvey band with me on upright bass, at the Town & Country Club, 1962. Milt Anderson, my arranging mentor, is the saxophonist, second from the right. Ned Harvey is conducting.

Above A self-portrait, adapting
a Beatles look. Brooklyn, New
York, 1963.

Right Tony Bennett, photographed
by me in The Town & Country
Club, 1963. Bennett wanted to
use it for an album cover but his
record company unfortunately
rejected it.

Above The Speedy Garfin quartet with, (*left to right*), Speedy Garfin (sax), Tony Demar (drums), Tony Visconti (guitar), (*below*), Buddy Monticelli (bass). The photo was taken by the famous show-business photographer James J. Kriegsmann, 1964.

Left Singing and playing guitar as part of the reformed Crewcuts, in the Philippines, 1965. Original Crewcuts singer Rudy Maugeri is on my right.

Right My official cabaret card with accompanying mug shot and thumb print; it was mandatory to have this before I could work in a nightclub in New York City. Frank Sinatra refused to be photographed and fingerprinted 'like a criminal' and boycotted New York until the law was repealed.

CABARET AND PUBLIC DANCE HALL
EMPLOYEE'S IDENTIFICATION CARD
DEPARTMENT OF LICENSES, 80 Lafayette St., New York 13, N.Y.

(RIGHT THUMB PRINT)

(SIGNATURE)

ISSUED BY

COMMISSIONER

N°P 3115   PERMIT NO. 542519

DATE ISSUED 9/12/62

NAME ANTHONY E. VISCONTI, JR.

ASSUMED NAME

OCCUPATION MUSICIAN

AGE 18 | HEIGHT 6'0 IN. | WEIGHT 152 LBS. | MALE

HAIR BROWN | EYES BROWN | FEMALE

NOTIFY DEPARTMENT OF LICENSES BY MAIL OF ANY CHANGE IN RESIDENCE

EXPIRES SEPTEMBER 30, 1965

Below In Central Park, New York, 1966, taken by my wife Siegrid.

Above Me with Liza Minnelli and Siegrid in the courtyard of The Olympia Theatre, Paris, 1966, where Minnelli headed a musical review called *The Young Americans*. The show ran for two weeks and was also performed in front of Prince Rainier and Grace Kelly at their palace in Monaco.

Left Siegrid Visconti, my first wife, on Fire Island, New York, 1966.

Above My Alien Registration book, required for all aliens who resided in the UK in the '60s. I was required to register at a police station annually for a new book but, after four years, I became a UK resident and no longer needed to register.

Above Denny Cordell, my boss and mentor, at his desk in Essex Music, Oxford Street, 1967.

unaware of the management's little scheme, as he does not receive a penny from it.

On another session for the Move, I was conducting some string players when a stranger walked in on the session. Denny quickly walked up to my podium where I was standing and whispered in my ear, 'He's from the Musicians' Union, cool your American accent.' I had not yet received a work visa and it was potentially a tricky situation. I proceeded to communicate with the string players in mime or very hushed tones. It seems so trivial now but I could've easily been banned from ever working in Britain if the M.U. representative had worked out that I was an illegal alien.

I gained a lot of confidence working with Denny and the Move. It was on those sessions that I learned how to get a great drum sound. At one of them Denny just couldn't get the sound to his satisfaction and he made poor Bev Bevan play his kick drum for three hours. Bev actually broke down in tears.

'My leg's so fucking tired I can't even play the song now.'

Denny seemed not to care, but we attended to Trevor Boulder's bass sound, which took almost as long, so Bev got a rest. All this was being committed to a 4-track machine so the sounds and balance of the entire drum kit and the bass had to be near perfect before both performances were locked onto one track. This was a great learning experience for me but I vowed never to put a drummer through the torture that Bev received on that day. I have since learned to get up drum sounds very quickly. Not that Denny was anything but a gentleman when trying to deal with a difficult situation. When he wanted to give advice he would say, 'Shall I tell you something?' Having asked your permission he would go on to say his piece. Even when it was uncomfortable for you to hear he would phrase it in a way that was perfect. But he was a man of few words, he wouldn't go on and on about something; but he wouldn't give up until he was satisfied. If Denny said, 'I think it could be better', that's all it would take for the musicians to run back into the studio, just to please the 'king'. He had a great skill.

The Move's album, simply called *The Move*, came out in March 1968. So much happened between recording much of that album and its release that it's almost possible for me to overlook how important it was for me. Besides the orchestral arrangements on 'Flowers In The Rain' and 'Cherry Blossom Clinic' I did 'The Girl Outside' and 'Mist On A Monday Morning'. On the latter track I played recorders, it was the beginning of my parallel career as a 'rock recorder player'. The album was moderately successful, and was the only one the band ever made that charted. It also marked the end of the 4-track era, a very tedious way to make complicated productions; the 8-track machine was to become the new standard.

Denny felt it was time to take on a project by myself. 'Tony, this is India's Elvis – his name is Biddu,' said Denny, as he was about to play a demo. A few days later we met up and I found him to be a very nice, affable guy. Back then George Harrison's love of Indian music led me to believe that everyone from India was spiritual, they meditated and they did yoga. The reality was Biddu was more Western than Eastern. My Indian 'mystic' turned out to like ham sandwiches and capitalism. Before we went into the studio Biddu and his friend Anil came round to my flat for a social evening. Anil rolled joints even larger than Denny Cordell – a true master. Anil could also make a chillum shaped cone out of a newspaper sheet and fill it with hashish mixed with tobacco.

Denny helped me get the musicians together for the session, including John Paul Jones on bass (he would later join Led Zeppelin) and Nicky Hopkins on keyboards. I wrote a very lush string arrangement for 'Daughter of Love', Biddu's first (and only) single for Regal Zonophone. Keith Grant, Olympic's finest engineer, engineered the recording and the rhythm section and the strings played live – and it was all over in 15 minutes. We recorded about three takes in that time and I listened back in the control and was flabbergasted that it had gone so well. As an arranger I wrote down every single note I wanted them to play; they were all fine readers. It fucking worked.

Everyone agreed it sounded great and once the string players were thanked and dismissed they were gone in minutes. The rhythm section stayed on to play the backing track for the poppy-er B-side, 'Look Out Here I Come'. When it was time for Biddu's vocals it was the first time I noticed that he sang so softly, his Indian jewellery he was wearing around his neck was very audible each time he moved; he had to take it all off, which took a bit of time as there was so much of it. He also had a very noticeable lisp that wasn't apparent on his demos. There was nothing I could do about it, except finish the song and mix it.

A few days later I realized that it was a bit ragged in parts, due to my hastiness and inexperience. But Denny seemed to like it. When it came out it got terrible reviews and that was that. Biddu eventually found fame as a songwriter and producer; his hits included the UK No 1s by Tina Charles – 'I Love To Love', and 'Kung Fu Fighting' recorded by Carl Douglas. He went on to become one of the most successful writers of Bollywood films and today is a far richer man than most rock producers.

Denny sensed that I wasn't the type of producer who could be assigned to do something I didn't appreciate musically. 'Visconti, you need to get out there and find something for yourself.'

For my part I was certain that whoever I 'discovered' would be no less than the next Beatles; being naïve is a blessing. I was a regular reader of the *International Times*. *IT*, as it was known, had started out in the autumn of 1966 as the counter culture's weekly newspaper and naturally bands that were a part of the underground scene were featured, along with adverts for gigs.

I had noticed adverts in *IT* in recent weeks for a band with a very intriguing name – Tyrannosaurus Rex. *IT* happened to list one of their gigs that very night. It was at the UFO Club, at 31 Tottenham Court Road, not far from our offices in Oxford Street. It was a 'Middle Earth' night, or so the ad said. I left our offices around 7 p.m. and went to the pub on the corner of Tottenham Court Road and Oxford Street to have a Scotch egg (a newly acquired taste) and half a pint of bitter (another newly acquired taste). Then made my way to the UFO.

This was my first time at the club and I walked from the street down a dark staircase. Music was wafting up the stairwell. I was totally unprepared for what confronted me. There were about two hundred kids sitting crossed-legged on the floor and there was a duo performing on a low stage, also sat in exactly the same way. The duo consisted of a very pretty man with dark curly hair, who was singing and strumming his guitar along with his partner, who was furiously banging on a set of bongo drums. The singer was dressed in a kind of ragamuffin clothes: torn jeans, a torn silk shirt, with a handkerchief tied round one upper arm and a maroon waistcoat. The bongo player was dressed in a similar fashion, but he had long straight hair past his shoulders. I thought they were the 'real deal', gypsy hippies that lived in a caravan somewhere in a wood on the edge of London. They were of course Tyrannosaurus Rex. Somehow I had it in my mind that the name implied they would be a loud band and the audience would be screaming kids; instead this was a 'happening' with an audience in the throes of an almost religious experience. The singer sang with an intense vibrato in his voice – a warble. The bongo player would occasionally interject with a supporting vocal. I had no idea what language they were singing in, it certainly did not sound like English and if anything I thought it could be French. As I was listening the hairs on my arm started to stiffen; somewhat against the odds I found myself thinking – this group is great. It certainly wasn't rock 'n' roll and then again it wasn't folk; it was eccentric and new.

When the set finished I approached the bongo player, I was too much in awe of the singer to speak to him. He said his name was Steve and he was a mumbler – he appeared to be stoned out of his brain. Amidst the mumbles I heard him say, 'Talk to him man, he's the leader.'

He pointed towards his partner. When I approached him, he first looked me up and down, as if inspecting me, and introduced himself as Marc Bolan, 'and he's Steve Peregrine Took,' said Marc pointing to the mumbler. He spoke in an affected posh accent.

I explained to Marc that I was a record producer and I was interested in working with them.

'You're the eighth record producer who has come to see us this week. John Lennon was here last night and he wants to produce us for his label Grapefruit.'

I was extremely impressed and at the same time disheartened because I thought I hadn't a chance in hell to record Tyrannosaurus Rex if Lennon was in the game. Nevertheless Marc asked me questions about my company and when I mentioned Denny Cordell his face lit up. He asked me for my phone number and said he would think about it. As it turned out, Marc was already working a number on me; the Lennon story wasn't true, it was just designed to wind me up. (From the first moment we met, Marc had to have the upper hand. Marc controlled those who worked with him by alternating genuine affection and deceitful intimidation. This was my very first taste of the latter. We have shared some of the greatest moments I've ever experienced in the studio and I'm extremely proud of our work together. After all these years I am finally able to let go of the anger I've harboured due to the way he mistreated his band and myself – which grew worse during the decline of his popularity.)

The next morning I was telling Denny about the 'group that got away', the one that John Lennon thought were hot and we'd never get them, when the phone rang. 'Hi Tony, this is Marc Bolan. I'm in a callbox. Steve and I just happened to be in Oxford Street and we were wondering if we could come in and meet Denny Cordell.' He was so full of crap I thought, but I asked him to hold, covered the mouthpiece and excitedly asked Denny if they could come up. 'Denny, this is them, this is that group I was just talking about.'

Denny seemed impressed and said, 'invite them up'. Five minutes later Marc and Steve walked into our cramped office. For a couple of guys who were just 'passing by' they had the small Moroccan carpet rolled up that they had performed on the night before, a bag of percussion instruments, and Marc had his acoustic guitar without a case. I noticed it didn't have a key on the G-string: Marc got out a pair of pliers to tighten the string in tune. They played their entire set. Denny smiled the whole time, often closing his eyes and swaying to the beat. His favourite listening posture was to sit with his hands clasped behind his head with his legs stretched way out under his desk. When they finished Denny told them that they were really great.

'Marc leave us your number and we'll get back to you.'

Denny was a fan of The Incredible String Band, a Scottish duo who played magical, mystical folk music with surreal lyrics and they were his point of reference for Tyrannosaurus Rex. After they had finished, packed up their stuff and left, Denny said 'All

right, I like them. We'll take them on as our "token" underground group. But I still want you to make some demos before
we actually sign them. It's one thing listening to them live, let's
see if it works on record.'

For a hard-core rock and roller like Denny this was off his
beaten path, but he did have a gentle side that appreciated folk
musicians. When Paul Simon came to England after recording
'Sounds Of Silence', and before it was a hit, Denny had
befriended him. Simon had a British girlfriend, Beverly (just
Beverly, no surname), who was also a folk singer. Denny did
some recording with Beverly. I called Marc to tell him the good
news. Strangely John Lennon's 'proposal' was never brought up
again. (Only recently I learned that Denny wasn't as convinced
as I'd thought him to be by the pair's potential; I was so trans-
fixed by the performance that I didn't notice Denny slip out the
door, as he'd spotted BP Fallon through the cracked opening.
Fallon, who later became the P.R. person for Marc, was visiting
Essex Music that morning; Denny grabbed BP from the hallway
and pulled him in to have a listen. He whispered that it wasn't
his cup of tea, but BP told him he liked what he heard.)

Just after meeting Marc and Steve I met someone else who was
to change my life. This was to be a more long-term relationship,
but it wouldn't improve my financial position in the short term.
Denny's continuing success meant a move for him and his
family from their basement in the Fulham Road to a top-floor
luxury flat in Cheyne Walk; two doors from Mick Jagger's
home. At the other end of the food chain I was on a £25 a
week retainer, and at that point no other source of income.
However, I could live with the lack of money – just as long as
the work opportunities continued to come my way.

One day in the autumn of 1967 David Platz called me into
his office: 'You seem to have a talent for working with weird

acts, I'd like to play something for you to consider', is the condescending way he framed it. After six months' working in London, Platz seemed to be irritated by my very presence. 'This is an album made by a writer I've been working with for some time,' he went on. 'We were hoping he'd be right for the musical theatre but he's become something quite different since he's made this record.' From the speakers came an amazingly mature voice, the phrasing and subtlety was something you'd expect from a seasoned stage or even a cabaret singer. The songs were humorous and dark; the backing was imaginative. But Platz was right – what was this? I listened to half the album and remarked that although it was all over the place, I liked it. 'His name is David Bowie and he's nineteen. Would you like to meet him?'

Behind David Platz's office was a small room with a piano; it harked back to the days, not that long before, when a publisher actually had a member of staff sit at the piano and play a song to a prospective singer, or songwriters would play their latest compositions to the publisher. Platz led me into this inner sanctum and there was David Bowie – nervous and shy. I realized then that this casual encounter was a set up. As I shook Bowie's hand I realized that he had two different coloured eyes. The only other person I ever met with two different coloured eyes was Jerry Lieber, of Lieber and Stoller. After a brief introduction, Platz wisely left us alone. I liked David Bowie immediately.

We talked for ages about anything and everything, like two people getting on really well at a party. David seemed obsessed with American music in the same way I was with British music. He told me he bought as many American records as he could. He adored Little Richard. He also liked American jazz – sax player Gerry Mulligan in particular. He said he also played baritone sax. He loved underground music like Frank Zappa and The Fugs; I had the same records in my collection. Another

album that we shared a mutual love for was Ken Nordine's
Word Jazz. He was a radio announcer from the American Mid-
west with a very deep voice. He made a spoken word album
with jazz music and some sound effects for accompaniment. It
was another album I had bought back in the States and David
had it too; we must have been one of a dozen people who had
bought it.

We decided to leave the stuffy office and take a walk and
eventually found ourselves on King's Road. We came across a
small cinema showing Roman Polanski's *A Knife In The Water*;
we watched it and discovered another shared interest – foreign
art films. If it was in black and white, made anywhere but in the
USA or the UK, and it was scratchy and had subtitles, we loved
it. I left David around 6 p.m. and went back home to Elgin
Avenue and told Siegrid about my new friend.

Within a few days David and I started working together. He
was signed to Deram but was on tenuous terms with them. His
debut album, the one I'd heard in David Platz's office, did not
do well – it certainly didn't chart. With its variety of styles it
didn't seem to fit anywhere and with no hit singles it didn't get
airplay. David played a wicked 12-string rhythm guitar and had
a flair for putting odd chords together but the LP was not very
youth orientated and seemed out of kilter with what was happening on the scene. But there was something that was consistently evident in his latest songs, a kind of acoustic folk-rock
style. One song especially, 'Let Me Sleep Beside You' sounded
very cool, almost American. On 1 September we went into
Advision Studios, in New Bond Street and recorded it along
with another of David's songs called 'Karma Man'. Its subject
matter alluded to Tibetan Buddhism, another fascination we
shared. The sessions went very well, with both Big Jim Sullivan
and John McLaughlin on guitars, but we were in trouble from
the start. Deram's A&R people said 'Let Me Sleep Beside You'

was too sexual in context and the BBC wouldn't play it. After this was put to David he reluctantly bowed to their wishes and punched in the line 'Let me "be" beside you.' Of course it changed the meaning and didn't have the same impact. Deram then dropped their concern for the suggestive original title and it went out that way. The BBC ignored the single.

My far from auspicious start with Bowie did nothing to enhance my reputation with David Platz. In a sense I was confirming his view that David was a 'weird act'. It was a good job that Denny appreciated what I did, and I had helped with the Move and Procol Harum, otherwise my collateral would have been at a severely low ebb. My hopes at this point rested on Tyrannosaurus Rex – I just hoped they could make the transition from a live act with a small but enthusiastic following into fully fledged pop stars – whatever that meant.

chapter 3
variety is the spice . . .

Our move from Elgin Avenue was hastened by a visit from Ellen Resch, our psychic teacher from New York. She confirmed that Siegrid and I had a 'presence' living with us in the flat; she said this immediately upon arrival. We told her that when we slept we could hear furniture being moved around in the middle of the night; when we woke up the furniture arrangement always looked a little different.

'I can see that an old lady used to live in this flat and she died here; her spirit has never left.' Just as Ellen finished speaking the three of us saw something move, out of the corner of our eyes; we simultaneously turned our heads in the same direction. We saw a spectre, an apparition of a small, hunched old lady slowly walking from one wall to the other; midway she turned and looked in our direction. She wasn't completely solid, we could see through her and then she faded away. It wasn't as terrifying as it might sound. Siegrid and I were just relieved that we knew what was moving the furniture.

'Don't worry, I'll talk to the lady and ask her to leave,' said Ellen with a smile.

Regardless of this comforting news we decided to leave the flat as soon as possible; more than anything else we needed a place that didn't have a shilling-guzzling machine. I was making a mere pittance as Denny's apprentice and we found it hard to make ends meet, as I learned to say. We couldn't afford to go out late – the tube usually stopped at midnight and I couldn't afford a taxi after hours. Siegrid and I could only partake of the free things London had to offer, Hyde Park, Kensington Park and, especially, Portobello Road, where we could just hang out with the coolest people and buy cheap, used clothing.

We found a lovely ground floor flat at 108 Lexham Gardens in London W8, both well decorated and furnished. It was in a building owned by an elderly gay antique dealer and his boyfriend; they lived on the top floor. There were a few valuable paintings and bits of furniture that were just 'visiting' our flat, a kind of warehouse for our landlord's merchandise. It cost £18 pounds a week, which made it tough because I was still on a £25 a week retainer. Fortunately I was able to supplement my frequently drained coffers with arrangements written for the likes of Billy Fury and Kenny Lynch; stars for a previous generation. One lucrative piece of extra work was an arrangement I wrote for a song that featured in *Here We Go Round The Mulberry Bush*, a film that said so much about these changing times in Britain. Traffic supplied much of the music, but I arranged a love song called 'It's Been A Long Time' sung by Andy Ellison; unbeknownst to me it was produced by Marc Bolan's manager, Simon Napier Bell. I also had no idea when I did it that Andy had been the singer with John's Children, a group that Marc had left shortly before teaming up with Steve Took. Months later, when the movie came out in January 1968, I heard my arrangement in the film but noticed that my name was absent from the credits; I remember making £40, though.

Shortly after recording David and moving to Lexham Gardens, Marc (with girlfriend Terry Mosaic in tow), Steve and I began making demos at the flat. They would sit cross-legged in my living room while I recorded them live with a stereo microphone into a stereo machine. Even before we moved, our flat in Elgin Avenue had been a magnet for social guests; my parents flew over from New York to stay for a couple of weeks and one night while they were there David and his schooldays' girlfriend Kitty dropped by. Also there that night were Stan Bronstein and Myron Yule from the New York band Elephants Memory, who would metamorphose into the Plastic Ono Band. For the life of me I cannot recall how come they were there – it was that kind of place. One weekend David showed up unannounced with his father, mother and brother Terry.

Marc Bolan and his new girlfriend June Child, a secretary in Pink Floyd's office, also started coming round very regularly; he had moved out of his mum's flat and moved to a flat in Blenheim Crescent, Ladbroke Grove that he and June shared. They also shared a W.C. in their hallway with the other tenants of the building and they asked to use my bath for one of their two weekly baths; they went to Marc's mum's flat in Wimbledon for their other bath. Marc would arrive with LPs under his arm; he would often arrive with a Ricky Nelson album because he was a huge fan of his guitarist, James Burton. We'd listen to the Beatles, but we loved the Beach Boys. If you listen in particular to *Unicorn*, Tyrannosaurus Rex is doing that kind of Beach Boys thing à la *Vegetables*. We listened to *Smiley Smile* a lot; the vinyl copy I have came out of the BBC library courtesy of either John Peel or Kenny Everett. There were a few nights when David came over and we jammed; Marc and David on guitars and me on bass. It never ever occurred to me to run the tape recorder, this was such early days and quite honestly I didn't have that much tape; it wasn't like it was big time. Also if I had bought tape it would have blown the food budget and we wouldn't have eaten.

We spent a lot of time at our flat or going to friends' flats because anything else made too big a dent in our budget. We didn't go out much to dine in restaurants or to the cinema; West

End plays were out of the question. Many of the friends we had came from the music business. Through Don Paul, who produced Billy Fury and Don Partridge (the busker who sang 'Rosie') I met Kenny Everett who had been on the pirate Radio London until shortly before I arrived in England; when we met he was working for the BBC. We had a few lovely evenings working our way through bottles of cheap wine and playing cool sounds on the gramophone. One evening I gave Kenny a back rub on the floor of his front room. He was groaning, moaning and cooing the whole time. Even though Siegrid was there he turned around and whispered in my ear, 'Are you gay?'

While most of my life revolved around music I also had a brush with a member of another area of the arts. My next-door neighbour was comedy actor Derek Nimmo, although we were never formally introduced. One night our fat cat Shoshone was stuck on the wall that divided our homes. As I climbed up it to retrieve Shoshone, Nimmo burst out of his side door, 'Are you trying to break into my house?'

'Of course I'm not, I'm trying to get our cat.' Of course by this time the cat was nowhere to be seen having bolted. 'Anyway, I'm your next-door neighbour.'

'A likely story, and even if you are my neighbour you're still trying to break in.'

I found it hard to keep a straight face because he made me laugh every time I saw him play a clergyman on TV's *All Gas and Gaiters*.

'I'm going to phone the police.' I couldn't suppress a smile; we never did get a knock at our door from the police.

We had got a TV when we moved to Lexham Gardens and to my American mind it was all rather surprising. For a start signing off at 11:30 p.m. while playing 'God Save the Queen' used to make me angry. I was amazed that it was all in black and white, I was so used to colour TV. There were only three shows that really interested me: *The Prisoner*, *The Avengers* and *Top Of The Pops*. *The Prisoner* because it was extremely confusing, full of unexplained subplots – in short, it was far out (psychedelic). We would sit around with a bunch of friends and get stoned before watching it; afterwards we would discuss the show and try to make sense of what we'd just seen. I liked *The Avengers* because it had class, and especially Diana Rigg; for me she and Patrick MacNee were worth the price of a TV licence. Of course I *had* to watch *Top Of The Pops*, but I was also a big pop fan. I was perplexed by the variety of music on the weekly chart show. When I arrived in London I had no idea that the British public could have such bad taste, while simultaneously nurturing the greatest rock stars in history – to me it was a baffling dichotomy. *Top Of The Pops* was live back then and so exciting things were bound to happen. The rest of British television left me cold.

Besides being a place of great fun and much laughter, Lexham Gardens was also the place that my marriage to Siegrid ended. Growing resentment about me working while she didn't led to frequent arguments. I made one whole-hearted attempt at making Siegrid happy about her talents. She decided that Tony & Siegrid as a recording duo was no more; she decided she would go solo – she fancied herself as a female Bob Dylan. Dylan's basement tapes, recorded in a Woodstock barn with The Band, were floating around in London and Manfred Mann had already recorded 'The Mighty Quinn'. Siegrid loved 'Ride Me High' and asked to record it. She wrote her own B-side – a cryptic message to Dylan. It basically said that he and she were the only two people in the world who understood each other. I got neither David Platz's or Denny's sanction but recorded her on the sly because I felt this last-minute attempt to save our marriage wouldn't float with them. The results were mediocre at best; Siegrid was no lead singer, although I always loved her lyrics. I got reprimanded for recording without permission and nothing came of Siegrid's solo attempt. There was something about Siegrid that rubbed him the wrong way. Whereas he tolerated me, he covertly disliked her and virtually ignored her.

Finally she packed her things and said she was going back to Arizona to see her mother for two weeks. After she left I looked in her part of the closet; she had packed everything except for one white sock. I knew she had gone for good. Two weeks later she sent a letter telling me that she was looking for a new home for us and that I should tie up my loose ends and leave. I wrote back saying there were no loose ends to tie up, I had found my home and I was staying here. It was to be two years before I saw Siegrid again.

I didn't stay single for very long. There was a secretary in the office called Janet and she started coming around with her girl-friend, Sheila Cane; I fancied Sheila with her blonde hair, pink cheeks, pale complexion and blue eyes. A lot of young British people must've had the same problem as Marc and June because Sheila asked if she could take a bath in my flat. While Janet was watching TV, with a drink in one hand and a fag in the other, I gently knocked on the bathroom door and asked Sheila if she would like her back scrubbed; to my surprise she said yes. Within a week Sheila moved in as my new girlfriend. Since this was the swinging '60s, my gay landlord didn't bat an eyelash, he just reminded us to take good care of his antiques. Sheila on one level was a very proper English Rose. She had a posh accent and had been raised in India, the daughter of an English Army officer, and from there attended a public school in England. Her father was wealthy; after his military career in India he'd become a successful businessman. By the time Sheila and I got together he had heard the calling and became an Anglican vicar; we spent some lovely weekends at the vicarage in Cambridgeshire – separate bedrooms, of course.

* * *

As I was developing things with Marc and Steve, Denny gave me another project to work on. He had signed a band and planned to release them through Regal Zonophone; a wonderful guitarist named Mick Wayne fronted the group. We recorded 'Subway (Smokey Pokey World)', which has since become something of an underground psychedelic classic, but at that point they hadn't even decided what their group was to be called. I named them 'The Tickle', a name they hated so much it was the first and last time I ever named a group. Today any song that's labelled an underground classic is as likely as not to have been a resounding flop, and true to their name Tickle didn't even manage to do that to the charts; they soon broke up and a few months later Mick Wayne formed a band he called Junior's Eyes.

By March 1968 I had finally managed to convince David Platz to let me have a budget to make a record with Tyrannosaurus Rex: the homemade demos had done their job. That was the good news, the bad news was that Platz agreed a budget of just £400; the equivalent to less than £5,000 today – that would barely get you a middle eight in one song today. It was to be recorded at Advision and, given the paucity of the budget, it needed to be made with military precision – a strange concept for a bunch of hippies. It was carefully rehearsed at my flat and the recording was planned to account for every minute of studio time. I used Gerald Chevin, a resident engineer. He had worked with me while I acted as Denny's assistant on *The Move* tracks and was a compressor freak; he loved to put sound through this automatic volume controlling device set at 'eleven' so that the sound is squashed, devoid of dynamics. Gerald had built several of Advision's compressors himself, so I guess he had to constantly impress me with how well they worked. I wasn't clued up enough about engineering yet, so I was at his mercy. The vibe in the studio was great. Marc was born for this moment – he and Steve performed as if they were in a stadium, they gave their all. We recorded the entire album in two days, including a single, 'Debora', which was not on the album. We overdubbed extra vocals and instruments, which Steve mostly played after each song was initially recorded as live guitar, vocal and percussion. In stereo you can hear Marc's live voice bleeding into his guitar microphone.

John Peel was Marc's great champion; he adored Tyrannosaurus Rex. He was the only one who played their music regularly and he would take them on his club DJ gigs. Peel thought that Marc was a very spiritual person and that all their songs were very magical. When John Peel walked into our studio I was really in awe of him because he was the only DJ playing really great underground music – the coolest, hippest sounds. He was really genuine, he was no phoney and he was very shy, painfully so, to the point where he mumbled when he spoke. It was towards the end of day two that Peel came in to read a children's story that Marc had written, which divided the last track of the album, 'Frowning Attahualpha'. We spent the remaining two days mixing the entire album, first in mono, then a quick adjustment of pan controls to make a stereo mix; the hastiness made the stereo very definitely an afterthought. This was a transitional period when stereo was being introduced slowly into the pop world. It was as if only classical music deserved the full stereo treatment, not us riff raff, rock 'n' rollers. Sonically, the album has always sounded thin and reeked from being a rush job. But at the core of its tinny exterior the album, with the abstruse title of *My People Were Fair And Had Sky In Their Hair. . .But Now Are Content To Wear Stars On Their Brow*, was all heart. David Bowie introduced me to his school friend George Underwood, whom I commissioned to do the cover artwork. He charged Denny £75, which puts into perspective the paltry recording budget;

but it was still £25 more than Denny had ever spent on an album cover.

Even with the extra money I made from my 'off duty' arranging gigs I still failed to make ends meet. And so when a cheaper, smaller flat became vacant on the next floor I practically begged my landlord to let Sheila and I have it. It saved us £3 a week, which was a big difference (equivalent of almost £40 in 2007). It was Sheila who introduced me to the joys of Indian food and the 'spare money' was put towards eating as much as possible. With Sheila as my first British girlfriend I felt that I really was becoming acclimatized to England – I'd gone native.

Another good friend and colleague was folk-rock singer/composer Tucker Zimmerman, a San Franciscan who came to London via a music conservatory in Naples, Italy. I made a very simple but effective album with him called *Ten Songs by Tucker Zimmerman*, with a single called 'The Red Wind'. I think this might have been the very first session I used Rick Wakeman on – possibly his first recording session ever. I'd met Rick on the premises of Essex Music; he was writing for Jon Fenton at the time. I always liked Rick, he had a refreshing 'just-one-of-the-lads' personality and could drink most of us under the table at the pub. There was also Dr Sam Hutt, who was recording as Boeing Duveen in those days (he later metamorphosed into Hank Wangford); Peter Jenner of Blackhill Enterprises managed Hutt/Duveen. Peter and Sam would come over with their wives and we'd have a spiffing, spliffing evening. On one night Bowie was there and tried to smoke one of the few spliffs he's ever had in his life, which resulted in much coughing and little else.

The big cinema event was Stanley Kubrick's *2001 – A Space Odyssey*. We went to see it with a friend and his wife on a widescreen West End cinema. He had been able to get hold of some cannabis tincture and made a tea with honey and lemon, which he put in a thermos and took to the cinema that day. We would take little sips of what he called 'the beautiful soup' and the film became more and more fantastic and intense as the drug took effect. We weren't the only ones watching the film in an altered state. Behind us were two people on acid and they were very freaked out by the intentionally psychedelic ending. I turned to them and tried to talk them down a few pegs. God knows what they were seeing, I'm sure it wasn't the same film we were watching.

In 1967 David Bowie had begun studying mime with Lindsay Kemp and by December he was earnestly rehearsing a piece called *Pierrot In Turquoise*. This fantasy starred Kemp and another artist, named Orlando, along with Bowie and a stunningly beautiful ballet dancer named Hermione Fotheringale. David was eager for me to meet Kemp to show him, of all things, my karate 'skills'. We met at a rehearsal in Notting Hill Gate. I showed Lindsay a flurry of kicks.

'Oh my dear, you'll do yourself an injury. You simply mustn't do that sort of thing without a proper warm up,' he shrieked, and quickly turned his head in disgust. Mime and martial arts didn't mix that day.

I went to see their performance at The Mercury Theatre in Notting Hill Gate in March and was a little baffled as to how Bowie's musical career would benefit by concentrating on a non-speaking role dressed in tights. Of course, his integration of mime into his Ziggy Stardust persona in later years is now legendary. Back then it seemed like his interests were simply too scattered. Bowie was charismatic and mime lessons were making him very aware of movement. I would watch him execute the ordinary task of walking to the fridge to get a pint of milk, but on his way there he would be working out in his head how he could do it gracefully and artistically as Kemp might do; he would make a little movement that would send a wave-like ripple through his body. Other times he would go to a mirror just to check a head angle, or he would brush his hair back in a particular way. At the time I thought that he was just incredibly vain; later I realized that he was always working on himself, constantly honing his stage persona.

Having finished the Tyrannosaurus Rex album and the single we were all frustrated by the long delay of its release. I was constantly trying to keep Marc happy, being his friend as well as his producer probably exerted just a little more pressure. My requests to Platz and Denny to record a second album, before the first one was even released, had been blocked. Having written what he inevitably saw as superior material, Marc was pressuring me to get back into the studio. I agreed it was better material, having heard it over many evenings in Lexham Gardens. I was totally sympathetic with Marc and I was angry with 'The Man', my mercenary company. I decided to take a chance and booked Trident Studios for two weeks in April, without written permission, or permission of any kind, from David Platz. I reasoned that the bills would come in the following month and by that time Platz would hear the fabulous new album by Tyrannosaurus Rex and say that it was money well spent. It didn't quite follow my script. Phrases like, 'This is tantamount to embezzlement', were bandied about in Platz's confrontation with me after he discovered my duplicity. I was almost fired. Looking back now I understand that it was insane to make another album before the release of the first one.

'Debora', the first single, was released in mid-April 1968 (while we were at Trident) and made an impact, even if some DJs only played it to make fun of Marc's voice or to pretend that they couldn't pronounce Tyrannosaurus Rex. It went into the charts just under a month later and finally climbed as high as No 34. Sheila had had the idea of painting plastic models of Tyrannosaurus Rex, bought at Hamley's toyshop on Regent Street. Sheila, Steve Took and I sat around the front room in Lexham Gardens and painted them in dayglow psychedelic colours. We sent them to the BBC and Radio Luxembourg in an early attempt at promotion; it was all very innocent and at the same time reflects how strongly we felt about that record. I was more excited by the success of this record than I had been about my involvement with the Move's 'Flowers In The Rain' or any of the other records I had a hand in since I moved to London; this was *my* project. The fact that it charted at all probably saved me from 'Basil Rathbone' Platz's wrath.

That second Tyrannosaurus Rex album proved to be a major turning point in my career. We were anxious to create a fuller sound – very challenging given the cheap guitar and trebly bongos that made up the band's sound. London studios, and the engineers that worked them, were primed to record the quintessential pop band: two guitars, bass and drums. For Tyrannosaurus Rex the basic elements of pop music just weren't there, yet Marc, Steve and I were determined to make a pop record. We were particularly anxious not to repeat the brutal experience of recording and completing the previous album in four days. Marc didn't like the sound we were getting at Trident and naively assumed that I could just sit at the enormous console and somehow create a fabulous sound. Malcolm Toft, who had designed the desk, was the chief engineer at the studio and he overheard Marc berating me and chipped in.

'Look, I don't "get" your sound at all, Marc, but I will walk Tony through the recording process and I'll stick around to help out whenever I can.'

While recording was no big mystery to me I had never attempted the role of engineer before, at least not in a commercial studio. (An engineer's job is to get the sound down on tape, and to tweak the gear in a studio to maximise the sound; a producer's job is to create the complex layers of a song, and to get the best performances out of the band.) The first couple of days were confusing, but I soon got the hang of it. I finished the recording of the album by my own hand and we mixed the album with just Marc, Steve and myself. This was a big breakthrough for me; I was now a recording engineer and I've never looked back. Malcolm Toft still builds fine recording equipment today and lives in Somerset. We are still friends.

We made some great sounds on this album; we overdubbed more layers of sound and made our first foray into backwards recording. 'Debora' was re-recorded as 'DeboraArobed', signifying that the song starts out forward and in the middle it goes backwards and ends at the beginning – it was very much 'of its time'. We were recording for our imagined audience of 'heads'. Although Marc did not take psychedelic drugs he knew that many of his audience delighted in listening to his records on strong hallucinogenic substances – they could 'see' sounds and 'hear' colours. We wanted nothing less than to blow some minds. We were finally having fun in the studio being creative and provocative. As strict vegetarians we would have lunch at the newly opened Cranks off Carnaby Street (Siegrid and I had become vegetarians while in New York; I fell off the wagon every now and again but I still prefer to be that way).

On 12 May, the day after 'Debora' went into the charts, Steve Peregrine Took crashed in the front room of my flat – a not infrequent occurrence. This is how Steve came to appear on a BBC radio session as a backing vocalist for David Bowie on 'Silly Boy Blue'. The BBC had an arrangement with the Musicians' Union that restricted the amount of records that could be played, to limit 'needle time' – recorded music. Prior to the birth of Radio One they were limited to just five hours per day for records to be played; it had been generously increased by thirty minutes after the new pirate-replacing national station had gone on air. The BBC's innovative solution was to record bands live in their own studios. For many people listening back then it was sometimes seen as a frustrating experience but at the same time it provided some wonderfully unique and innovative broadcasts. Bowie was to record a session for John Peel the following day at London's Piccadilly Studios. Besides Steve, David's band was billed as the Tony Visconti Orchestra – fame at last. These were almost always very quick sessions and we had to be completely professional, recording up to five songs in three hours, complete with one overdub per song. Having written arrangements for several days we showed up ready to be put through the BBC's highly unionized recording machine. It was always a rushed, wham-bam-thank-you-ma'am experience, with two of their technicians overseeing the sessions. They were charged with performing any task related to electricity; you weren't even allowed to plug your own guitar amp into the mains socket, or adjust a microphone to your height. Any transgression of the rules threatened a union walk out.

A week after the session David played an unusual show at Middle Earth in Covent Garden along with Tyrannosaurus Rex, the Edgar Broughton Band, Tales of Justine, Third Ear Band and Junior's Eyes – the 'son of' Tickle – led by Mick Wayne. For this appearance David had written a mime piece called *Jetsun and The Eagle*, a commentary on Chinese oppression of the Tibetan people after 1959. Marc would only have David on the bill if he did a mime piece and didn't sing. Two weeks later David reprised the piece at the Royal Festival Hall; Stefan Grossman opened the show, followed by Roy Harper and Bowie was on right before Tyrannosaurus Rex. For *Jetsun and the Eagle* David and I prepared a soundtrack containing what we thought might pass for Tibetan music, played on a Moroccan guitar-like instrument I'd bought in Portobello Road. We added improvised sound effects with saucepans (they were the ceremonial cymbals) and I read a narration written by David. For some reason he decided my American accent made it sound more like a documentary – maybe it was Ken Nordine's *Word Jazz* that influenced his thinking. At the performance it was not all peace and love; as the tape began, David came out and mimed the whole thing. He portrayed the Chinese going into Tibet and banning everything, including kissing; David had just learned how to turn his back to the audience and pretend he was two people kissing, then he tapped himself on the shoulder as if he was a Red Guard. This was the point at which the audience lost it; Communist sympathizers booed David. During this heckling two Asian gentlemen, standing at the side of the audience, dressed in smart suits and looking remarkably like Japanese businessmen from TDK or Sony, fled quickly. David later told me that they were Trungpa Rinpoche and Chime Rinpoche – Tibetan Lamas in civvies. Years later I would study meditation with Chime.

Playing live was now David's only music outlet at this point following an abortive session for Deram a couple of months earlier. We recorded at Decca's studio in West Hampstead; ironically our engineer was Gus Dudgeon, who was soon to work in our office when David Platz made him a partner. Bowie recorded 'In The Heat Of The Morning' and 'London Bye Ta-Ta' (the first of three versions I produced), but they were never released. I was in a second-hand relationship with Deram as I never met or discussed any recording ideas with anyone there; David was my point person. Deram then decided to drop David in favour of another singer/songwriter on their books, Cat Stevens.

*   *   *

Working with Bowie and Bolan was my preference but I still took assignments from Denny Cordell. Mick Wayne's Junior's Eyes had been signed by Denny and I went into the studio with them to begin working on some tracks. The first two, 'Mr. Golden Trumpet Player' and 'Black Snake' came out on Regal Zonophone in June; the single didn't get a lot of airplay and while they were a band 'on the scene' they were not getting the attention I think they deserved.

In an attempt to be a 'proper' record label Denny hunted for potential releases on Regal Zonophone recorded by other artists. Denny secured the rights to release Johnny Nash's 'Hold Me Tight'; he and I loved that record. When I first got a preview copy I played it to Marc and June and we immediately learned it; Marc and I jammed on the chord changes and we sang it for fun in my flat.

With the huge success of *A Whiter Shade Of Pale,* Procol Harum suddenly became a major band and central to Denny's attentions, but, and there was often a but with Denny, his attention had been captured by another artist, named Joe Cocker. This led to me being asked to oversee the Procol Harum sessions while he worked across town on the Cocker album. Unlike my bad experience with Manfred Mann, Procol Harum accepted me, and as a band they were very committed to what they wanted to accomplish. It was from working with them that I learned to listen carefully to what artists stated as their goals. We worked on *In Held 'Twas In I,* a very long suite of side two of their album. I bravely asked Keith Reid what the title meant (Reid was a scary, laconic character) and he candidly told me that each word in the title was the first word in each of the five songs used in the suite – of course, stupid me. I had a great time working on this opus. Denny, being a singles man, wouldn't have had as much fun as I did working on this 'theme' side. On ''Twas Tea Time At The Circus' I joined the band in the studio to scream and shout as part of the crowd. For me the crowning glory was to record a complete track all by myself; it was the oddly charming 'Magdalene, My Regal Zonophone'. The title and lyric were too surreal for a mere mortal like me to ponder. Who is Magdalene? Why is she regarded as the patroness of their record label? While these were questions few people other than myself wanted to know the answers to, many others questioned why the album bombed so badly. Like Procol Harum's first album, this album, which they called *Shine On Brightly*, didn't chart in the UK, although it's considered by most people to be a far superior effort. To many people's surprise it made the US album charts, reaching No 24. We were fortunate that it did, as the effort we'd put into recording that album needed some reward.

Sometimes good fortune, however, does fall into your lap. I have rarely received an unsolicited demo that was worth considering, let alone worth raving about. Just before recording the second Tyrannosaurus Rex album a small package arrived in the office postmarked Sheffield. In it was a 4-inch reel of tape containing just one song; on it was a label that said 'Marjorine' and the name Joe Cocker. There was a note inside that explained that Joe was a steel worker and part-time pub singer. When Denny, publisher Jon Fenton and I listened to it we were dumbfounded, it sounded incredibly professional for its time. Joe's number was on the note and so Denny called him immediately and asked him to come to London with a view to recording the song. Denny had always wanted to make a Stax Records-style recording in London; Joe was the way to fulfil his dream.

When Cocker and his partner Chris Stainton arrived in London they were wide-eyed and acted as though they were in the Land of Oz. We found it fascinating that they had recorded their demo in Stainton's home. Denny teamed Joe and Chris with a London session organist named Tommy Eyre. Denny spent ten days in the studio trying to recreate the home demo – compared to the four days I had to do the whole of the first Tyrannosaurus Rex album. Although a slicker version of 'Marjorine' was eventually recorded, Denny admitted that the demo was far superior to his production. Their demo was a little too grainy to release commercially (today I would just use a piece of software such as a Pro Tools plug-in and have it sorted in no time). Joe and Chris made their demo by bouncing back and forth between two mono tape recorders, which gave it a charming primitive compression; Denny just couldn't get that with the professional gear, it was too clean. (It's one reason why I don't try to make great demos; sometimes the 'vibe' just can't be recreated, or the sonic quality is too poor.)

'Marjorine' wasn't well received and it was hard to get airplay – radio programmers didn't get it. Shortly after it came out Jon Fenton invited the actor Terence Stamp to our offices. Stamp was dressed from head to toe in a brown, pinstriped 'city' suit complete with a brown homburg and brown umbrella. The odd choice of colour, for this otherwise conventional outfit, made Stamp look like a character from a *Batman* movie. Stamp took out a vial of extremely strong marijuana and got Joe, Denny and myself to take one toke each from a small pipe. 'There's no way you'll be able to take a second one,' said Terry. In minutes the four of us were laughing hysterically and when it subsided Jon played 'Marjorine'; Stamp loved it.

'You're in the minority Terry,' said Jon.

'Really? I'm amazed. Why don't I speak to the producer of *Two Way Family Favorites*?' suggested Terry. This weekly radio show gave shout outs to British listeners' relatives in Commonwealth countries. Next thing Stamp was on the phone.

'Hello, it's Terry Stamp, and I have an auntie in Australia called Marjorie. Could you dedicate a song to her this Sunday? I'd love it if you could play 'Marjorine' by Joe Cocker?'

'Yes, and I'm the Queen of Sheba,' said the producer before he hung up on Stamp. We were all laughing uncontrollably as Stamp called a second time. This time the producer was even ruder and ended the call abruptly with some expletives.

During much of the summer of '68 we were recording more tracks for what became the debut Joe Cocker album. I was Denny's assistant for much of this and contributed the brass arrangement for the cover of Lennon and McCartney's 'With A Little Help From My Friends'. I also played 'chop guitar' on 'Bye Bye Blackbird'; the other guitarist, Jimmy Page, played his solo on a different day, I missed out on my one and only chance to meet him. Still, I'm very proud of that credit: Guitars, Jimmy Page and Tony Visconti.

Like Joe's first single, 'With A Little Help From My Friends' gave Denny similar anxieties; especially as he absolutely lived for Joe Cocker from the moment they met. Cocker would go on to become a significant artist in Denny's future, after he formed Shelter Records with Leon Russell. Denny recorded at least two versions of John and Paul's song from scratch. It ended up with Procol Harum's B.J. Wilson as the final drummer, Jimmy Page as the guitarist, Chris Stainton played both the bass and organ parts, and Sue and Sonny along with Rosetta Hightower were the backing singers. This was an 8-track recording and seven of those tracks were crammed with musical information. There was only one track left for Joe's immortal vocal; Denny drove Joe for eight hours to get what he needed. Every time Joe did a new vocal the previous one had to be erased. I will never forget watching his veins popping in his neck, his face almost purple as late one night he finally recorded the 'perfect' vocal. And even though we were all exhausted and more than a bit insane – we knew it. We had it.

All that was then needed was the right mix. Denny flew to the USA and spent two weeks attempting to perfect the perfect mix; in his quest he used ten different engineers. While in America Denny decided the backing vocals needed to be more authentic and so he put the 8-track master on the new, experimental 12-track machine and crammed 'genuine' Black female backing singers onto the song. Denny had tried to get a mix done in London before he left; I also had a go. Denny kept sending mixes back to London until one day in September a desperate Platz came to me and said, 'I have no idea what a good mix or a bad mix is. Can you listen to them all and chose one? We have to release this single, it's going to be a big hit and we can't release it in November because the Beatles, The Stones and every other big pop group is going to release their Christmas singles.'

I spent the day listening to all the new American mixes, which to me sounded progressively worse. I went back to all the British mixes and picked one of mine. It was mixed to all of Denny's dictates – it was the best mix. Platz told me to get it mastered and the single was released before Denny returned from America. He was initially upset but when it went to No 1 in no time it made him feel a whole lot better.

Denny was not good at mixing, at least not technically. He didn't know how to express things in technical terms but would instead say things like, 'Could we have more slam on the kick drum?' I quickly learned that slam meant about 3 more decibels at 2000 hertz and compression of 4-1. When I started mixing the Joe Cocker album I said to Denny, 'We're going to have to do a stereo mix.'

'Oh right, okay.' But I could hear in his voice that he was very unsure, because he couldn't really understand the process. When we started mapping it out I said, 'I'm going to put the guitar on the left and the organ on the right, is that okay?'

'Wait a minute Tony. I don't see stereo as a straight line where you have things ranged from left to right.' Denny then explained that he saw it as a big semi-circle; he even drew a big semi-circle showing the drums in the middle, but not in your face. 'I see it more like an amphitheatre.'

That was a good start and I was soon interpreting Denny's vision; I was trying to get the effect of the drums a little further back. I think the album's well mixed and there's a lot of depth in it for one of the earliest pop stereo mixes. Denny and I worked it out. The big issue for me mixing this album was that I had to do it during the night as I was also working on my other projects during the day. By the end of mixing Joe Cocker's album I was completely frazzled; exhausted from lack of sleep and so much pressure.

Denny was a recording manager, when no such term really existed back in 1967/8. I was brought over to be a musical director and to translate his ideas. We were really a great team and it was always mutual admiration; he adored me and I adored him. People have been unkind to his memory. Apparently he was tight with money but that's the common gripe of not just a few rock stars – 'I was robbed, I was ripped off.' I will always be grateful to Denny; I was getting paid to do work that I loved to do and I was living in London.

One of 1968's big stories was the Beatles starting their own record label; it was the epitome of musical success and laid down a marker for every band that followed as a way of showing they'd really made it. The first two releases on Apple were in early September; the Beatles, 'Hey Jude' and 'Those Were The Days' by Mary Hopkin. Like everyone else in Britain I had fallen in love with Mary watching her on TV's *Opportunity Knocks*; she won seven weeks in a row. Mary had just turned 18, I thought she was cute, and she had a great voice. I was glad that Paul McCartney had signed her; it was like a fairy tale unfolding before the eyes of the nation.

Apple had also signed an American singer named James Taylor and a curious group from Liverpool called The Iveys; curious because they sounded almost exactly like the Beatles. Denny, being the hottest producer in town was asked to produce The Iveys and as his trusty assistant I tagged along. It was in early September that we recorded backing tracks for 'Your Daddy's A Millionaire' and 'Maybe Tomorrow'. He was in top form, getting his signature drum sound, but he was nothing less than appalled by drummer Mike Gibbons' time keeping. Denny expected British drummers to play with the in-the-pocket groove of American drummers but Gibbons was for the most part up and down with his timing. Things were not helped by the fact that The Iveys were very young and seemed slightly terrified at finding themselves in the inner sanctum of their idols' world. Denny was also on edge, trying to juggle his time between Joe Cocker and Procol Harum. In the middle of the second day Denny had had enough, and as he was walking out the door he said, 'Visconti, you can take over. I'll never work on a session like this again!'

Considering that they had been abandoned and were stuck with me we got on very well and I finished the two tracks we had begun with Denny. I added a string section to 'Maybe Tomorrow' and surprisingly it became a minor hit in America. I was then asked to finish the album with Glynn Johns as the engineer on these sessions. I begged him, almost on my knees, to teach me how to 'phase' and 'flange', one of the most well kept secrets of British recording techniques. I kept badgering him for three days during The Iveys' sessions; he finally relented and taught me.

You can hear the swooshy effects of phasing and flanging in 'Itchycoo Park' and 'Lucy In The Sky With Diamonds'. It was discovered in the 1950s by an engineer who was making a tape copy on two separate machines simultaneously; he accidentally listened to the two machines playing together and discovered this severe sound akin to a short-wave radio being tuned in and a jet plane taking off. The first time the public heard phasing was on a song in the '50s called 'The Big Hurt', by Toni Fisher. In the '60s, engineers could harness this sound by putting a variable speed control on one of the two machines and turning the knob during playback: when the speeds matched very closely the effect is called phasing, when the speed is further apart it is called flanging. A primitive way of flanging, without a vari-speed control, was by placing a finger on the reel of tape of one machine; the metal reel is called a flange, hence the word flanging. Nowadays these effects can be made without tape recorders in digital sound effects boxes in every modern studio and guitar pedals. But it's not the same or as deep in character.

One day I was busy mixing a track called 'I'm In Love', and there was a spoken part that was meant to be very subliminal, although I was not at the point in the mix where I had yet established a level. My head was buried in the line of volume faders but I suddenly detected a change of mood in the control room. I looked up and saw Paul McCartney staring at me about a foot from my nose; I practically jumped out of my skin. Dressed in an all white suit he gave me a big show biz smile; it was very, very intimidating and I was at a loss for words.

'I'm sorry, but I thought me and the lads were recording here today. I guess we're at Abbey Road,' beamed Paul.

'Oh, that's okay,' I mumbled.

We didn't shake hands or exchange names (as if I didn't know who he was) but he was quick to offer advice: 'You know that spoken word bit? I think it's too loud. You know that bit on 'Good Day Sunshine'? It should be lower in volume, like when John says, "She feels good".'

'I know that, I'm not up to that part yet!' I defensively snapped back. McCartney raised his eyebrows in surprise, apologized for barging in, made his excuses and left for Abbey Road.

I later thought that this little 'accident' was planned. The Iveys thought that the interaction between McCartney and me was extremely funny. Pete Ham, who did the speaking part, said that he would like to do that voice again. He went into the studio and got in front of the mic and asked me to roll the tape. When his cue came he shouted as loud as possible in his strong Welsh accent, 'I'M IN LOVE.' We all cracked up. When he came back to the control room he said, 'Now mix that fucking line as loud as possible.'

As it turned out McCartney had other plans for The Iveys. Having written a song for the movie *The Magic Christian* he for some reason did not want to record it himself or with the Beatles, despite Ringo acting in the film alongside Peter Sellers. McCartney picked The Iveys to record 'Come And Get It'; if you listen to Paul's demo and The Iveys' record, who by this time had been renamed Badfinger, they are virtually identical. In January 1970 some of my Iveys' tracks made their way onto *The Magic Christian* album; McCartney had not produced an album's worth of material. Some people thought that the tracks on that album were a side project with Paul and John singing, but it was always Pete Ham and Tom Evans. The success of Badfinger came at a great expense. Through bad management they hardly earned a shilling. Pete Ham committed suicide in 1975; eight years later so did Tom Evans.

In early 1968 David Bowie had long finished with his school-days' sweetheart Kitty and love blossomed between him and Hermione Fotheringale while appearing in *Pierrot in Turquoise*. By August they had moved into a flat in Kensington, 22 Clareville Gardens, where they seemed blissfully happy; they were also frequent visitors to 108 Lexham Gardens, a short walk away. Hermione's parents had a beautiful home in Edenbridge, Kent. It was in the middle of a field surrounded by trees. On one of our day trips to the country David, Hermione, Sheila and myself sunbathed in the nude – we were naturists for the day.

David and Hermione formed a group called Turquoise, probably in homage to the mime they were in when they met, along with Tony Hill, a seasoned London folk musician, as their third member. After a few gigs as Turquoise they renamed themselves Feathers, and continued to play gigs including Middle Earth and another in support of the Strawbs at the Wigmore Hall.

They were very enthusiastic about one song they had written and were anxious for me to record it with them. It was called 'Ching-a-Ling' and, after I'd heard it, I begged Denny and David Platz to let me record it. But Denny was explicitly anti-Bowie: 'You know I've never "got" him' was Denny's take on things. 'I'm not about to finance another of Bowie's follies', was how a slightly less than generous Platz put it. I was slightly baffled because it was he who had initially wanted me to work with Bowie. Once again, I did my 'embezzling' gambit and booked Trident Studios in St Anne's Court in late October to record 'Ching-a-Ling' and a second song written by Hill, which was called 'Back To Where You've Never Been'. Unfortunately within a few days Hill was out of the band and David's friend John 'Hutch' Hutchinson was in. I needed another day in the studio to take Hill's voice off and put Hutch's voice on. I thought Platz would be over the moon with the results of this session.

'What's this? Who's Feathers? I didn't know we had a group called Feathers on the label?'

I thought that Denny recorded so much bullshit stuff, wasting so much time and money in the studio I could just slip this session through. I wasn't a great 'embezzler' because I didn't think of writing 'Joe Cocker' on the work sheet. Yet again I was severely reprimanded and almost fired. the Beatles' 'Hey Jude' had been recorded at Trident a few months earlier, but none of their magic rubbed off on us.

I was lucky that my contributions to Joe Cocker's success were there to balance my lack of hits with David and the less-than-stellar start to Marc's recording career. I knew myself that I was improving, gaining experiences in the studio that were helping me to make better records. At the same time I was slowly becoming a better producer, consciously trying to offer a real contribution in the studio, rather than just doing the obvious things.

chapter 4
it's all hype, man

After two albums with Tyrannosaurus Rex, we had probably sold 40,000-plus copies, and given the cost of making them, art work, and everything else there was no question that they had made a little bit of money for everyone. Certainly David Platz and Denny Cordell had turned a profit for a minimal outlay. The deal that I had from them was to receive a 2 per cent royalty, Marc and Steve shared 3 per cent; given that it was still early days in the life of the band the flow of money was a trickle, not a flood.

After the disappointment of *Prophets Seers & Sages* failing to make the album chart Marc and Steve began working on the next album in November 1968. We also recorded a single, 'Pewter Suitor' with 'Warlord Of The Royal Crocodiles' on the B-side; unlike the previous single, 'One Inch Rock' that scraped into the Top 30, this one failed to chart. Despite its lack of success 'Pewter Suitor' had a more expansive feel than our previous efforts; it was a pointer as to what would evolve into the T.Rex sound. *Unicorn*, the band's third album, came out in May '69 and narrowly missed making the Top 10; its stay on the charts was sweet but short, which once again showed that we had a hard-core fan base but the band didn't have enough support to break through. Marc and I had sharpened our studio skills and had a much clearer idea of what we wanted to achieve; we also felt we'd done a good job. For me this is the quintessential Tyrannosaurus Rex album. Both the Beach Boys and Phil Spector influenced our thinking in the making of *Unicorn*. Everything is bigger on this album, which includes the first use of proper drums, albeit a child's Chad Valley kit bought at Woolworth's, detuned and played by Took. I became the first 'outsider' to play on a Tyrannosaurus Rex album when Marc asked me to play piano on 'Cat Black (The Wizard Hat)'. In his belief that I could do anything I consented and was relieved that it was in the key of C – the all-white keys. John Peel returned for a spoken word part; he was still the band's champion on the radio.

Besides working with Tyrannosaurus Rex, the first few months of the year were spent in a variety of different studios, and guises. I continued to work as Denny's assistant; I was also concentrating on producing my own projects, arranging and even occasionally playing live. For the first time since arriving in London it felt like I wasn't scraping a living; I was regularly and gainfully employed. Joe Cocker's debut album also appeared in May; I mixed most of the tracks, with the exception of 'Feeling Alright', which was produced and mixed by Island Records' owner Chris Blackwell, a friend of Denny's.

One of my outside projects was very different from what I had been doing. I got a call from David Platz, who was acting as an interim director for Apple, asking if I would be available to work with one of their artists. Mary Hopkin, the 18-year-old Welsh songbird who'd had a massive hit with 'Those Were The Days', wanted to record something a little different. True to her Welsh upbringing she wanted to record a song in her native language, 'The Sparrow' written by Gallagher and Lyle, but translated into Welsh. I was told that if I did a good job recording her vocal she might take notice of me and I would work with her on her next project. Apparently she took no notice of my coaching – although for a boy from Brooklyn who never heard Welsh until that day I thought I'd done okay – and that distinction went to Mickey Most.

May 1969 provides a perfect snap shot of my eclectic working life. Gus Dudgeon was by then based in our Oxford Street office, one door away from me, and he asked me to orchestrate The Strawbs' first album that he was to produce. The week it came out I went with David Bowie in his father's Riley to perform at the Strawbs Arts Lab at the White Bear pub in Hounslow; it was a dress rehearsal for a TV recording. A few days later we went to record our performance for BBC2's *Colour Me Pop*; I played recorders, two at once, while David mimed to the Strawbs' song 'Poor Jimmy Wilson'. I also continued working with Junior's Eyes in what proved a vain attempt to come up with that elusive hit single. However, we made an album together called *Battersea Power Station* – my first rock album – it's one I'm proud of and in retrospect it has become respected, but it failed to do anything for the band's career. They were victims of Regal Zonophone's non-existent marketing plan; they just put it out and hoped for the best. Midway through the month a song I had recorded with Marsha Hunt made the charts; hers was arguably one of the most interesting projects that I worked on in the first half of '69. The gorgeous black American singer, who was appearing nightly in the London production of *Hair*, and I recorded 'Walk On Gilded Splinters'. The song composed by Dr John entered the chart at No 46, but dropped out two weeks later when it stopped getting any radio plays. Marsha had appeared on *Top Of The Pops* and – shock horror – one of her breasts dropped out of her loose-fitting halter top; it was live TV and so the nation was divided – viewers sent letters both pro and con (she beat Janet Jackson by 25 years doing the same stunt). The BBC, however, was united in condemning Marsha; I think they may have banned her for life.

Life for me was far from all work, there was a good deal of play; London was as much fun as it had ever been and I had more than my fair share. Marc and David, along with their girlfriends, continued to be frequent visitors at our flat. Marc was still living with June, but David had had a break up personally and professionally – Feathers were no longer a band and he and Hermione had also split up. David had met Angela Barnett early in 1969 and they had started to go out together. I too had split with Sheila and was now living with Liz Hartley, a Scottish girl from the Isle of Arran; she was the quintessential skinny, long-legged hippy girl you'd see dancing in the audience at free festivals, with flowing long hair, wearing colourful clothes made in India. Liz and I hosted many an impromptu social evening. I'd met Liz at a friend's house; she was my friend's girlfriend. My friend was a hashish connoisseur and I found myself seriously astral travelling after a couple of hours. The party was in his garden and I tried to make my way to a bedroom to recover but collapsed in the dark stairwell. I swear my consciousness sprang about thirty feet above the house and I was looking down at the garden party and then at myself lying on the stairs. Liz discovered me and comforted me by holding a wet towel on my forehead as my head rested in her lap. I don't recall how she got my address but she showed up on my doorstep the next day. She wanted a dalliance, and we did dally, as Sheila was visiting her parents that weekend. Liz and I hit it off immediately and within days both her boyfriend and Sheila were shocked when we said we were leaving our respective partners. Liz lived her life where it led her. She took odd jobs as a salesgirl, but she became very interested in art, took courses in an art school and paid for them by posing nude for the students. She was so comfortable with her long, slender body it meant nothing to her.

We didn't go out to see live music much; I was always disappointed by the quality of the sound. My life was the studio; music for me was all about records and making records. I'd left New York two years before Woodstock and I never went to Reading or the Isle of Wight either. It never appealed to me to sit in mud and smoke dope and not be able to find a toilet. I loyally went to concerts by my artists. I remember coming back from a Jimi Hendrix and The Experience concert saying, 'Shit, he's way better live than on record', but hardly anyone believes me.

The night that David first met Angie he came to my flat. They'd been introduced to one another at a club by Calvin Mark Lee, a mutual friend. David was living at home in Bromley and Angie lived in a student dormitory, so neither had a place they could go back to spend the night. They came around to our one-bedroom flat where Liz and I made them up a bed on the living-room floor. Liz was a good seamstress and she had made some beautiful voluminous cushions, which we had spread on the bed to make it nicer for them. Before retiring I told the anxious couple, 'Please don't cum on the cushions.' For months after that I had a new nickname: Uncle 'don't cum on the cushions' Tony.

When we had guests there was almost always a spontaneous jam; we watched the 'cool' TV shows and we nearly always shared a couple of bottles of wine. Both David and Marc had an aversion to hashish so it was never present when they came around. Our idea of 'cool' TV included Spike Milligan's *Q* and the extremely 'radical' *Monty Python's Flying Circus*; even the children's programme *The Clangers* was new and fresh; added to which television was in colour now. This was sadly the last year of *The Avengers* with Diana Rigg; her character was replaced by Linda Thorson's 'Tara King'. It was still a great television spy series, albeit a little harder for Patrick MacNee as John Steed to swing his cane.

In June, David Bowie recorded 'Space Oddity' with Gus Dudgeon. I thought the song was a cheap shot to capitalize on

the first moon landing. I also thought it was too vocally deriva-
tive in style of both John Lennon and Simon and Garfunkel. I
had already started to work on the material for David's first
album since he had signed to Mercury and his style was char-
acteristically in a folk-rock vein; 'Space Oddity' was totally out
of the bag. David said to me. 'It's a condition of my contract
that I record the song.'

'Okay, but I'm not the one to do it; I'm afraid I don't think
it's right for you.' (I was a very principled hippy back then.)

I suggested Gus, who had after all involved me in the
Strawbs' recording; he also wanted to work with David very
badly, and he adored 'Space Oddity' after I played it for him.

'Tony are you absolutely sure you want to pass?' asked Gus.

I was adamant, so the session went ahead without me. Gus
used my current favourite guitarist Mick Wayne, and I also recommended Rick Wakeman for keyboards (Rick had to play a
Mellotron, which he'd never seen before that day). Rather than
using the rest of Junior's Eyes, who backed David on the
remainder of the album, Gus used two respected session men,
Herbie Flowers on bass and Barry Morgan on drums. (David
later told me that Gus had very little to do with the recording:
it was all Bowie's arrangement and his ideas, as his original
demo will support.) The recording was a complete success and
my first reaction was to assume that David would continue to
work with Dudgeon. To my utter amazement David came to me
afterwards and said, 'Well, I've got that out of the way, now
let's carry on with the rest of the album.'

I couldn't believe this act of loyalty, but I needed no second
invitation, I wanted to do it. Ironically 'Space Oddity' was not
an immediate success as a single, but would prove to be a hit
with a subsequent re-release. My mistake was seeing what was
wrong externally with this song – the subtle rip-offs. What I
didn't realize at the time was that the music was just window

dressing for a subtler subject – alienation – and the setting was outer space.

Recording David's album was interesting, although I was not sure that Junior's Eyes was the best choice for all the songs. We eventually used some session men to finish the album; I also played bass, recorder and added some backing vocals. The highlight of this album was the re-recording of 'Wild Eyed Boy From Freecloud'. I didn't like the throwaway B-side version that Dudgeon recorded, with Paul Buckmaster playing avant-garde cello to David's simple 12-string guitar accompaniment. I heard a Wagnerian orchestra in my head. I convinced Mercury to allow me to use a fifty-piece orchestra for just this song and then spent five days writing an arrangement. It was based on David's guitar chords and would require him to sit in the middle of the orchestra and play guitar without singing (we recorded his vocal afterwards). On the day of recording we started rehearsing at 10 a.m. in Trident studios. It was very stressful, made more so by the fact that Trident's new 16-track machine wasn't working well at all. Our 1 p.m. deadline for the orchestra's departure was fast approaching, and any extension was out of the question as overtime was too expensive. With ten minutes to go the tech staff made the machine work a little better and we were able to record just one take to tape. We listened to it just once as the clock showed one o'clock; we had a harrowing happy ending.

At the end of July, with me still working with Bowie, the latest Tyrannosaurus Rex single, 'The King Of The Rumbling Spires', was released. It's another that gets closer to the T.Rex sound and features drums, bass, electric guitar and backing vocals; despite that it only stayed on the charts for a week. One reason, perhaps, was that along with the sound Marc's image was not quite there either. It proved to be the last single to feature Steve Peregrine Took. The split up was provoked by

Took's arrest for possession of hashish; Marc was very much against Steve using drugs. Liz and I had to borrow a suit for Took for his court appearance and tuck his very long hair inside his collar to make it appear shorter. Not that any of this did much good; Steve was in court for two minutes and he was given a month-long sentence. I had previously found Steve, who was a frequent guest at my flat, face down on the floor in the hallway one morning – he admitted he had taken opium. I warned him never to touch the stuff and never to frighten me so much in my flat again; I was wasting my breath. When Steve got out of jail he started making a play for having his songs included on the album. This was too much for Marc; he fired him on the spot. As we had already begun working on the next album, which became *A Beard of Stars*, the timing of Steve's firing was something of a problem.

In the end, finding a replacement was not too difficult. June even said, 'We just need someone who looks like Steve, the fans will never know the difference.' Enter Mickey Finn, who certainly looked the part, but as Mickey proved to be far from a consummate singer I had to remove Took's voice from the tracks we had already recorded and replace him with Marc. Sometime after the album was released a very bitter Steve Took confronted me: 'I swear I can hear my voice on "Blessed Wild Apple Girl".' He thought I was lying when I said that Marc re-sang his parts. Steve later played with the Pink Fairies for a while and tragically died when he choked on a cherry stone in 1980; he was 31 years old.

I continued to work with David on his album, and in mid-August I played bass and John Cambridge (from Junior's Eyes), played drums at the Beckenham Free Festival; it was free but it was barely a festival. It was very small and disorganized and John Peel introduced the bands that included the Strawbs; for a laugh we performed a reggae-style 'Space Oddity'. David was so taken with this festival that he later wrote 'A Memory Of A Free Festival'. We recorded the song a week or so later, rather badly, I felt, for the *Space Oddity* album using Junior's Eyes. David's album came out in mid-November and promptly sank without trace. In the month before he had opened for Humble Pie, as a solo artist, on their UK tour. After the album came out, David, backed by Junior's Eyes, set off on his own tour. Ten of the gigs, well over half the total, were in Scotland. Although these gigs did little to promote the album, a re-released 'Space Oddity' became his first ever hit single; it reached No 5 as David played his opening gig at Perth's Salutation Hotel. What does that say about my ideals? I'm happy to say that I became a little less principled from then on, as the success of 'Space Oddity' has proved me wrong. (Years later I was at a Bowie concert and he sang it and the audience went berserk. I told David that I have since regretted it and he said, 'I knew you'd come to your senses one day!')

While David was away gigging I started work on the rest of *A Beard of Stars*, it was the fourth Tyrannosaurus Rex album. Mickey Finn by this time was being fully integrated into the duo, but he was not as versatile as Steve Peregrine Took; added to which Finn could hardly carry a tune so Marc had to do all the vocals. On the upside Mickey was incredibly good looking and played percussion very well. This is not as trite as it sounds because his looks generated more interest in the band. The album was made in a really good atmosphere, helped no end by Finn's positive spirit, which all led to the sessions being very creative and experimental. A combination of Marc's growing proficiency on rock guitar and my engineering chops getting better helped the duo sound more aggressive. Something was definitely happening, we knew we were getting closer to what we wanted.

It was around this time that I realized that the more I stroked Marc's ego the better he performed. He needed this and surreptitiously demanded it; his ego had the appetite of a Tyrannosaurus Rex, or a bottomless pit. When he was in public (and an audience of one would be considered 'the public') I had to pose my comments to him very carefully, so that they couldn't appear to be criticism. In the recording studio I couldn't say his guitar was out of tune because, even in the eyes of Steve Peregrine Took or Mickey Finn and the recording engineer, Marc had to appear perfect in every way. So I learned to say that I thought his B string 'slipped' a little. The situation would be even more tense if a real outsider happened to be in the studio. Marc was one of the most difficult people to produce purely on a psychological level. I had no expertise in the field of psychology, of course, but I remembered certain bullies I had encountered at school and that prepared me for the likes of Marc. Even on a casual evening at my flat in Earls Court, when we played records for each other, I had to be careful not to give too much praise to something I liked. Quite often Marc brought over an armful of the latest singles and LPs and played them to me. After each selection he'd ask, 'What did you think of that?' and I would say I liked it. He'd grimace and say, 'It's crap!' to which I would respond with a meaningful frown; to disagree with him would be an affront to his 'good taste'. Once I was raving about a recording of the classical guitarist John Williams playing Rodrigo's *Concerto de Arunjuez*, the cadenza was played with flawless virtuosity. I turned to Marc and asked him what he thought and he hesitated slightly and said with not so much conviction, 'Oh, I can play that!' For once I confronted him and said, 'Here's my guitar, let's see you play that.' He quickly responded, 'Well, I could if I wanted to, but it would take me maybe two weeks.' The purpose of playing the piece was simply to share the beauty of one of my favourite recordings, but Marc quickly turned it around to be about him.

Most artists have some degree of uncertainty about their level of talent and success, but tend to be more realistic and confident in their uniqueness. Marc was totally unique and had specific talents that would be the envy of anyone aspiring to be a pop star. But in his head he also had to be things that he wasn't. It wasn't enough that he was Marc Bolan of T.Rex; he seethed with contempt for David when he came up with Ziggy Stardust. When Bowie's album came out he made some very petty and nasty comments.

It had been during the making of *Unicorn*, when Marc would come over for his bath, that things began to change. I had a Fender Stratocaster that Marc would pick up and plug it into my little amp and then play for hours. The ready availability of my instruments and the spontaneous jamming led to a series of happy accidents. Our social soirees certainly helped in the evolution of his music. If I hadn't had a bathtub he might not have come over so often, it was just one of many seemingly unrelated factors that contributed to him going electric. But even on his beaten-up old acoustic you could hear Marc playing the little rock riffs on the early albums. It was my Stratocaster that appeared on a track on *A Beard of Stars*. Marc's move to electric was helped by another stroke of good luck. June had previously dated Eric Clapton and she remained on good terms with him. One weekend during this transition from acoustic to electric she took him to Eric's place in the countryside. Marc sat cross-legged on the floor in silence watching Clapton play. According to Marc: 'I sat at the feet of the master and I watched his hands the whole time.' This brought Marc one-step closer to becoming a pop guitar wizard.

Within a day or two of using my guitar on *A Beard of Stars* Marc bought his famous white Stratocaster. I had bought my girlfriend Liz an enamelling kit from Hamley's on Regent Street and we both used to sprinkle powdered glass on flat pieces of copper and bake them in a small electric kiln. When we ran out of the pre-cut copper pieces we enamelled pennies and even old large pre-decimal one-penny pieces. On one of our evenings at Lexham Gardens, Marc asked Liz to make something to stick on his Stratocaster. He was delighted with a piece that she made, a multi-coloured tear; I glued it to his guitar where it remained; it's very visible in stage photos and the film *Born To Boogie*.

Just before Christmas 1969 Liz and I moved from Lexham Gardens and headed south. In the spirit of 'let's have an artist's commune and all live together', Angela and David proposed that we join them in sharing a place in Beckenham, Kent. They had found a huge flat in Haddon Hall, a large Victorian mansion on Southend Road; it was about a 10-minute walk to the train station and from there it was about a 45-minute journey to London. The front door of the beautiful old build-ing opened directly into a vast hall; at the far end was a stair-case leading to a wrap-around 'gallery'. In the gallery were sealed up doorways, which once led to the bedrooms of the family that had originally lived there when it was first built; these had been converted into seven separate flats. To the right of the entrance was a small kitchen and bathroom. Just beyond that was David and Angela's bedroom; Liz and I took the back bedroom. On the left was our sparsely furnished communal living room; we were always short of furniture. Soon after we moved in Angela flew to Cyprus to spend the holidays with her parents. It was quite cold; there was no central heating and we would huddle round the big fireplace in the hallway. Our land-lord, Mr Hays, a charming septuagenarian, allowed us to create a rehearsal space in the basement. While it was a splendid setting for a commune, we all had the distinct feeling that it was haunted. And it was.

Living together drew David and me closer, both as friends and as professionals. Besides being his producer I became the bass player in David's live band, which was a fun thing to do. In a way it briefly fulfilled my dream of being a rock star, as I always knew I wasn't a front guy. When I had met David and Marc I was both impressed and intimidated by their fashion sense. Even as poor working-class London kids Marc and David were stylish. Eventually I went to Portobello Road and got a military jacket and I thought I started to dress with a bit more style, but I never really got it right. It was self-evident that I would rather spend my time in a studio in a t-shirt and jeans, creating new music, than driving up and down the M1 motorway playing the same songs night after night.

Nevertheless I enjoyed dipping my toe in the water, and on 8 January 1970, David's twenty-third birthday, we played the Speakeasy club, on the very same stage I had seen Jimi Hendrix jam while sitting next to Kit Lambert during my first week in London. David used John Cambridge on drums and guitarist Tim Renwick, another member of Junior's Eyes who had also played on the *Space Oddity* album. David also played some solo gigs locally. He regularly played The Three Tuns (now bizarrely named the Rat and Parrot), a pub with a room reserved for entertainment, which was a 10-minute walk from Haddon Hall.

A month later David, myself, John and Tim played the Marquee Club; Junior's Eyes were the support band – a strange turn of events as John drummed for both. Junior's Eyes disbanded after the gig and John became our official drummer. He moved into Haddon Hall, the first lodger to sleep in the creepy gallery. David briefly named us as – Harry The Butcher. Two days later David, John and myself recorded a session for the *John Peel Sunday Show* before a live audience at the BBC's Paris Studios in Lower Regent Street. During the making of the *Space Oddity* album John Cambridge introduced us to a guitarist, his former band mate from Hull, Mick Ronson (their band had been called The Rats). Mick had come back down to London a few days earlier and David suggested he played the radio show with us – we were very under-rehearsed which was plain for all to hear.

'Is this your regular band?' asked Peel.

'Err, I don't think so after tonight,' said Bowie.

Amongst the songs we didn't quite nail was 'A Memory Of A Free Festival'. Bowie always had a hard time playing the organ and singing part one of that song. On this occasion it was a disaster. A few days later Mick Ronson had moved into the gallery. In the next week or two we acquired an Australian roadie, who was known as Roger the Lodger – if he had a surname I have no idea what it was. Two months later in mid April we re-recorded 'A Memory Of A Free Festival' as a single with Mick Ronson on guitar, John Cambridge on drums, myself on bass and a classically trained keyboard player, Ralph Mace – a middle-aged executive at Phonogram records. We rented a huge Moog synthesizer, one of only two in Great Britain, and hired a young Chris Thomas to program the beast for us. Thomas later became a well-known producer, working with The Pretenders, Elton John and Procol Harum amongst many others. For me this second version is a wonderful record, the precursor to everything good that I've recorded with Bowie.

After the near disaster at the Beeb we rehearsed almost every day for two weeks for what was our most important gig as David's band; we were opening for Country Joe and The Fish at the Roundhouse on 22 February. Musically we were getting very tight. One night as we sat talking at Haddon Hall the chat moved on to the fact that we had nothing decent to wear on stage. Angela, who had theatrical training, and Liz, as a creative seamstress, were the solution; they designed some outrageous stage wear. We gave ourselves names, like cartoon characters.

I was dressed as a superhero comic-book character and called 'Hype Man'. David had inadvertently come up with a name for the band during a telephone conversation with his manager, Ken Pitt; we had become The Hype. I wore a white leotard, silver crocheted briefs and a green cape with a red H on my chest. John Cambridge's pirate outfit, complete with an eye patch, became 'Pirate Man', while Mick Ronson was dressed as 'Gangster Man'. Somehow David acquired a gold lamé suit and a gold fedora for Ronson, and with the rest of the small budget we got several diaphanous scarves that the girls sewed on David's shirt – David donned a leotard under that and was 'Rainbow Man'. Musically it was a great gig, although we were heckled initially, and called a variety of homosexual epithets.

This was the time when rockers had long shaggy hair, some wore beards, and the dress code was check flannel lumberjack shirts and torn jeans. In contrast we were glamorous. For me this will always be the very first night of Glam Rock. I didn't know it at the time, but when we saw photos taken of us by Ray Stevenson, Marc Bolan was visible resting his head on his arms on the edge of the stage, taking it all in. Bolan never admitted he even went to the gig. When we got back to the dressing room we found that the clothes and winter jackets that we had arrived in had all been stolen. Roger the Lodger drove the gear back to Beckenham in his heated van, but we all piled in David's small hand-cranked Riley, wearing our thin costumes; the car's radiator was broken and we kept warm by sheer body heat.

We did more gigs as David Bowie and Hype, although when we played Dave Cousin's Basildon Arts Lab we were billed as David Bowie and his New Electric Band. On 6 March we drove up to Hull and played Hull University to a small crowd. We never did a gig in 'drag' again. A week later Mercury released another single, 'The Prettiest Star'; it had been recorded in January, having been started during the day of the evening that we played the Speakeasy. It was finished a few days later, along with an old chestnut, 'London Bye Ta Ta'. This is the third time I recorded the song, once for Deram, once for the BBC and now, possibly the quintessential version, with myself on bass, Marc Bolan on lead guitar and Godfrey McClean on drums, who was in a London soul band called The Gass. For the B-side of the single it was decided to use an out-take from the *Space Oddity* album, called 'Conversation Piece', it was a 'lost song' that should have been included on the *Space Oddity* album, in my opinion. (Thirty years later I re-recorded this with David in New York for what was going to be an album called 'Toy' – it didn't get released.)

Despite being liked, although not loved, by the music press 'The Prettiest Star' was a huge disappointment for David, and for me; it probably sold less than a thousand copies. Considering how well the 'Space Oddity' single had done it was a double blow. It would be another two and a half years before David had a hit single in Britain. This wasn't the only time that Marc recorded with David, but it's the only one that's been released. I thought they'd get on great, but June's comment that Marc was too good for David at the end of the session put a cap on that possibility. I censored Marc when he said nasty things about David; David, on the other hand, was always happy for Marc. But I saw a great opportunity to unite them for 'The Prettiest Star' because I knew Marc fancied himself as a lead guitarist. David never returned the favour; as much as fans swear that they hear David play sax on this or that T.Rex track, it never happened. There is a bootleg cassette of Marc and David writing a song in a NYC hotel room which is the real thing; Marc's death stopped the possibility of them recording together. Towards the end their friendship was better, and they spent quite a lot of time socializing in NYC around the time that cassette was made.

We had a gig the end of March at The Star Hotel, Broad Green, Croydon. One afternoon, a few days before the gig, David and I went over to check it out and see the size of the stage. We stood at the bar having a shandy (we weren't really drinking much at the time, and there was no drug taking while we were at Haddon Hall) and started talking to two pretty girls. David was a master at chatting up girls and he was winning them over for us.

'Who are you?' Asked one of the girls, looking at me.

'I am The Light.' I cleverly quipped, not to be outdone by David.

'Sure, light and bitter,' David quickly added.

This turned out to be the last show with John Cambridge on drums. Although he had introduced his mate Mick Ronson into our band, Mick confided in David and I that he knew a far better drummer in Hull – the one that had replaced John when he went off to join Junior's Eyes. David and I were considering replacing John anyway, but this was a surprise coming from Ronson. We liked John very much, his presence was very uplifting, but he wasn't the adventurous drummer we needed to go to the next level. It was done very quickly and before John's spot on the gallery floor cooled off, Woody Woodmansey moved into Haddon Hall.

In an interview at the end of March, David said, 'Although we're all happy with the set up, I can't see it becoming a really permanent thing. I want to keep Hype and myself as two separate working units whereby we can retain our own identities.'

This was more than significant. While Hype had been formed to be Bowie's backing band, finances were severely low. A very enterprising Angela Barnett marched into Phonogram Records and persuaded them to sign Ronson, Woodmansey and myself as a separate entity; she had negotiated this directly with the company's head, Olaf Wyper. We had no real plans to make an album, but the cash advance of £4,000 gave us the funds to buy some new equipment, and petrol to drive up and down Britain. Ever so distrustful of each other, we made a mandate with the bank to only accept cheques with all of our three signatures on them. To fulfil our contract we managed to record three songs, 'Clorrisa', 'Invisible Long Hair' (written by me, but not as a homage to my earlier duet with Siegrid) and 'The Fourth Hour Of My Sleep', which was written by my buddy Tucker Zimmerman. These tracks have since emerged as bootlegs. Bowie did not partake in these sessions.

During this time David and Angie got married. Unfortunately I wasn't able to get out of my Tyrannosaurus Rex session to attend. Eleven days after David's wedding there was a severing of another longstanding relationship. On 31 March Bowie fired his long-time manager Ken Pitt. In his auto-biography Pitt calls me a 'draft-card-burning pinko' and blames me for the break up, but it wasn't the case. Shortly after I had met David two years earlier he had told me that he had grown disenchanted with Pitt's ideas for him, based on old show-business models, and he felt that a split was inevitable. For my part I don't recall fuelling these thoughts.

In April we carried on gigging and started work on the album that would become *The Man Who Sold The World* at Advision Studios on Gosfield Street. We set up in our gigging positions with Woody in the middle and Mick and me on either side; David was in front of us facing us, singing and sometimes playing guitar. When we started the album David hadn't yet written enough material and this was about to become a new, angst-ridden (for me), style of working. We had been playing 'A Width Of A Circle' live, but we felt like it needed another section. We ended the first half with a dreamy interlude on acoustic guitar as played live. But after one take we broke into a spontaneous boogie riff. Afterwards we listened to a playback of the boogie jam for a laugh, and we decided to make this a permanent part of the song. We worked on it for another hour or so, without melody or lyrics, but just some vague 'la-las' as a guide. We put the track 'to bed' with the promise that David would come up with lyrics and melody at a later date. This caused me to feel some apprehension as we were on a tight schedule. But it set the tone for the rest of the album and I constantly asked myself, 'Will he or won't he finish these songs on time?' This, however, worked like a drug for David and most of the songs on the album, like 'Black Country Rock', 'The Saviour Machine', 'She Shook Me Cold' and 'All The Madman' were written well after we'd recorded the backing tracks. 'Black Country Rock', for instance, was actually its working title, which simply described the styles of music we'd used. David cleverly incorporated those words into the song.

The last week of recording was quite tense for me, as David and Angie had taken a fancy to Art Deco and Art Nouveau and were often sneaking away to visit antique shops on the Old Kent Road. David had some pocket money from *Space Oddity*, but these shopping sprees were eating into his writing time. Once I got quite upset when I found Angie and David billing and cooing in the studio's reception area when he should've been writing lyrics. When I softly chastised him for being away from the studio for so long he took ages to separate himself from Angie and get down to work. It took everything to hold back an explosion of Brooklyn wrath. On the very last day of the very last mix, the song we had up on the tape deck was 'The Man Who Sold The World'. I tapped my fingers anxiously on the recording console as David feverishly finished the lyrics in the reception area. I didn't even know the title of the song was

'The Man Who Sold The World'. When he finished the lyric he sprang into the studio and sang the new song. Within an hour we were mixing it and the album was finished that night, just a few days over schedule.

In April 1971 *The Man Who Sold The World* was released to complimentary reviews. Lacking a hit single, in fact no single, it failed to sell. But this has become one of my top three Bowie albums in my personal chart. It brings back fond memories of Mick Ronson goading me to listen to Jack Bruce's bass playing and emulate him. If you have complaints that the bass is too high in the mix, blame Ronno. And even though Bowie threw me for a loop in his newly formed unorthodox method of song writing, his writing and performances were ultimately stunning. To this day he often comes to a session with just chord changes and ideas in addition to maybe one or two finished songs – and I don't panic anymore.

Roy Harper, who was managed by Peter Jenner, was a frequent visitor to Haddon Hall; David, Marc and Roy knew each other. Harper employed me in my capacity as 'rock recorder player' on 'Tom Tiddlers Ground'; a song on his *Flat Baroque and Berserk* album. Unbeknownst to me the tape recorder was constantly running as Harper and I sat in the cavernous Studio 1 at Abbey Road (the symphonic studio). We sat in the dark but for one floor lamp to illuminate us and Roy engaged me in a conversation, part of which can be heard at the beginning of the song; my Brooklyn accent (with a hint of British vowels) was a source of fascination to Roy.

Marc Bolan and I continued to grow as colleagues and friends. At the time when Bowie's career was so nebulous, Bolan was extremely focused and driven in the studio and his career. With *The Man Who Sold The World* completed I went back and concentrated on the bopping elf's career. In January

'The Light Of The Magical Moon', had been the first single to feature Mickey Finn as a member of the band. Like most of its predecessors it didn't do very well, and failed to even make the charts. Two months later when *A Beard of Stars* came out it was well received; it didn't reach as high on the charts as *Unicorn* but stayed there twice as long, which showed a big improvement on former sales. Mickey Finn was definitely a bonus to the line up and at the same time Marc's songs were becoming more pop flavoured. Marc was not playing as many gigs as David but in mid-April Tyrannosaurus Rex appeared at the Roundhouse as part of a series of the 'pop proms'. Also on the bill were the Pretty Things, Elton John and Heavy Jelly. The critic Chris Welch wrote a wonderful review of the evening:

> *As Marc Bolan gave vent to one of those curiously*
> *defenceless bleats and Mickey Finn entangled himself in*
> *his collection of rhythmic pots, one warmed to their mixture*
> *of innocence and audacity.*

Soon afterwards *Beat Instrumental* had an article and interview with Marc. It was full of half-truths about other people making bad choices for him (he never listened to anybody) and hardly ever acknowledged me in interviews. I was astonished when I read these early articles. Bowie would always come over as introspective, intelligent and honest. He'd give credit where credit was due. Marc, however, was creating an alternate universe where he was the omnipotent deity of the Tyrannosaurus Rex cosmos. Like a Hindu god, he had many arms and faces; he did everything. Privately he was extremely complimentary to me, but he felt that he needed to do an unnatural amount of self-promotion, laced with fabrications, to focus attention in his direction. I never confronted him, except in later years when I thought enough was enough. But even this early on Marc under-estimated the journalists he'd try to seduce, so much so that the British rock press soon caught on to his vanities; even John Peel was growing disenchanted with Marc's new egocentric ramblings.

David Platz encouraged me to work with the Strawbs again, but this time as producer rather than arranger. I really liked them; they were such an affable bunch of guys. During the spring I flew to Denmark to record the album that was called *Dragonfly*, which came out that summer. We recorded it at Rosenberg Studio in Copenhagen, which was built to the side of a stage in a cinema; we couldn't record when a film was being shown in the evening. This gentle album was fuelled by Carlsberg's Elephant beer (it's about the same strength as wine) and pornographic magazines obtained from vending machines on the street, to dispel loneliness. You'd never believe that when you hear the gossamer beauty of this album and the spiritual songs that dwell within. This was the first album I'd engineered from beginning to end.

Dragonfly was promoted by the group touring. One such concert was recorded as their next album. On 11 July I was in a mobile recording truck outside London's Queen Elizabeth Hall engineering and recording the band's performance. The brilliant Rick Wakeman had joined the Strawbs as a permanent member. This was very gratifying because I had given him a big boost when he first started doing session work. It was a revelation to realize that I had 'the best seat in the house' in the van. I never heard a live performance with this kind of control. The main difficulty recording live is that mistakes are often unheard by the audience, especially when the sound is almost deafening. You are feeling sonic energy more than hearing individual notes. But when a live performance is recorded and you hear it at a more normal home listening level, you can hear flaws that you can't live with. Sometimes it's easy to fix these flaws by replaying the area with the mistakes in the studio (a common practice). But sometimes the mistakes can be heard if they leak on another musician's microphone. The only alternative then is to edit from one performance to another, which is much trickier. Hopefully the tempos will match otherwise the listener will hear a 'jump', cold hard evidence of doctoring. What you pray for is that the group is very well rehearsed and they give you more than one show to edit between. *Just A Collection Of Antiques and Curios* was only one recorded show, but the boys were well rehearsed – and reasonably sober!

Setting up for a live show isn't very different from a recording session in the studio. Ideally I would love to have set up my own microphones, but that would double the amount on stage, which is a no-no. So we use splitter boxes. The one microphone goes into the box but the two outputs are routed to the stage mixing board and to my remote van respectively. If the mics are placed very close to the instruments you can get amazing separation between them and it is easier to make fixes in the studio. What *is* extra special about a live recording, of course, is the audience and the physical characteristics of the venue. So we add as many as six extra microphones above and beside the audience, capturing their response and the inherent reverb in the venue. This is an exciting aspect of live recording and absolutely breathtaking in the new Surround Sound format. You really get a sense of being in the room. Four months later *Just A Collection Of Antiques and Curios* by the Strawbs came out and was their first album to make the charts.

With no hard feelings, Gus Dudgeon continued to hire me to play bass, recorder and to arrange strings on *Seasons*, Magna Carta's second album; it was a very chummy experience because my mates Rick Wakeman and Tim Renwick were also on the sessions.

Shortly after recording the Strawbs, Liz and I decided that life in our idyllic hippie commune was wearing a bit thin and we decided to decamp to Penge – we became 'Penguins', a word that David invented to describe the residents of Penge. It was a parting that had nothing to do with artistic differences or anything similar. In true 'flat sharing' scenario we had arguments about mundane things like grocery shopping and whose turn it was to take the rubbish out. But Haddon Hall had also become overcrowded with not just us, Angie and David, Mick Ronson, Woody Woodmansey, and Roger the Lodger, but also a constant stream of visitors staying late into the night. I was the only member of the 'commune' who had a steady job. I was still answerable to Cordell and Platz. Moving to Penge and still maintaining almost daily contact with David was the only solution.

As we were moving out a strange single that I had made back in March came out. 'Oh Baby' and 'Universal Love' by Dib Cochran and the Earwigs was a rather brilliant idea of Marc Bolan. I played bass, arranged the strings and sang lead vocals as 'Dib'. John Cambridge played drums, Marc played guitar and sang backing vocals, and Rick Wakeman played piano. Mick Ronson, who had just joined Bowie's band, came along to watch. David Platz had some extra free time at CTS in North London and gave us a whole six hours to do whatever we wanted. The Earwigs project was an experiment to see if Marc could write and record a hit single. But just in case it didn't work he wouldn't put his name on it. Marc specifically wanted me to sing lead, as his voice was so recognizable. As it was, the single didn't really do anything in the shops.

Marc decided that his band's name needed to be shortened, especially for the syllabic-challenged DJs on Radio One. Around September we started recording the tracks for the next album that would eventually be called *T.Rex*. I would often write just 'T.Rex' on my calendar in the office to show what days were blocked out. Marc came to the office one day and admonished me for shortening the name,

'Hey, it's TYRANNOSAURUS REX, man!'

'Marc, I've been doing this for a long time since I don't want to write out sixteen characters when four will do.'

Many years later I met up with David Enthoven, who managed Marc, who also takes credit for shortening the name of the group. He probably had the same problem of writing the group's name in full on his calendar too. The truth is a lot of people in our circle were shortening the name and it was Marc himself who decided to change the name officially and started to use it for gigs in October, and of course for the first *T.Rex* single 'Ride A White Swan'.

Whether it was the record, the name change, a combination of those two or something else altogether it changed our lives forever. The DJs loved the record, they loved the name change and we made the right choice in hiring an independent record plugger by the name of Anya Wilson. She was smart and a beauty that would rival Marilyn Monroe. We were in the studio finishing tracks for the new T.Rex album when we received a call from Anya.

'The record is number TWO in the charts.'

That day, like any other day, we went to Cranks, and we ordered our nut rissoles, salads and carrot juice – as we always did. We ate in a trance, although every now and then one of us would just say 'Wow'. It was only as we walked back to Trident Studios that we got really excited about having the No 2 record in the nation. I was 26 years old, and I finally had my first real hit record.

The fact was that Marc had had enough of not having hits, and 'Ride a White Swan' was a conscious decision to truly 'have a hit'. We all knew it was from the moment it was finished; even David Platz thought so. In the studio when we had finished mixing we realized that we had made one simple mistake, the single was under two minutes long. To stretch it to nearly two and a quarter minutes I made half a dozen tape loops of a section in the fade out to elongate it. The loop begins on the 'Dah-dah' of 'Da-da-dee-dee-daaaah, Dah, dah'.

During the making of *T.Rex* Marc invited Mark Volman and Howard Kaylan, the former vocalists with Turtles, who were calling themselves Flo and Eddie as part of Frank Zappa's band (who was playing in London), to sing backing on some tracks; they came to Trident Studios to overdub vocals whilst they were there. In the studio they proved to be possessed of an extremely acerbic sense of humour. The engineer on these sessions was Roy Thomas Baker (later to produce extraordinary recordings for Queen). He and I were under constant verbal attack, all taken well until we started to return the jibes – from there it escalated to blatant insults. Bolan found all of this extremely amusing and so did we once we all calmed down. Flo and Eddie must've picked up some defensive behaviour from working in the Mothers of Invention, as every time I said something on the talkback microphone they'd say, 'Who the fuck was that? Is it that asshole who doesn't know what he's talking about?' When Roy would announce a take they would come back with something equally insulting like, 'Who needs to know it's take twenty-seven, dick!' Once Marc felt that we were too much under fire and said, 'That's Roy, he engineered "It's All Right Now"', to which Mark Volman replied, 'Oh really? Big fucking deal.' I was thinking I could've taken this type of chiding three years earlier in NYC, but now I was so Anglicized, I was actually shocked. Marc was thrilled no end that two of his teenage heroes were actually singing back ups for him. When the dust settled we had excellent vocals from Mark and Howard on 'Sea Gull Woman'.

T.Rex continued playing live in November at various middle-sized venues to a mixed response. The part of the show when they went to electric guitars (with Mickey Finn on bass) was well received. I joined the duo on bass for one show at Guildford Civic Hall on 24 November. Marc had asked a guy called Steve Currie to observe me from the side of stage.

'I'm auditioning Steve to join the group,' he explained to me, 'and I want him to observe "The Master".' (See? Marc could be real sweet to me when he wanted.) Afterwards Currie became an official member of T.Rex. (Steve was an unabashed steak and burger eater, so the vegetarian Marc nicknamed him 'Beef Curry'.) Although Marc privately appreciated me, he still fell short of mentioning my name in press interviews, even when talking about using strings on 'Diamond Meadows', which I had arranged entirely on my own. Marc said he 'heard' them in his head when he was writing the song and it was implied that he wrote the string parts. It was the beginning of his long 'I Did It My Way' period.

Since I wasn't living in Haddon Hall, or playing any gigs with David, we were not spending much time together. David was being 'romanced' by a potential manager named Tony Defries. Angie, who had been managing David's career in the interim, did a good job, but admitted that she was out of her depth in the cruel world of 'cigar-chompers'. With no plans for promoting *The Man Who Sold The World* from any quarter David's career seemed to be in a state of limbo. Defries was promising the moon and Bowie wanted nothing less. One of the first things Defries did was ask David to drop Hype, which he did. Mick and Woody went back to Hull (but not gone forever).

Defries also wanted to manage me, as a producer. I wasn't so enamoured with the idea and didn't like his style so I was not easily seduced. I needed proof that he could do what he'd say and set him a task to recover an arranger's fee long overdue for me. He never did, but sent me an invoice after I grew tired of waiting for action and got it on my own. I told this story to David and said I was very wary of throwing my lot in with his if Defries was at the helm.

History proves that Defries was extremely effective for Bowie's career, but it was something David regretted when the financial structure in the MainMan camp came under scrutiny. Every major and minor expense was charged to David whereas Defries had assumed no liabilities.

But before that was to happen, on the corner of Argyll Street and Regent's Street, outside the office of Tony Defries and his partner Lawrence Myers, David and I had a parting of the ways. As I turned to walk away from David, the look on his face just seemed to say 'Why, oh why?' I felt terrible, but Marc was about to become almost a full time job for the next two years of my life.

Above At my flat in Elgin Avenue, Maida Vale, London, 1967.(*Left to right*) Stan Bronstein, Myron Yules, Tony Visconti Sr., Tony Visconti Jr., David Bowie, Kitty, Siegrid, Josephine Visconti.

Above Marc Bolan and Steve Peregrine Took recording demos for their first album. This image was taken in my apartment in Lexham Gardens, Kensington, London, 1967.

Above Biddu, the 'Indian Elvis', in my apartment garden, 1967.

Above Joe Cocker, Chris Stainton and Tommy Eyre at Essex Music, London, 1967. Joe and Chris had recently arrived from Sheffield at the behest of Denny Cordell, who introduced them to Tommy Eyre, a London session musician, who later joined their band.

Above Small *Tyrannosaurus Rex* models purchased at Hamleys toy shop in London, assembled and painted by me, my girlfriend Sheila Cane and Steve Peregrine Took. These were sent to DJs and their producers at the BBC to promote Tyrannosaurus Rex's debut single *Debora* (it was misspelled on the models).

Above Hermione Farthingale and David Bowie at my apartment in Lexham Gardens, 1968. David is playing a Moroccan stringed instrument.

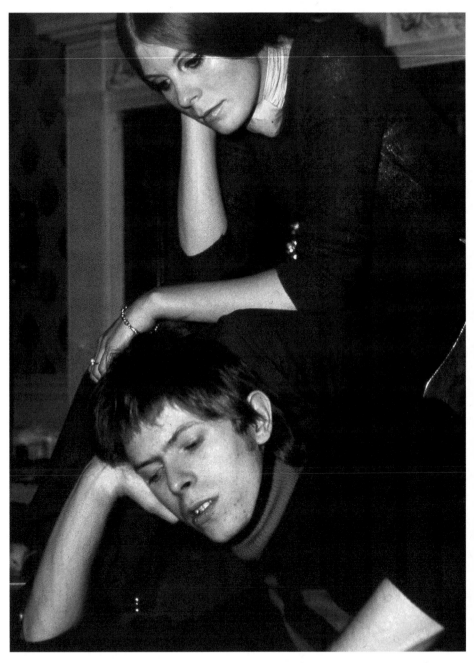

Above David and Hermione at a soirée which included Marc and June Bolan, at Lexham Gardens, London, 1968.

Above An intentional double exposure, Marc Bolan at a Tyrannosaurus Rex photo session in the garden of Hermione's parents' home in Edenbridge, Kent, 1968.

Left Steve Peregrine Took of Tyrannosaurus Rex outside my apartment in Lexham Gardens, London.

Above David Bowie wearing a fez in my apartment in Lexham Gardens, 1968. The photo was taken with off-camera flash, a favourite technique of mine.

Above June and Marc
Bolan on a break during
a Tyrannosaurus Rex
photo session in
Edenbridge, Kent. They
had just held a service
for a dead bird and then
buried it.

Left David Bowie at a
party in my apartment
in Lexham Gardens,
1968.

Above Me, relaxing on the balcony of Lexham Gardens, 1968.

chapter 5
myths and legends

Towards the end of 1970 I produced two acts managed by Gerry Bron; they couldn't have been further apart, either musically or culturally. Osibisa was a group made up of Africans and West Indians who created an infectious form of music; a fusion of tribal drumming, jazz and rock – think Santana without the Latin. While they were incredible live they were extremely difficult in the studio. Almost from the first moment things were steadily slipping down hill; their bubbly live sound was not surfacing under the scrutiny of microphones or the studio vibe. I was getting to the point where I wanted to throw in the towel.

'Is there anything I can change to make this more happening for you guys?'

'Well man, what it is you see is that we're not used to being separated from each other. These boards in the studio between us just don't work. I'm used to standing next to him, right up close when we are on stage,' said one of them.

The boards were in fact baffles, there to help to get a clean sound in the studio. I turned to Martin Rushent, the engineer, and said 'Fuck the separation, let's set up for a live recording.'

By the end of that memorable day we had several tracks recorded to everyone's satisfaction. While I thought things were going along fine the group managed to find all sorts of things that were wrong; I was served barbs like, 'As a white person you don't understand our music, but you're doing a good job anyway.' Added to which there was infighting; one of the members walked out during the recording.

There was even a short but ominous visit from the Black Panthers warning us about making stereotypical remarks on tape. Of particular concern was a phrase that Teddy Osei used during his opening monologue. He was sternly advised to remove 'darkest' from the phrase 'Darkest Africa'. Teddy briefly argued the point saying, 'I address the audience this way every night, but now that it's going to tape I can't use it?' There were about six Panthers, very tall muscular men, and they were all dressed the same in military clothes with berets and dark glasses. They were very intimidating. The group was visibly shaken by this visit. Despite Teddy being Black and African, the Panthers were the 'official' voice of Black radicalism and would hear no dissent.

When I finished the album I thought, enough's enough; the strain of organizing a disenfranchised group (Africans vs. the West Indians vs. me) was not worth repeating and I told Gerry Bron of my decision. I was as surprised as many others when the album made the charts in May '71; a couple of weeks later it went Top 20. I was invited by Gerry Bron to attend a post album release gig at Ronnie Scott's Jazz Club in Soho. The band carried me around the room over their shoulders.

'What's this, you don't want to work with us again?' Teddy Osei said, somewhat mockingly.

'Oh, okay,' I said, almost sheepishly.

The second Osibisa album, *Woyaya*, was released to great reviews in January 1972. This album was just as difficult to produce as the first one. There was still tension between the African and West Indian contingencies. One evening the West Indians – Wendell, Spartacus and Robert – stayed behind and wanted to start an alternative album. They told me that the others were holding them back from being more melodic and harmonic. This was around midnight and I did not fancy an all-nighter. Besides, I had to explain to them, it wasn't in the budget. To make matters worse, Lofty the baritone sax player left the band and we finished the album without him. As we were mixing he rejoined the band but was upset to hear that the drummer Sol also played his percussion parts. Lofty demanded that I record him and I told him that, again, the budget was all used up and we had to get on with the mixing; it was the truth – and my nerves were frayed.

I am proud of the album; it was a great sonic improvement over the first one. I also learned an important lesson from the experience. A producer has to be more than a technical or musical adviser. The producer's role is ever-changing; sometimes things go very wrong in the studio and I have to think on my feet. A row might be developing in the band and I have to squash it before it comes to fisticuffs or a walk out. I might have to settle big arguments about the tempo of the song, the guitar solo, the backing vocals, etc.; sometimes I even have to put a limit on the length of a break and watch the intoxicant intake with a sharp eye – the band can get too relaxed and lose their edge and I lose valuable studio time. Working with Osibisa was great grounding for many later projects, and I could have got a job at the U.N.

At the other end of the musical spectrum was Bron's other band, Gentle Giant – they were made for me. As a student of music their allusions to Bach, Brahms and Bartok fused with jazz and rock were extremely appealing. The band had metamorphosed out of Simon Dupree and The Big Sound, a pop band that had a hit with 'Kites' not long after I arrived in Britain. With Prog Rock taking a firm hold of the album charts, however, a name like Simon Dupree didn't say credible. I was in heaven working on their concept album. I was challenged to punch in vocals on a 15/16 bar; something studying music in high school prepared me to do. (I would count 1-2-3-4-5, 1-2-3-4-5, 1-2-3-4-5, *PUNCH* – believe me, that's not easy.) In August '71 the second Gentle Giant album came out; for me it's even better than the first. Once again there were few sales, but it's this record that established Gentle Giant's cult status. They had used a statement of mine on the sleeve of their first album; it was one that they came to regret, as it became a self-fulfilling prophecy. 'It is our goal to expand the frontiers of contemporary music at the risk of being very unpopular.' Gentle Giant never had a hit but ever since I have been amazed by just how many people have brought them up in the course of a musical conversation, as they still have some hard-core fans.

Having drifted apart from David Bowie, living close to Beckenham was no longer a necessity. For a while I commuted to London almost daily, either on my trusted 50cc Vespa Moped, or by British Rail to Victoria. The Vespa was frequently stolen from the alleyway next to our flat and then abandoned about a mile away. It was such a regular occurrence that the same constable would ring my bell and sometimes even give me a lift in his Panda car to collect it. The flat was small and dreary, with a bathroom out in the hall, but it was a welcome relief from sharing amenities with five others. But by March we could stand Penge no longer and moved to Oxford Road in Putney. We found a delightful unfurnished flat on two floors; the ground floor had a bedroom and a living room, with a wrought iron staircase leading into a garden.

I was able to have my own workshop studio in the basement; I painted the walls black and the woodwork bright, glossy red. Marc and June Bolan were regular visitors, as he still loved to make demos in my studio. We would use these sessions to discuss the procedure for new recording sessions; this is also where we recorded the demo for the *Children Of Rarn*, his 'unmade' rock opera. My neighbour from across the street, Roshan Sadri, would make us the most delectable Indian meals; she bragged that she had a different recipe for every day of the year – I believe she did. In return I used to do odd home improvements for Roshan; I installed some lights over her bed and put up some shelves. One day while Marc was at the flat and we were working, my doorbell rang. It was Roshan. She didn't know who Marc was, or for that matter anything about pop music. A shelf had fallen off its brackets and she asked if I could fix it. I looked at Marc and he winked. 'Sure, we'll help you,' he said.

It was really funny because he was wearing his chartreuse jacket with music symbols embroidered on it; as he held the shelf up, I screwed it back in place. When 'Get It On' went to No 1 and Roshan heard it mentioned on Radio One, she ran across the road to my flat screaming, 'Tony, Tony, it's NUMBER ONE!' She knew who Marc Bolan was after that.

'Get It On' also marked the end of my relationship with David Platz. Denny Cordell had already broken with him and gone off to America to start Shelter Records. Gus Dudgeon had 'replaced' Denny as Platz's premier producer and I was still very much the junior member of the team, despite my success. I had a year to go on my contract when he called me into his office; I expected he would make me an offer to be a partner with him in a production company, instead he said he was letting me go. He tried to sound altruistic and told me that as I was doing well I'd have no problem getting work as a freelance record producer. I brought up the possibility of a partnership and he said, 'I don't understand the record business, I'm a publisher.' I felt that I could at least duplicate, if not surpass his success with Denny if I had his corporate support. It wasn't that I needed the paltry £25 a week, I was making far more with royalties from

T.Rex by now, and that would always be coming to me (and does so to this day). I felt that he was relieved to be finally rid of me, this anarchic hippy American legacy from his Cordell days. I was out on the street, free as a bird but somewhat shocked.

The *T.Rex* album had come out just before Christmas 1970 and by the middle of January it was in the charts and on its way towards the Top 20. This, our fifth album together, garnered some good reviews and became our most successful so far. The transition from Steve Took to Mickey Finn was almost seamless, and on a personal level my string writing, a new thing for a Marc Bolan album, was receiving some praise. Flo and Eddie were noted as a welcome addition to the sound of T.Rex. Everything we consciously set out to do seemed to be appreciated.

In the autumn of 1970 I had been approached by David Knight, the former bass player with Procol Harum, and asked to produce a group he was managing. Called Legend, as was their eponymous album, their leader and singer was Mickey Jupp, something of a local hero in Southend. His gutsy voice and earthy writing had been shaped by singing blues and old R&B songs at the top of his lungs in pubs; he nursed his torn vocal chords with whisky. *Legend* is often referred to as the 'Red Boot album', so-called because of a red 'winkle-picker' in flames on its cover. It was another record I made virtually live in the studio. The band was very tight from playing countless pub gigs, but the drummer, Bill Fifield, was magnificent.

Marc, having found a bass player in Steve Currie, wanted to use a proper drummer on the follow up to 'Ride A White Swan'.

'What about using Bill Fifield from Legend? He's got the feel of Ringo Starr and even the tom-tom fills kind of spill over slightly into the next beat à la Ringo.' (I was thinking of the drum fill after the first chorus of 'With A Little Help From My

Friends', as well as the snare drum fills in 'Happiness Is A Warm Gun'.)

Marc agreed and had him play on 'Hot Love'; he did a wonderful job. Marc was so impressed he made him an offer he couldn't refuse. 'Bill, why don't you join my band?' With the success of 'Ride A White Swan' dangling in front of him Bill reluctantly left Legend, his long-time friends, to join T.Rex. For Marc there was only one problem.

'Fifield lacks rock and roll pizzazz and so from now on you will be – Bill Legend!'

'Hot Love' was released on 19 February 1971, four days after Britain went decimal; a single cost 50p. Marc always felt that the fans should have more for their money and included two B-sides, 'Woodland Rock' and 'King Of The Mountain Cometh', for the price of one. The reviews were great although one mistook Flo and Eddie for females.

When I left for a three-week vacation in New York, basically to see my parents, 'Hot Love' was No 1 and when I returned it was still there; it spent six weeks at the top in all. This was the first time I could afford a plane ticket home, and then only thanks to Freddie Laker and Laker Airways, the man and company that pioneered cheap transatlantic flights. The flight that Liz and I took was diverted to Bangor, Maine for no given reason – maybe we ran out of fuel. Liz was unceremoniously strip-searched in customs and then we took a six-hour coach trip to New York City; we had to stand most of the way.

Coincidentally, T.Rex was doing the first American tour and we met up in New York City. My parents hosted a dinner for the band; Mum made all her Italian specialties – lasagna, manicotti, sausage and braciole. Dessert was a chocolate layer cake with 'Hot Love' spelled out on top in sliced almonds; Marc loved it. He decided he wanted to record in New York as he had some freshly written songs, we knew we were going to need a new T.Rex album with the new line up. I found Media Sound on 57th Street between Broadway and 7th Avenue in Manhattan (it is now a nightclub called Le Bar Bat); *The Boxer* by Simon and Garfunkel was recorded there. Our engineer was Malcolm Cecil, a member of Tonto's Exploding Head Band. He had a very large Moog synthesizer in the control room, which was very impressive, but we didn't use it. The Moog had blown us all away when it was first introduced. When we overdubbed a Moog on 'Memory of a Free Festival', the re-recording for the Bowie single, we hired George Martin's Moog, a four-medium-sized module affair. It came with the only person in the UK who knew how it worked, Chris Thomas (who later became the record producer for The Pretenders); this set-up was about six feet wide by three feet tall and it could only produce one note at a time. The set-up we saw at Media Sound in NYC was more than twice the size of Martin's.

A few days earlier I introduced Marc to a commercial artist friend of mine, Barbara Nessim; they hit it off instantly. That night Marc, Barbara, Liz and myself went out to dinner and around midnight I said,

'Liz and I have to leave, do you want us to take you back to your hotel Marc?'

He grinned and said, 'No thank you.'

Next day Barbara attended the all-day session at Media Sound where we recorded 'Jeepster' and 'Monolith'; it was the start of the *Electric Warrior* album. The studio was huge, a sound stage for recording motion picture scores. The band set up around the room and all of us agreed it felt like the big time making a record in New York. The natural reverb of the studio can be heard in the opening bars of 'Jeepster' with Marc banging his platform-shoe heels on the floor. The atmosphere that day was electric, with two big hits under our belt and a tour in America it made all of us feel like heroes. Marc was inclined not to wear underpants and during a very exuberant take of 'Jeepster' he split the seam of his pale green satin trousers, exposing his bare bottom. Unabashed, he removed his trousers and Barbara, who conveniently had a sewing kit with her, mended them as Marc leaned on the studio piano with his back to us, naked from the waist down.

In sharp contrast to the great recording session, the first gig at the Fillmore East was disastrous. The truth is that the band didn't have enough of a repertoire yet; Marc was trying to flesh out his two-and-a-half-minute songs with five-minute guitar solos. The audience was actually quite hostile, added to which the sound was bad. I shrank in my seat, disassociating myself with the group, but we met afterwards and commiserated after the show – we blamed it on the sound system.

Even though I was originally in New York City to see my parents the Media Sound session had turned out so well Marc asked if I would fly to Los Angeles with him to do more recording. The plan was to meet up with Flo and Eddie who were going to book a studio for us. There wasn't enough money for Liz to go with us (even at this stage I was still living hand-to-mouth), so she stayed at my parents' home. Arriving in LA in the late winter was a rare experience for me. Traditionally the weather is cold in March/April but there I was walking down Sunset Boulevard, wearing shades and sweating in my t-shirt. I went to Tower Records; at the time it was the largest record shop in the world, where I heard Bowie's *The Man Who Sold The World* blaring out from the loudspeakers. In the middle of the almost empty store a sales clerk was playing 'air bass' to my bass part on 'She Shook Me Cold'. I couldn't resist it: 'I'm Tony Visconti, the producer and bass player of that song.'

'No way!' I had to show him my driver's licence before he would believe me.

Before going into the studio we rehearsed the new material at Howard Kaylan (Eddie)'s Laurel Canyon house. All his windows and doors were open and we could smell the orange trees that surround his pool. I'd never ever met anyone with a swimming pool in his back yard. Mickey Finn and Steve Currie staged a fake slow motion gunfight by the pool, which I filmed on my Super 8 cine camera, before we retired inside to routine the back-up vocals for a new song called, 'Get It On'. Rehearsing in such a lush house, close to a private swimming pool was a surreal experience. Marc was a prolific songwriter. He had a lined schoolbook chock-full of lyrics and chord symbols. He would open the book at the beginning of an album, and then when we had enough tracks recorded – say about 17 – he'd close the book. 'Get It On' was just one of about 50 or 60 he had in the book at the time. When I first heard it, only the day before we recorded it, it sounded like a hit to me. The next day we drove what seemed like miles and miles (typical of journeys in LA) to Wally Heider Studios and recorded 'Get It On' – the sunshine seemed unbearable to us, with our maggot-like complexions from grey London. Our engineer was a very helpful, and eager, Rik Pekkonin; I'd seen his name on many record covers. We did it in one evening, complete with overdubbed backing vocals from Flo and Eddie – we knew we had our next single.

Before we left LA, Marc played a gig at the Whiskey-A-Go-Go and once again the band's performance wasn't everything it could be, and was not as well received, as any of us would have liked. Marc was continuing to pad out the songs with extended guitar solos; some were as long as ten minutes and they were somewhat ragged. In the audience was Bruce Johnston who had joined the Beach Boys in 1965 to replace Brian Wilson who had decided he did not want to tour any longer. After the set we all went backstage, when Bruce, the archetypal Californian surfer guy with a smile to match, came by to see him. This gentle, well-meaning man was not prepared for the wrath of the Cosmic Punk.

'Hey man you're really groovy and I enjoyed it, but I think you should keep the set shorter and drop some of the extended solos.'

'Fuck off, get out of my dressing room, you're not even a real fucking Beach Boy.'

Bruce was so embarrassed and so was I. With Bruce was Terry Melcher, the producer of the Byrds; they looked at one another and high-tailed it out of there.

In an interview with one of the music papers Marc said, 'Britain's much tighter than America, because it's such a small country.' Bolan elaborated: 'Everyone knows everyone else, and if you want anything done, all you have to do is go and ask someone to do it. I needed some piano on a track the other day, so they just asked Elton John to do it.' He was by this time escalating his fabrications and in his mind he somehow confused the more accessible Rick Wakeman, who played piano on *Electric Warrior*, with the now mega-star Elton John. I'm not opposed to name-dropping but Elton never dropped in. That wasn't to happen until the filming of *Born To Boogie*, two years later.

Back in London we were adding my string arrangement to 'Cosmic Dancer' in Trident Studios when a thought occurred to me. 'Marc, you do realize that both the last two singles have strings on them and there are none on "Get It On"?'

He went pale on the spot. 'Tony we must have them, can you write something?'

With the string players patiently sitting in their seats I quickly dictated the three notes the strings were to play on the chorus. Without a score to read from I simply pointed to them when they were meant to play the three notes and repeat them when necessary. They had to watch me carefully to stop playing the three notes because the repetition was different each chorus.

When I was in NYC I had received a call from David Platz: 'Tony, would you meet with Mary Hopkin when you get back to London with a view to producing her new album?'

I told him I still had a bad feeling about not making the slightest impression on her when I did her Welsh vocal overdub two years earlier. But I relented, and on 4 May 1971, the day after Mary's twenty-first birthday we met for lunch. We got on really well; so well, that I fell in love with her.

Over lunch Mary talked about how it upset her that Apple saw her as just 'a pop star'. 'They make me record rubbish,' she said. 'I won *Opportunity Knocks* as a folk singer for seven weeks in a row and that's what I am.' We spoke about recording an acoustic album with strings; she was particularly fond of the cello.

'Why don't we use my mates Ralph McTell and Dave Cousins on guitars and Danny Thompson on bass.' Mary's eyes lit up because she knew them by name. The British folk scene was fairly small but already had its icons in those days: Danny Thompson was the first-call bassist for virtually all British folk recordings, he also played for The Incredible String Band and Sandy Denny. Ralph McTell was a stalwart voice of the folk movement and an icon by virtue of composing the immortal 'Streets Of London'. Mary said, 'I adore *Dragonfly* by the Strawbs, Dave Cousins' songs are great.'

After the lunch I contacted Ralph, Dave and Danny and they were more than thrilled to work with Mary. We all felt that she possessed one of the most unique and beautiful voices in the world. But before we were allowed to do the folk album Mary was asked to do another pop single for Apple. I had found a beautiful song called 'Let My Name Be Sorrow' and we recorded it with Richard Hewson as the arranger, who had already arranged much of Mary's solo album that had been produced by Paul McCartney. The song was pure art, a kind of Chopinesque piece, not the bland song that Apple was expecting. Mary defiantly recorded this song as a gesture of 'I'm going to do it my way.'

My instant feelings for Mary had just knocked me sideways. After I came back from a later meeting with Mary, with an unmistakable glow about me, my girlfriend Liz said to me, 'You love her, don't you?' I admitted that I did and Liz moved out that day.

A few weeks later, in late June at a press conference for the release of 'Let My Name Be Sorrow', Mary and I were 'outted' as a couple. I remember being impressed with the way she fielded questions from Fleet Street's worst. She was asked if we were living together and she honestly replied we weren't, but that she believed in living together before marriage – this innocent statement was front-page news the next day. When I was asked if we'd get married I replied, 'I'm not sure if one album is the basis for a marriage – but maybe three . . .' In that moment I admitted to myself that I wanted to marry her.

The album we started was called *Earth Song, Ocean Song* and became one of the most gratifying albums I ever made – a sharp contrast to the raucous rock music I usually worked on. It was recorded in the first flush of romance, with songs lovingly handpicked from about 200 from publishers in New York City and the rich folk catalogue at Essex Music. Mary and I would ride to and from the studio most days on my motorbike; I'd often stay the night with her in her rented house in Queensway. When the album was finished she had one last commercial commitment to play, a summer season in Margate that co-starred Lonnie Donegan. Mary had to sing her hit singles, which now seemed so lightweight compared to her newly recorded folk album.

In between finishing the tracks and mixes for *Electric Warrior*, I would speed through Kent on my motorbike into the arms of my beautiful Mary. She would dismiss her dresser from her room and asked me brush out her long blonde hair instead, and help her with costume changes on those days I managed to make it to the theatre. We befriended another couple in the show, Mark Goodwin, Lonnie Donegan's drummer (also Welsh) and his girlfriend Ondrea, a chorus girl in the review. We spent the summer blissfully and whenever I could I stayed with Mary in the house she rented from comedian Ronnie Corbett. Mary and I would go for long walks on the beach with her mad Irish Setter Barney. Life was lovely and I had never been happier and, I think, nor had she since she'd turned professional.

The counterpoint to working on T.Rex was brought into even sharper focus in July with the release of 'Get It On'; it was the beginning of T.Rextasy. Although the two big hits had catapulted Marc and the band up several rungs on the ladder, 'Get It On' took them to an altogether different place; it become universally the most popular T.Rex song. While I say universal, America was not easy for Marc and some US critics also had a go at me. When the *T.Rex* album was released in America it met with lukewarm reviews; my string writing was attacked in *Rolling Stone* – the opposite to the compliments I'd received from British journalists. Not that everything in the UK went entirely smoothly. An album called *The Best Of T.Rex* was released in August, but it was almost entirely made up of Tyrannosaurus Rex tracks – David Platz was attempting to cash in on the single successes, as well as the band's change of name. The fans weren't fooled so the album failed to even make the Top 20.

Sometimes it felt like I was immersed in the mania that was beginning to surround T.Rex, but at the same time I was also working on other projects, although my empathy with Marc had always been the strongest, including even Bowie at this point. In the late summer of '71, having worked on 'Walk On Gilded Splinters' two years earlier, Marsha Hunt's album finally came out. She had started work on this album with Gus Dudgeon, as producer; he had used me as an arranger. I ended up producing some of the album over an extended period; Marsha's theatrical commitments helped in making it a protracted affair. Gus had asked me to find some material for Marsha and I offered two early Tyrannosaurus Rex songs, 'Stacey Grove' and 'Hot Rod Mama'; Marsha loved them both. Marsha and I immediately hit it off; she came from California and appreciated my laid back personality. I ended up taking over the producer's duties from Gus and I got Marsha to sing 'Woman Child', written especially for her by my friend Tucker Zimmerman.

Marc heard about her recording. 'You've got someone else who wants to record my songs and that someone is Marsha Hunt. I have to meet her.' Marc came to the studio during an overdubbing of 'My World Is Empty Without You Babe' and was enlisted to sing a backing vocal, the nursery rhyme 'Hickory, Dickory Dock' in the interlude section. After the session Marsha and Marc walked out of the studio hand in hand and into the night, and weren't seen for three days. June Bolan would frequently remind me that I did her no favours by introducing Marc to Barbara Nessim and Marsha Hunt.

One night, very late, Marsha was doing a vocal in Trident Studios mix room. It was one of the last vocals she had to do and it was a song from *Hair*, the musical in which she was appearing. We recorded late at night because she could only record after the show; most nights we started at 11:30 p.m.

Marsha was in the vocal booth off to the side of the mixing console and the recording assistants and I could see this smoking hot woman sing through the booth's window. This particular night she was having a problem 'feeling the song'. Finally she said, 'I've got it! I usually sing this song naked on stage every night. It feels really weird singing it with clothes on. I'm going to get nekkid.'

We three blokes simultaneously had a rise in our pulse rate.

Marsha soon threw cold water on our collectively rising temperatures. 'I'm not going to get nekkid in front of you lot, though. It's enough I do that every night on stage. Can you please tape sheets of newspaper to the window?'

Professionally, but begrudgingly, I complied with her wishes. From inside the studio, via the microphone, we could hear articles of Marsha's clothing being pulled over her Afro hairdo and drop to the floor.

'I'm ready. Let's roll the tape.' Marsha started singing a lot better – talk about method acting. The three of us, engineer, assistant and I, couldn't help making sly comments like, 'Maybe I should go in there and adjust the microphone.'

'Sure, and then I'll go in there and check your work.'

On and on it went.

Between takes we heard Marsha light up a cigarette.

'Oh damn, there's no astray in here. Can one of you pass one in?' You've never seen three men move so quickly, almost bumping heads in the process. I got to the door handle first and pulled it, only to feel a lot of resistance. Marsha was a strong lady.

'Hey, no taking a peak. I'll just open the door a crack and you can slide it in sideways.' Funny, that thought crossed my mind too, but I think we were talking about two different things.

Marsha was very smart; she approached her music very intellectually. She was totally confident in her innate beauty but she was into how we could interpret the material for her album in a very hip, almost psychedelic way. She wanted to make a credible 'guy' record, and not come off as a Black Marilyn Monroe, which is how the record company saw her. When she became pregnant with her child Karis, by Mick Jagger, she would call me sometimes just to talk about it, feeling insecure and unsure about her life. We've remained friends and I hear from her from time to time.

On 25 September *Electric Warrior* was finally released. Because of the success of 'Hot Love' the band spent much of the time making the album while they were touring. I had to pull them into the studio whenever I could. We spent no more than six weeks in all in the studio but it was over a three-and-a-half-month period. Despite reviews that were somewhat less than laudatory it was a huge success, climbing to No 1 where it stayed for six weeks. It was on the charts for the next ten months. 'Jeepster' from the album was released as a single in November. This was not Bolan's choice nor did he want another single taken from the album, it was David Platz's edict in an attempt to make even more money from T.Rex. Although it was released against his wishes, Marc reluctantly promoted the single, but this was the beginning of the end of his relationship with Platz. Marc wanted a higher royalty. The fact that I had a 2 per cent royalty had rankled with him, but that situation had partially been alleviated after Steve left; Marc got to keep the full 3 per cent on subsequent recordings. He put Finn and the others on a weekly retainer of £75 (about £1,200 in today's money) with a promise that it would eventually increase (it never did).

In November Mary and I got married at a registry office in New York City (she wanted a low key wedding away from the British press) and moved into a flat on the top floor of a house in Courtfield Gardens in Kensington. It was the nicest place I had ever lived in up until then, with four bedrooms (one was my home studio), a big kitchen, dining room and living room. We lived there as a kind of sublet. Mary's manager and brother-in-law (married to her sister Carole) took the apartment in his name because Mary didn't want anyone knowing she lived there. Marriage prompted Mary to want to take a breather from full-time recording and performing. With our friend Ondrea we formed a group for one single, the 1950s song 'Summertime Summertime', a rock and roll madrigal (and one of my favourite pop songs). It was a real homespun production; the basic track was made on a 2-track Revox. On track one I hit a cushion with a wooden spoon as the bass drum track, and then I overdubbed an acoustic guitar on track two. We took the tape to Sound Techniques in Chelsea (where a lot of folk records were made by the legendary Joe Boyd) and transferred the 2-track tape to a 16-track; we then multi-tracked the vocals. For the B-side we sang an early nineteenth-century madrigal, the exquisite 'Sweet And Low', which I heard on an Alfred Deller album (the most famous counter-tenor of the twentieth century). We were emulating the Mamas and Papas, I guess, (the papa being me) and to our surprise the bouncy four-part harmony song was a minor hit in several countries, and especially so in Holland. We intended to do more stuff like this, Mary loved being part of a group rather than be a soloist, but pregnancy followed in December and Mary wanted to record less and less and devote more time to home-making and planning for mother-hood. We were two months into our marriage when Mary became pregnant. I was thrilled as I privately thought that I had altered my genes so much by taking LSD I was infertile. I was even a little worried about spawning a mutant.

Life for Mary and me as a married couple was lovely; we did all the nice things that newlyweds do. I was making good money by this time, we could enjoy the 'good life'; living in Kensington there was no shortage of places serving excellent food within walking distance. We also enjoyed the cinema. We saw and fell in love with *Death In Venice*. I had never seen a Visconti film before and I admit sharing the same surname made me curious. The film was cinematic poetry and Dirk Bogarde delivered a painfully flawless performance. Woody Allen's *Bananas* had us almost falling out of our seats. It had an absurd premise, with Allen almost successfully impersonating a Castro-like dictator. It also gave birth to the anthem, 'Rebels Are We . . .' which re-emerged in the futuristic comedy *Sleeper*, also by Allen. *Carnal Knowledge* and *Duel* were both nail-biters. *The French Connection* had me back in the cinema at least twice, having the best car chase scene ever. *A Clockwork Orange* was the must-see film of the year but we didn't see it, and I still haven't. I refused to see it because of what I had read about it; although it's commonplace in films today, extreme violence and rape depicted graphically in a film was new in 1971 and I simply did not have the stomach to sit through a film like that.

At home I often watched Open University because nothing else was on British telly after midnight. *The Old Grey Whistle Test* debuted this year and I appeared on the show, playing guitar for Tom Paxton. *Monty Python's Flying Circus* was still running and I would never miss it.

On 26 December Mary and I flew to New Zealand, where she was to share the bill with Tom Paxton on a tour that also took in Australia; it was also our honeymoon. We played with another guitarist, Brian Willoughby; I played acoustic bass and conducted a local string quartet, replicating the sound of *Earth Song, Ocean Song*. When we rehearsed in a hotel room in Rotarua the rumble of a passing truck turned more intense until we realized we were in the middle of an earthquake. It didn't do any damage to our hotel but houses were reportedly flung into the air about 25 miles away. Ironically, all the New Zealand gigs were outdoors and subject to very changeable weather; all but one of the Australian shows were indoors – on beautiful days. Mary was extremely well received in both countries, although we had one bad show in Melbourne; Mary was booked to substitute for a local favourite rock band that cancelled at the last minute. We were booed at first but the audience eventually calmed down and loved Mary's music. I stepped on a five-inch beetle that was walking towards Mary onstage; it crunched like a hen's egg. I only told her about it when the show was over as she was terrified of creepy-crawlies.

We had celebrated Christmas before flying to New Zealand and Mary cooked her first turkey. We naively left it on the kitchen table when we went to the airport. When we returned, weeks later, there was a horrible odour in the flat; searching through the flat with our fingers pinching our noses tight we realized it was coming from the turkey. Suddenly Mary screamed, and I confess I shuddered too as the turkey appeared to shift into life. We watched in horror as the carcass slowly moved along the table under its own power. A quick investigation showed that the mobility came from thousands of maggots playing 'pass the turkey beach ball' over their heads. This was a nauseating crash course in food management for us.

It was strange, given everything else I worked on, and especially T.Rex's newfound electric rock fame, that I was involved in a number of folk projects in 1971 besides Mary's. I played bass for Magna Carta, again, with a very forgiving Gus Dudgeon producing *Songs From Wasties Orchard*. Also for Gus I arranged strings on the Ralph McTell album *You Well Meaning Brought Me Here*. It was always a pleasure to work with Ralph (and Gus) and this album inspired McTell to ask me to produce his next one, *Not Till Tomorrow* (with Mary on backing vocals). As an arranger I wrote string parts for two songs by former Zombies member Colin Blunstone on his *One Year*; although not folk it was a lovely gentle album. Despite being work I took on to pay the rent I was lucky that there was quality projects like Colin's for me to do. The two songs were the haunting 'Caroline Goodbye' and, ironically given that we did the album early in the year, before Mary and I got together, 'Mary Won't You Warm My Bed'.

I think the eclecticism that began to appear increasingly in my projects during 1971 was the beginning of a thread that has stayed with me ever since. I've always had issues with a low threshold of boredom and that was certainly a factor in my taking different work. Even though I am probably regarded as a British rock record producer, my roots come from several different sources. Due to my varied background and exposure to different types of music, I feel equally comfortable with jazz, standards of the 1930s, '40s and '50s, rock and roll, pop, classical and opera. I think that may be why David Bowie and I have always been such a creative team – he's never limited himself to one style of music either and he could've felt equally at home on stage in the musical theatre as he does in a rock concert.

chapter 6
it's the same ol', same ol'

In early 1972 T.Rexstasy reached new heights with Marc the centre of just about everyone's attention with page after page of the UK pop press devoted to his antics, his thoughts and his image. 'Get It On' was released in America as 'Bang A Gong', a changed necessitated by an R&B single of the same name being released at the same time. It became Marc's only single to make the top ten of the Billboard Hot 100. He had told the rest of the group and myself a few months earlier that if it got into the American Top 10 he would buy us all a Harley Davidson each; he never did. There were no bonuses for the band but for me, being on a royalty at least meant that I was comparatively well off as the cheques kept coming in; it all added to a big upswing in my standard of living. I felt for the others who were just earning a wage. In Britain 'Telegram Sam' was released in the third week of January, but not on the Fly label; Marc had left David Platz to start his own label, a rarity in those days. the Beatles had Apple, and the Stones had RS Records, but it was very unusual for an artist to get their own label. The single went to No 1.

Three No 1s in the UK, and a US Top 10 single had an effect; this was the beginning of the 'ruthless' Marc Bolan. I soon felt a cooling in our relationship when his new lawyer asked me to lunch.

'Marc is now at a stage in his career where he doesn't need to pay a royalty to get his records produced.'

I was jolted by his words. 'Marc promised me that whatever Platz was paying me he would double it when he got his new label. Now, instead of receiving a four per cent royalty you're telling me I'm to get nothing?'

'Of course not Tony,' said the lawyer. 'We're offering you a guaranteed retainer of £10,000 per year.'

This was a paltry sum compared to a 4 per cent royalty. Royalties are for life but a retainer could be discontinued at anytime – there was no security in this offer. We were selling 35,000 to 50,000 copies of 'Get It On' a day during this period; let's say a single sold for 50p – one day's royalty at 2 per cent would be between £350 and £500. Over a year that would amount to a large sum of money. On top of that album sales would increase my annual income to a figure way in excess of what they were offering; the retainer that was offered was an insult.

To the lawyer's shock and probably his amazement I said 'I quit', got up from the table and walked out of the restaurant. As I walked along the street I just kept thinking to myself, Marc's growing arrogance is increasingly difficult to cope with and now they want to buy me off cheap. Within the hour of getting back to the flat I got a tearful phone call from June Bolan asking for forgiveness.

'Tony, Peter [the lawyer] made us do it. We didn't want to offer you a retainer.'

I played along though I detected some insincerity in her tearful voice. I was right, because she segued into how money was tight now that Marc was his own boss and all they could offer me was 1 per cent, half of what David Platz had been paying me. I didn't commit until I sat down and thought about my new life with Mary and the expenses that we were incurring.

There was a very real incentive to take the offer; Mary was pregnant. There were no other superstars on the horizon for me to produce. So I called June and accepted the offer. I was too young and inexperienced to know that I had some collateral – within the recording industry I was as well known as Marc Bolan. I opted to bide my time, make some more singles and albums until the time came when I could get out of what was increasingly becoming an unpleasant situation.

My wounded pride never recovered from this, and my 'friendship' with Marc became an empty shell. Many of the decisions he'd made after his chart success had begun to alienate him from those who'd supported him on the way up. Marc surrounded himself with emerging talents in his band, people who'd had no previous success; he always acted like T.Rex was the biggest thing that had happened to them. The band had enormous talents as individuals, but Marc handpicked them not only for that, but also because they all had timid natures. Marc wanted people in his group that he could control and this went beyond his band to include his roadies and managers, all very subservient in nature. I played this game up to a point because the larger picture was making hit records and my former deal with Denny Cordell and David Platz made me the only person in the entire T.Rex camp who got royalties apart from Marc. He promised the band a huge wage increase and presents of motorcycles and cars, but their wages never increased from the initial £75 a week nor did they ever share in the record sales. They never complained to him, but I heard all about the resentment. It was hard enough to fend for myself against Marc, I couldn't stick up for the band. As Marc got more successful he also got more 'people' to look after him, so it was impossible to negotiate with him directly after a certain point.

While Marc was playing his celebrity for all it was worth, David Platz still tried to capitalize on T.Rex's success by releasing back catalogue on which he had the rights. 'Debora', the Tyrannosaurus Rex debut single from 1968 made it all the way to No 7 in April '72. T.Rex fans, especially those that had only just discovered them, were hungry for anything by Marc Bolan. Platz then started re-releasing Tyrannosaurus Rex albums, for which he didn't need Marc's permission. I was not complaining because I still received my 2 per cent royalty. *Bolan Boogie*, a compilation album that Platz put out, reached No 1. Ironically it is made up of the same songs that were virtually ignored when they were first released. I couldn't help feeling a sense of vindication. Marc wouldn't have complained either; the 3 per cent from his early material would have helped boost his bank balance too.

Marc went on a spending spree; he went from nothing to having so much that he needed to find things to spend his money on. This included the trappings of a '70s rock star – cocaine, champagne and limos. Marc had also turned into a guitar God (well, maybe a minor deity); he could now afford a Les Paul '48, a Les Paul Special 1961, a 1958 Fender Stratocaster, a Fender Custom Telecaster, two Japanese acoustic guitars (an Aria and an Astoria), a Gibson Special and a 1969 Epiphone. Nowadays, even without having belonged to Marc, some of the guitars in his collection would sell for over £60,000 – maybe as much as £100,000.

I introduced Marc to Tony Zemaitis, the guitar maker. He made Marc a guitar, as well as an acoustic guitar for Mary and an electric 12-string for me, with Tibetan Buddhist symbols engraved on the metal front. George Harrison saw it and asked Zemaitis to copy it exactly, except he had a 6-string made instead. Ironically Marc hardly played his Zemaitis, maybe because even though a few existed they were instantly recogniz-able, as Ronnie Wood played his all the time for the Stones.

I began to get a little recognition from the press, not just a passing reference in a review or in someone else's interview.

This was very helpful in building my own profile and career. In my first ever interview, Penny Valentine from *Disc* did her best to put me at ease when she interviewed me, but I was so nervous; I got 'cotton mouth' throughout the entire thing. Still she did me proud and the title of the piece was both ominous and flattering: 'Dark Visconti Strings'. Another early interview for *NME* was again very favourable; I had gotten over my shyness by then and when I was asked by the interviewer, 'What about the suggestion that all T.Rex records sound the same?' I got on my high horse.

'That's a load of crap. Tony Blackburn sounds the same day after day. T.Rex have a style, and if artists have a style then it's the same voice and same guitar playing each time you hear them. If you don't like their style, you can listen to someone else. Marc has a style that's different.'

T.Rex had become something of a touring machine. So intense was their schedule that I had to record them on the run, again, during this period. One night they played a show in Copenhagen and Marc swung a mic around his head à la Roger Daltry, but it became unattached and was launched, missile-like, into the audience. It banged into a girl's forehead and she bled all over her white dress. Afterwards the girl and her boyfriend were brought backstage, he was very belligerent, and rightly so, about his girlfriend's injury and ruined dress. Marc was stressed and nervous that he was going to get sued, and expressed concern for the girl by being very charming and conciliatory. He was extremely apologetic and said he'd pay for a new dress (not bothering to address the head injury and the medical attention it required; mind you, neither did the boyfriend). He took his roadie/tour manager, Mick O'Halloran, aside and instructed him to give the couple 'a hundred quid', which oddly seemed to put things right. This put a damper on what had been a really great performance. Towards the end of the show, I had been called out from the wings to play a second bass guitar for the encore of 'Get It On'. The next day we recorded a couple of songs in Copenhagen, one was 'Thunderwing', the B-side of the band's next single, 'Metal Guru'; the other song we did in Denmark was 'Telegram Sam'.

The Slider, the new T.Rex album, came out in July. We had made it earlier in the year during three days of wall-to-wall recording at the Château d'Hérouville. The fame and the tour schedule had all but driven Marc mad. We had a most uncomfortable limo journey from Orly Airport to the studio. Marc started swigging from a bottle of Courvoisier while making up a blues song, 'I'm an old bull dog . . .' singing and drawling that phrase over and over. We were all very embarrassed when Marc yelled, 'Come, everybody sing, "I'm an old bull dog . . ." come on you cunts!' We all squirmed and looked out of the windows instead. Marc demanded Mickey Finn should sing; he looked terrified and complied with 'the leader's' demands. It was probably the most demoralizing experience we had as a group. I felt especially sorry for Mickey. I was scowling thinking I was going to lose my temper any second.

When we arrived at the château we were shown to our rooms. Within moments of being shown into my room I heard Marc running along the corridor and down the stairs, yelling at Mick O'Halloran,

'I want to be in the star's bedroom. Why aren't I in the star's bedroom?'

'That's the owner's room, he'll be back later and I'll sort it out,' said Mick.

Marc then began screaming at Mick, 'Throw his shit out of the room! That's my room!'

Mick pleaded with Marc to wait for the owner to return, but Marc was adamant that he wanted the room that instant. For the first time Mick cracked and yelled back, 'I am not a fucking animal. I do not want to be spoken to like I'm an animal. I do not want to treat anyone like an animal and throw his clothes in the corridor!'

Marc turned pale, but instantly calmed down (there was a nine inch difference of height between the two men). He then begged Mick in a very soft and apologetic tone to come into another room so that they could have a talk. Later that night at dinner Marc excused Mick's behaviour to us as 'his ego thing' and that it was all sorted out.

On the second night, after laying down about five backing tracks during the day, we spent about two hours having dinner and enjoying some lovely French wine. Marc had left the table about twenty minutes earlier but returned furious that we hadn't immediately followed him. 'I'm not paying you to come here and eat. I'm paying you to make a record! Now get back to the studio.'

It was no way to address a band that was still only earning £75 per week and a producer whose royalty had been cut in half. The mood for the rest of the album was horrible, although the rest of us pulled together and shared some humorous moments, with Mickey Finn acting the clown. Despite the oppressive atmosphere we recorded seventeen songs in three days. The main reason for Marc's angst was because he, not David Platz, was for the first time paying production costs, and so was aware what the bill was going to be. Later, when David Bowie recorded *Pinups* at the same studio he would bring a chef and spend a leisurely four weeks at this beautiful country retreat, the 'Honky Château'. Several years later I was back there with David to make the groundbreaking album *Low*.

The Slider was the first T.Rex album not to list everything I'd done in the liner notes. I was only credited as the producer, although I was also the mixing engineer and the string arranger. When I asked Marc why he said, 'Tone, if I list all of what you did then your name would appear more times than mine. We can't have that can we?' If I had had the guts back then I would've responded with, 'And your point is?'

When *The Slider* only reached No 4, there was an uneasy feeling in the T.Rex camp that Marc was losing his grip on his creativity since taking over the business side. He was also running foul of the music press as they had started to realize that he had been feeding them so much hogwash and hyperbole for years. Journalists had begun to ridicule him in return; it was a situation that got worse over the next year and did nothing for Marc's peace of mind. Ironically Marc said in one interview that he felt he didn't have much longer to live. For some it was another statement to ridicule, but it was chillingly prophetic in retrospect. In another he said,

I sit here and think, I've sold 18 million records in a year and two months . . . I've worked eight years for what I've got now, but in the end I don't know what it's worth, how I'm gonna come out of the whole thing . . . The gods are strange, they take it away baby so fast.

A touching sentiment, but it was more like 3 million records. Equally ironic, given my feelings and the state of the T.Rex camp, the next T.Rex single, 'Children Of The Revolution' is one of my favourites. It's a simple recording of just the band and a string quartet, with Marc and me doing backing vocals; it has since become a sort of anthem for certain types of television documentaries with either youth or revolution as their subject.

Ringo Starr and Marc Bolan became fast friends around the time of the first wave of T.Rextasy. One of the first creative results of their friendship was when Marc played lead guitar on

tony visconti: the autobiography

Ringo's biggest solo hit in April '72. It was called 'Back Off Boogaloo', a title suggested by Marc, who always had a great turn of phrase. The senior and junior pop idols began working on the film *Born To Boogie*. Ringo even told the press that T.Rex were bigger than the Beatles in their heyday (at least in Britain) and he wanted to get right with it. Ringo was known as the 'acting' Beatle and now he wanted to make his directorial debut with a 'rockumentary' (although the term didn't yet exist) of T.Rex. A live concert was filmed with five cameras at Wembley Stadium on 18 March 1972; it showed the band at their absolute peak.

A few days before the concert I was asked to record it using the Rolling Stones' mobile recording truck. This was probably the best available at the time, having 8-track and 16-track tape recorders, along with a Helios desk (which produced a specific sonic personality, kind of sweet and full, that engineers loved). This was a complicated recording because there was the risk of tape running out in the middle of a performance. I conferred with Marc about the song running order and it was agreed that he would put a short acoustic set in the middle of the concert. That allowed me to record the band performances on 16-track and the acoustic performances on 8-track; we switched the 16-track reels during the acoustic set.

Very long cables were sent onto the stadium stage and each microphone feed had to be 'split' with a lead to the front-of-house mixing desk and another to my console in the truck. This took many hours of work, often resulting in arguments with the different teams (Marc's crew, Ringo's film crew and the RS mobile crew). Things were further complicated by the intricate camera set up, which included a railroad-type track to allow one of the cameras to travel quickly in a semicircle around the perimeter of the stage; Ringo was to personally work this camera.

There were two shows, the evening performance had sold out quickly and an afternoon show was added. Our plan was to record both, using the first show as a run through. The thought was that footage could be inter-cut between the performances if mistakes were made in the evening, but Marc blew that idea by wearing different clothes for each show. Steve Currie couldn't hear his bass during the first song of the afternoon show, and so the T.Rex roadies frantically pulled out all of his cables, which cut the sound to me in the mobile. As this was before closed circuit TV and walkie-talkies were in common use, my assistant and I had to make a mad dash from outside the arena to the stage and fix the problem; chastising the roadies who pulled the cables. Recording the evening performance went very smoothly and we had all the material we needed. If Marc seemed to be on fire during previous concerts, he was an absolute volcano during this one; the film captures him at his absolute best. When he was hot he was steaming, and the crowd went crazy. He would sit cross-legged and sing some acoustic songs solo. Marc would be very communicative with the crowd and talk to individual audience members. He was beautiful in appearance, as well as generous in spirit to his fans.

Mal Evans, the hefty Beatles roadie, was put in charge of security and the task of getting Marc out of the arena into a waiting *ambulance*. The limousines were a decoy and only for the band's use. The fans went berserk when they saw Marc appear at the stage door with only Mal at his side. The commotion made me come out of the mobile and I could quickly see that Mal and Marc were in trouble. I pushed through the crowd and remembered a story I'd read that in a similar situation Mal had picked up tiny Ringo and threw him over a crowd to the arms of Neil Aspinall, the other Beatle's roadie. But Mal was facing a crowd far more hostile than Beatle fans; they wanted to tear Marc apart. He was in an advanced state of terror and couldn't hear me or understand me when I shouted, 'Throw Marc!' The 500-plus crowd of mainly teenage girls were behaving like a pack of wolves at this point and were trying to drag Marc into the crowd. I pushed through the mob and got to the other side of Marc and shouted to Mal, 'Let's go.' We threw our arms around Marc and shuffled towards the ambulance, which was maybe 25 feet away, but we had a wall of crazed teenagers to penetrate. We managed to get closer and closer as we were being kicked and scratched; many hands with sharp fingernails were trying to unclasp our grip on Marc. Some girls were getting in and ripping pieces from Marc's clothes; some even managed to uproot some curly locks from his scalp. We finally got to the ambulance and Marc and Mal fell into the back. Mal was still petrified, but Marc was holding his stomach and laughing hard, totally unaware of how he'd probably have been torn limb from limb if we had let go of him.

At various points during the year work was done on the film. Marc went into Apple recording studios at 3 Saville Row and recorded and filmed two songs for inclusion in the movie. We did 'Tutti Fruitti' and his own 'Children Of The Revolution'; Ringo played drums on a second kit alongside Bill Legend and Elton John guested on piano.

From this point on, the film was less about T.Rex and more about Marc Bolan. Ringo and Marc spent several days shooting Fellini-esque comedy scenes. One scene was shot at Tittenhurst Park, John Lennon's home, although John and Yoko were not there the day we filmed. I was in South Wales visiting Mary's family when the call came from June Bolan to get back to London the next day. I didn't really want to go because it was the beginning of a short vacation. But we had already planned to shoot a Mad Hatter-type scene, with Marc playing a medley of T.Rex songs with a string quartet in the background – only we never set a date. Weeks earlier Marc and

I worked out an exact medley arrangement and I wrote the parts. This last-minute call for the shoot was a great inconvenience but I left for London after telling June my clothing sizes. The thing that made it really worthwhile (because I wasn't getting paid) was that Geoffrey Bayldon, the actor that played Catweazel on television, was going to be in the scene.

The following day was overcast but we went ahead as planned. Most of the morning was spent setting up the tea party and working out camera angles. I dressed in the hired tail suit, with a waistcoat, bowtie and white gloves, a hippie in concert conductor's clothes. Besides Ringo and his camera crew, there was only Marc and Mickey Finn from the band, the other two members were conspicuously missing. June Bolan, Chelita Secunda (Marc's PR lady) and a bearded Hilary Bluebyrd (an Apple executive) were to be in the scene dressed as nuns, a blatant ripoff from Frank Zappa's *200 Motels*. Also there was Geoffrey Bayldon, so out of context, but the true stroke of genius to bring class to this event. He was every bit the Shakespearean actor, cut from a different cloth from the rest of us. I overheard him telling Ringo, 'I usually do not work without a script', but he went off a slight distance away and rehearsed his only written lines that Marc had provided, 'Some people like to rock, some people like to roll, but a-movin' and a-groovin's gonna satisfy my soul.' It was a joy to witness.

The only real snag, given that it was to be filmed live, was that we didn't have time to rehearse the music that had been agreed weeks earlier with the string quartet. Marc completely forgot the arrangement. After a few abortive attempts to play together we agreed that Marc would play anything that he felt comfortable with, the quartet would pretend to play and I would re-score the strings and have them overdub in a studio later on. That's why the strings look out of sync in the film – we were all clueless. When the filming was over Mr Bayldon and

I shared a limo back to London and he invited me to have dinner with him, which I politely declined, as I wanted to get back to Mary.

Some time later I was asked to mix the entire film, including the Apple studio performances. I also wrote some incidental music that was performed by the same string quartet in the film. It galls me that I am not credited for any of this; my role is noted simply as 'recordist' in the film credits. It became abundantly clear during the mixing sessions that the live performance was very ragged, something we tried to put right with a second and sometimes third electric guitar. The band did not sing backing vocals live, so Marc and I sang backing vocals where needed. Marc's guitar got progressively sharper during the performance (as a result of tuning up and up and up), so Steve Currie sounded flat on 'Get It On', the final song of the show. Steve had to replay his bass in the mixing studio tuned to the higher pitch of Marc's guitar.

I shot the cover photo for *The Slider* during the long wait for the Mad Hatter's tea party scene in the film. One of Marc's new toys was a motorized Nikon F camera. Marc had always liked my photography and so during a lull in shooting he asked me to take pictures of him with his new camera. I clicked my way through three rolls of 35mm, 36-exposure film. He made a specific request for the back of his head to be photographed, wearing the iconic top hat (which was, incidentally brown and made of leather – not black as it appears in the photo). I asked why, and he said it just might be the front and back cover of the new album sleeve. I was actually pretty buzzed with the thought of shooting a T.Rex sleeve.

A few weeks later I visited Marc at his flat and noticed contact prints on his settee. 'Tony, why don't you initial any photos you've taken and if I use any of them you can get a credit,' he suggested.

'Easy, I'll initial the three sheets since they're all my photos.' When *The Slider* came out my photos were the ones used but they were credited to Ringo. It was a typical Marc ploy; the publicity hound he turned into prompted another lie. When I confronted him after the release of the album he simply said, 'Oops, I forgot.' Ringo did not take a single still photo of Marc that day, as he was overwhelmed with setting up the movie shoot.

An interview I did with the *NME* revealed an interesting issue that would be a major factor in my ongoing relationship with Mary. I was already starting to apologize for her not wanting to work any longer.

We're going to just make folk records and she's going to sing in Welsh quite a bit. It doesn't matter to her if she has mass acceptance or not. She wants to be personally happy. She's cutting out all live performances because she hates going on stage. She's so very frightened. Two or three years of Palladiums and pantomimes is enough to drive anyone crazy.

Mary also relied heavily on pregnancy as an excuse for not wanting to sing in public. This precipitated a 'farewell concert' (for the time being, but this would be the last performance ultimately). On 20 May she opened for Ralph McTell at the Royal Festival Hall, London, but it nearly didn't happen. It was at first difficult to get Mary to agree to do this concert, which was not helped by a falling out with her manager, Joe Lustig, over the fact that we had announced her pregnancy to the press without telling him first. Joe was quite a puzzling character – a coarse-spoken, yet sensitive Brooklynite. He was very hurt and yelled at her on the phone on the day of the announcement; shortly afterwards I rang him back and dismissed him as her manager.

The stage fright that Mary developed after her hit record success kicked in violently backstage; it was no doubt exacerbated by pregnancy. She went onstage looking pale, yet unworldly beautiful. As soon as the first few notes came out the evening became a magical, mystical event that none of us present would ever forget. Brian Willoughby and Danny Thompson played for her and I conducted the string quartet. The audience applause was thunderous and they gave her a standing ovation. Backstage I tried to affirm this great success by telling her that she surely would not give up performing now. She was, however, adamant that 'this was it', the last time she would ever sing on stage. Mary felt strongly that as a mother she would be remiss in not staying home and raising our child. It never dawned on me that the pregnancy would have such a profound effect on Mary's attitude to work; whereas our plans had been of building our own recording studio and recording a follow up to *Earth Song, Ocean Song*, we now switched to talking about decorating the nursery, ready for the big event. I adapted to her wish to cease performing live, but there was a growing resentment inside me that never stopped as our lives had less and less music. As callous as it may sound, I felt trapped by the thought of a family.

At the same time, with all the mayhem and madness in Marc's world going on, I continued to work with folk artists, I guess for the soothing effect they had on my psyche. As a result of hanging out with Tom Paxton 'down under' I produced his album *Peace Will Come* in the summer of 1972. I decided to let this legendary folk singer go wild in the studio and make the folk equivalent of a modern rock album; Tom overdubbed several guitars and his own backing vocals. Mary was thrilled to sing back ups on this album as she did on *Not Till Tomorrow* by her idol, Ralph McTell.

We made McTell's album on a shoestring budget but I tried to do all kinds of experimental recording, all with Ralph's approval. We explored lots of multi-tracking effects and we 'phased' the guitar, the effect heard on the Small Faces' *Itchycoo Park* and on much of *Sgt. Pepper*. I used a cheap Tandy microphone that suited McTell's voice better than any expensive studio mic. Ralph was an intense foot-tapper when he played and instead of asking him to take off his shoes and tap on a thick carpet (normal studio procedure) I had him tap as loud as he wanted on the hollowest part of the studio floor. The other musicians were drummer Laurie Allan, bassist Danny Thompson and myself on various instruments. It was a fun album to make as all of us were great friends and the camaraderie was improved by frequent visits to the pub. Producing a folk record is very different to making a rock record. It doesn't take a long time or a lot of money to make a folk album. Rock 'n' roll and pop, on the other hand, rely on creating new, radically different soundscapes. Their very nature requires experimentation and more things are left off a rock album than left on. *Sgt. Pepper* took nine months to record compared to the four days it took to make the first Tyrannosaurus Rex album (essentially a folk music duo) made during the same period.

I had had no contact with Bowie since we parted on the street corner but watched as his career deservedly gained momentum. *Hunky Dory*, the follow-up to *The Man Who Sold The World*, was a much-applauded album that charted at No 3. In July of 1972 *The Rise and Fall of Ziggy Stardust and the Spiders from Mars* made the charts and eventually made it to No 5; this performance was enhanced by the fact that it stayed in the charts for over two years. To capitalize on Bowie's new-found success the *Space Oddity* album and *The Man Who Sold The World* were re-released; they had a lot more chart and sales success than the first time around.

I decided to form my own production company and called it Good Earth Productions. It was named after the book *The Good Earth* by Pearl S. Buck. I was so impressed with the spirit of the central family in the story, how they survived disaster and made a success of their lives – attributing the gamut to the Good Earth. Unfortunately many Chinese restaurants took this name, so we often had tourists in Soho ringing my studio's doorbell late at night asking to be let in for dinner. Roger Myers, a business adviser and accountant, and brother of Laurence Myers, the manager of David Bowie, convinced me that he could generate far more income for both of us than I could make on my own. His idea was to buy into the business as an equal partner, an offer I accepted. He made a label deal with Essex Music, and in a nice piece of synchronicity the first Good Earth production was released on the Regal Zonophone label. It was by a group I saw in a folk club at the William IV pub in Leyton, North London. Gasworks were incredibly funny live and that's the way I decided to record them, but with a new technique I coined as 'Live Plus'. We made no secret on the record sleeve that the duo was embellished by further overdubs in the studio. I hired the Marquee Club for a day and recorded two performances, editing between the two. They were part northern comedic wit with a smattering of Woody Allen deadpan delivery. I think the verbal introduction to 'Verbalise Your Pre-Orgasmic Tension' is one of the best introductions to any song in recording history. Unfortunately I was in the minority and it bombed.

The year ended with 'Solid Gold Easy Action' by T.Rex being released on 1 December; it reached No 2. Mary and I decided to put out a Christmas single, the traditional 'Mary Had A Baby'. It was recorded just before our first child, Delaney Jay, was born on 22 November 1972. We had first heard the name Delaney (as a first name) through the singing duo Delaney and Bonnie. Delaney officially changed his name to Morgan by deed poll when he was 15 years old – he did it all by himself. He was always being teased as 'Delaney's Donkey' in school. Val Doonican recorded a comedy single by the same name in 1967 and Mary and I were completely oblivious to that reference. I'll call him Morgan from here on to avoid confusion.

The other big event of the year's end was the release of Marc's movie. In December, Mary and I attended the premiere at Oscar's cinema in Brewer Street and an after show party at Tramp; we were photographed and, oddly, the photo was used on the back of the sleeve for Marc's next album, *Tanx*. It was one of the few occasions that we went out socially during the year. Pressure of work, Mary's pregnancy and the other things that crop up for newlyweds all played a part in curtailing our nights out. We did manage to see *The Godfather*, but we missed *Deliverance* and *Cabaret*. Woody Allen's *Play It Again, Sam* was the most innovative comedy in ages and we loved it.

We enjoyed cooking and entertaining. Mary, being the youngest child, was never allowed to do any housework or cooking when she was growing up. Being a homemaker was new for her, and an exciting challenge most of the time. The domestic VCR became available and we bought a very early model; a clumsy recorder made by Philips that could only record for 30 minutes on a bulky cassette. This was perfect because I was busy amassing *Monty Python* shows. After I had about eight hours of shows we had a non-stop *Monty Python* marathon at our flat and invited Marc and June Bolan and many other friends over to get stoned and watch all the shows I had on tape. We did have one break for food but only June Bolan was together enough to order Chinese food delivery for thirty people; we had five deliverymen bring the ten carrier bags to our flat. I remember the bill being nearly £300. I think I paid for it all, but then again, this was the first time in my life that I could. For me the other most hilarious comedy show at this time was definitely *Are You Being Served?* They milked the double entendre to death. I never stopped loving Molly Sugden's comments about her 'pussy', one of the most outrageous risqué things you could get away with back then.

Shortly before the end of the year T.Rex had started recording once again at the Château d'Hérouville. Marc felt, for some reason, compelled to rush into a new album hard on the heals of *The Slider*. He was also anxious to record it abroad to avoid paying taxes on income that was earned outside the UK. Marc had a company named Wizard Bahamas to take care of his 'overseas' work.

Fortunately the atmosphere was a little more relaxed than during our previous visit to the château. Maybe Marc had less anxiety over money, whatever the reason we recorded at a more leisurely pace. One of the tracks for the album that would become *Tanx* was 'Left Hand Luke and the Beggar Boys', a blatant homage to 'Montague, The Magnificent', a 45-rpm single I bought as a teenager in New York. Montague was a NYC DJ who would sermonize over a backing track; he was like an R&B version of a southern preacher. Marc and I loved it and would listen to it over and over again – it was great music and Montague's rap was so uplifting. At the beginning of another track, 'Mad Donna', you hear a young French girl announce, '*Donna la folle, par T.Rex.*' Marc then gives her a big kiss and the track begins.

Back in London we overdubbed female backing singers; we also rediscoved the Mellotron (made famous on 'Strawberry Fields Forever') and used it on many tracks. I am the Mellotron player and you can hear my warm-up just before the opening track, 'Tenement Lady', begins. As seemed to be the custom by now I'm only credited as the producer, I got no credit for mixing, arranging or conducting the strings. One nice touch was using a fantastic tenor sax player named Howie Casey, a Liverpudlian who played for the Beatles on 'Good Morning, Good Morning'.

I enjoyed making *Tanx* very much; I thought it was the first really cohesive T.Rex album. However, despite Marc feeling more confident with this body of work, it proved to be something of a watershed. We were criticized as being 'samey' and formulaic; *Tanx* made No 4, the same as *The Slider*, but failed to stick around as long in the charts. It was the last of Marc's albums to make the Top 10, other than greatest hits and compilations. The press also continued to snipe at what they saw as Marc's attempts at manipulation; today it would be called spin. One reporter took him to task for putting down his teenage mate David Bowie, which he did, and pointed out that Bowie was always gracious towards Bolan in his interviews. The piece finished with a real jibe at Marc, 'just makes him seem like a be-glittered Don Quixote loudly tilting against windmills.'

The press took the view that T.Rex were on the way out and that Bowie was 'poaching' the hip T.Rex fans. I could all too clearly see the writing on the wall. There were new kids on the block doing the Glam thing and some were doing it much better than we were. The teenyboppers had Slade and Gary Glitter, but the cool kids were listening to Bowie and Roxy Music. I tried to encourage Marc to take some time off and rethink the whole thing. My suggestion was met with one of Marc's determined statements: 'Tony, we have to make one more album for the kids.' For me it revealed that Marc had gotten out of touch, and was removed from his fans. Those kids were growing up and growing out of T.Rex and no one was replacing them.

My next project for my Good Earth company was an excellent band. I got a call from a manager who said he represented a rock-flamenco group from Los Angeles; I was fascinated by the idea and asked if I could meet them. They were called Carmen and I adored them from the second they walked into our offices in Museum Street wearing facial makeup and their hybrid rock/flamenco outfits. When they opened their mouths to sing I felt like I was gloriously transported to an alternative universe. They did two numbers, unplugged. Paul Fenton was seated, drumming on his thighs. John Glascock and David Allen played acoustic guitars, Angela Allen (David's sister) and Roberto Amarel sang and danced; in fact they sang in slick four-part harmony. They were my first really big signing for my company; there was certainly nothing like them on the scene, which may have worked against them. But I was excited about them and confident they were one of the next big things.

As I was finishing their album, *Fandangos In Space*, in the summer, Bowie and I had just got back on speaking terms; David had rung me, and we talked over the phone a bit before agreeing to meet one evening to see Peter Cook and Dudley Moore live. I invited David to meet Carmen when I was mixing their album at Air Studios in Oxford Circus and I was thrilled when David invited them to appear with him at the Marquee Club as a part of a TV project.

David asked me to write some string arrangements for a side project of his, The Astronettes, who consisted of Ava Cherry, Geoffrey McCormick and Jason Guess. They were a vocal group that looked incredible and sounded unusual. I wrote some very different arrangements for songs such as 'God Only Knows' and 'I Am A Dodo' (which was rewritten as 'Scream Like A Baby' for Bowie's *Scary Monsters* album). I also wrote strings for '1984', a theme song for Bowie's television special, which was in the early stages of development. The 'God Only Knows' arrangement features mandolins playing what would normally be for violins; I thought I would have to persuade David to accept it, but he did so without hesitation.

The *1980 Floor Show* was videoed at the Marquee Club in late October 1973. Besides Carmen, and the Astronettes, there was Marianne Faithful and Reg Presley of The Troggs. Although Mary and I were invited as guests, David, at the last minute, asked me to help out in the recording truck to keep an eye on things; Ken Scott was the engineer. I was happy to volunteer, but I was a bit upset that I missed a special moment. 'It's a pity you were in the recording booth. You missed Marianne Faithful's bum,' said Mary on the way home. A very stoned (and pretty) Marianne Faithful had turned her back to the audience, revealing that she was wearing nothing under her nun's habit as it fell open.

David and Angela invited us to the theatre to see *Behind The Fridge* written by and starring Peter Cook and Dudley Moore. When they arrived to pick us up in their limo, David took the lift up to our flat to collect us. I was giving the babysitter instructions about how to feed our infant son when David walked into our kitchen dressed in full Ziggy Stardust regalia, with orange spiked hair and shaved eyebrows – how long must have it took him to get ready to go out? The babysitter, unbeknownst to me, was a Bowie fan; she dropped the pan filled with warm water that contained the baby's bottle on the kitchen floor and shrieked. David was amused (no doubt he was used to having this effect on people) and I laughed hysterically. The stretch limo was an American left-hand drive car and as we got into the narrow streets of Covent Garden the driver wedged the limo in between cars parked on either side of the narrow lane. We had to squeeze out of the narrowly open doors and walk the rest of the way to the theatre.

In his post-Beatle career Paul McCartney had made some interesting albums that spawned some hit singles. In search of a new

direction, and possibly to give an injection of something different, Paul and Linda, along with Denny Laine, had gone to
Lagos in Nigeria to make their next album. In late September,
shortly after they returned we got a phone call at our home
from Macca. After he talked briefly to Mary she handed me the
phone.

'Hi Tony, I love the strings on T.Rex records, did you write
them?'

'Yes,' I replied.

'Can you really read and write music?'

'Yes.'

'Oh right, in that case will you write strings for the album
I've just finished?'

'YES!'

The next day, a Sunday afternoon, Mary, our ten-month-old
son and I made the short trip over to the McCartneys' home in St
John's Wood. Mary and Linda sat in the living room with the
McCartney children making a fuss over our little Morgan. In
the same room Paul sat at the piano with me sitting next to him
and played me snippets of songs on a portable cassette player,
while on a second one he recorded his comments and his piano
doodlings for string ideas. Some ideas he wanted me to strictly
adhere to and some were just sketches that I was asked to improve
upon. For a song called 'Drink To Me (the Picasso song)' he said,
'Just do your thing, but in the style of Motown strings.'

I was thrilled to be doing this for one of my idols but not so
thrilled when he told me he needed all seven arrangements by
Wednesday.

I hardly slept for two days. I also had to book and strategize
the session, starting with the sixty musicians needed for the
title track, 'Band on the Run', down to the string quartet for
'No Words'. When I arrived at Air Studios I'm sure I looked
bedraggled, I definitely felt it. I was greeted by Paul, Linda and

Denny along with their great engineer Geoff Emerick. The sixty musicians are already there and I braced myself to begin the tedious arm waving (my bad style of conducting) and note correcting. The very first thing we did was the interlude between the first and second parts of 'Band On The Run'; it proved to be very difficult because the first section is in an entirely different tempo from the next. We just kept doing take after take until we got the transition to work smoothly. Only some of the sixty musicians were wearing headphones, so it was a genuine job of conducting to bring them in and to keep them together. The rest of the day went a lot smoother. For the most part Paul acted the jovial perfectionist, which made it all seem like fun.

The afternoon reunited Paul with Howie Casey; they knew each other from Liverpool. He was one of the sax players that we used on 'Jet'. It all went very smoothly until Paul wanted to add a sax solo at the very last minute. He sang it to Howie, but the melody started higher than the upper limit on the tenor sax, added to which it was in concert B major, a very difficult key for saxes. I solved the problem by writing out the phrase and gave the first half to the alto sax player. The first half was easy on alto sax but ended lower than the alto's range. Paul would not accept alternative notes once he had this part in his head, but he liked the idea of Howie playing the final handful of notes on the tenor sax. After several tries, the two sax players made the transition perfectly and helped make the song's end so much better.

About a month later I got another call from Paul, asking if he and Linda could come over and play the mixes to Mary and me. I was excited to hear them.

'I hope you don't mind but a band I'm working with called Carmen are at the house this evening . . .'

'No problem, Tony, we'll be right over.'

He arrived and handed me a reel-to-reel stereo ¼ inch tape I could play on my Revox. 'Oh goodie, I can't wait to hear my arrangements.' I exclaimed.

Paul immediately cut in, 'I can wait to hear my arrangements.'

This was slightly off-putting and I was slightly embarrassed in front of Carmen. The arrangements were cooperative efforts. Little did I know I wouldn't even be credited on the sleeve, I was just mentioned in the column of 'Paul, Linda and Denny would like to thank . . .' We listened and I made comments on the mixes and Paul took some of them well and some he defended. I don't recall if he went back and remixed any of them. Carmen left afterwards and the four of us retired to the dining room where we ate vegetarian lasagne that Mary had adapted from my mother's recipe. When the 25th anniversary reissue of *Band On The Run* came out, Paul acknowledged my orchestrations on the new sleeve and sent me a personal handwritten note saying, 'You got your credit.'

chapter 7
abroad and at home

We went to Munich in October 1972 to work at Musicland on the new T.Rex album; once again I asked Marc if he wanted to do something a bit more experimental. Once again 'We have to do one more for the kids,' was his reply.

The studio was very slick and Mack, who ended up as Queen's favourite engineer, worked the place like clockwork. It was in a huge complex that housed a bland, Hilton-type hotel, but the accommodation was, for the first time, first class for all of us. On our first night Mickey Finn, Steve Currie and I decided to have a sauna after work. We opened the door to the health spa's pool and discovered nude Germans of both sexes lounging around as if this was normal – which it obviously was for them. We were confused having walked through the door marked 'Herren'; it made me question my grasp of German. Undeterred we got into the spirit of the place as we removed our towels and joined in the nudity. The three of us sat in the extremely hot sauna for far longer than we should so that we could seriously contemplate the two attractive blonde females lying prone before us. The next night everyone, including the roadies, had to take a sauna.

The sessions went fine, but it was the same ol' same ol' and I was convinced it wasn't what the kids wanted at all. Back in London we added Gloria Jones and her friend Pat as the new, official, T.Rex backing vocalists. During the London sessions my parents, who happened to be staying with Mary and I, came to the studio during the string overdubs for 'Teenage Dream'; Marc, who always adored my parents, made a big fuss of them. They were in the control room as I was in the studio conducting the strings. The engineer was playing the track very loud at Marc's request and he was wildly running from wall to wall posturing for the benefit of my parents. He held my mother's shoulders and shouted in her ear, 'Money, MONEY!' as if the music wasn't loud enough. Marc was becoming more and more irrational.

Another nail in our professional coffin came when Marc invited some groupies to the studio to watch the session, something completely out of the norm for him. T.Rex sessions were usually closed ones (no outsiders permitted), but as well as the groupies there was an abundance of cocaine and cognac. It all seemed to encourage Marc to be his teeth-grinding, egotistical worst. Both alcohol and cocaine are serious impediments for being able to tune an instrument or a voice, and I noticed that Marc's guitar tuning was growing particularly sharp; he never would refer to the ubiquitous stroboscopic guitar tuner that is found in every studio. He would just tune up higher and eventually became much sharper than concert pitch, which was problematic when overdubbing orchestral instruments, especially the piano.

'Marc your guitar is out of tune.' It was a big mistake in the presence of the groupies. I was assaulted with by a verbal lashing.

'Fuck you! My guitar isn't out of tune – I just tuned it.'

Everyone froze and Marc stormed out – my cheeks went slightly rouge. I quickly moved from the control room into the studio and tuned his guitar properly, as I'd done many times in the past. I had been through countless tirades like this in the studio, and even on the phone when record sales weren't good, but I had come to the end of my tether. I'd given him my all, but being a team player to a maniacal leader wasn't my idea of a rich, creative experience – or a so-called friendship.

During the making of the album June left Marc for having the third affair in their marriage. This time it was backing singer Gloria Jones. June could not take one more paramour coming between them. Gloria and Marc had first met in Los Angeles during the week we recorded 'Get It On'. I didn't realize that something more than a musical interest had passed between them and now Gloria was in London with her friend 'Sister' Pat Hall; both were accomplished singers and very nice people. Even on these overdub sessions I was still not quite sure what was going on, because Marc was now living alone.

During the overdubs I spent an evening at Marc's flat at Marble Arch along with some of the band, including Carmen's drummer Paul Fenton, who had played on Marc's session earlier in the evening at Air Studios. There were copious amounts of cocaine available courtesy of Marc and his fridge contained about twenty bottles of champagne and, oddly, one cold boiled chicken left by June; Marc had ceased to be a vegetarian. Besides the cocaine and champagne we were also swigging cognac from the bottle. Several Polaroid's were taken that night and made their way to the double sleeve of the new album *Zinc Alloy and The Hidden Riders of Tomorrow* (an album title not unlike *Ziggy Stardust and the Spiders From Mars*). Marc was now, not so obviously, chasing Bowie. Incidentally, earlier in the year we'd recorded a demo of a song called 'Truck On Tyke' and Mary, my wife, did a backing vocal. When we made the final recording, Marc's new girlfriend Gloria, the future mother of Rolan Bolan, sang the final back up vocal.

Again, I dutifully wrote all the string parts, played Mellotron, mixed the album, tied up all the loose ends and left

Marc for good. I made my decision midway through the making of the album; I wrote him a letter of resignation as we were finishing up. In it I said I was leaving because his behaviour towards his band members and me was rude and insulting, and that he showed no signs of wanting to progress musically. I can't remember the exact wording; he never responded. When the album came out I was surprised to see on the cover that the band was now called Marc Bolan & T.Rex and that the album was 'co-produced' by Marc, downplaying my roles even further. Technically, because he was paying the bills, he could call himself a co-producer. But he did no more on *Zinc Alloy* . . . than he did on former albums. Apparently he remixed '(Whatever Happened To The) Teenage Dream' and credited himself as the sole producer – possibly his way of getting back at me.

Despite the patchiness of this album, it has an attractive dark quality, and I really like three of the tracks: 'The Avengers', '(Whatever Happened To The) Teenage Dream' and 'Interstellar Soul'. It was surprising that any of it was good given the fact that the band and I were so demoralized and Marc was at the peak of denial; the reviews were terrible. I heard nothing from Marc; Steve Currie told me at Marc's funeral that Marc simply said, 'Tony's not working with us anymore', and said not another word about it. Several months later Mick O'Halloran phoned and asked for the demo of 'Children Of Rarn'; I told him that I'd lost it. I actually couldn't locate it, it was buried somewhere in a moving tea chest. But I wasn't going to go out of my way to find it.

It was to be a year of change that was in part the result of our landlord discovering that Mary and I were not Mr and Mrs Stan Sherrington, Mary's brother-in-law and sister. We were nearly kicked out, but it encouraged us to find a place of our own to buy in London. We bought a house at 9 Melrose

Terrace in Shepherd's Bush. Even on a 1 per cent royalty from T.Rex I had been earning a considerable amount of money, and the earlier stuff on Platz's label was still selling strong. This presented me with a dilemma: either pay a lot of tax or invest my earnings in a state-of-the-art home studio; gleefully I opted for the latter. My business partner Roger Myers at first objected, saying that as an accountant he'd seen rock stars do this and lose interest later, finding the technology and upkeep daunting. Mary was for the home studio, however, because she still wanted to be a recording artist, just not one who sang live. The ground floor of the house was already converted to a long front-to-back photographic studio. It 'screamed' to me, 'RECORDING STUDIO!'

The owner was a very hip, well-connected London fashion photographer. After we were shown the house we were invited to a party that evening in the house. It was one of those very trendy parties that had liberally sprinkled models in every corner and copious amounts of cocaine and champagne were served. Cocaine was the social drug of the '70s, replacing hashish almost entirely. A lot of the popularity of the drug was based on the myth that it was not habit-forming. Some sweet young things at the party were going out of the way to get me to try their own 'Charlie' in little glass bottles with tiny spoons attached to the lid – as if they each had a special 'vintage' (Mary would never touch the drug). Mary and I fell in love with the size of the house. There was plenty of room for the studio and a long back garden for our son to safely romp around in.

Transforming the photographic studio to a recording studio meant soundproofing it and adding adequate ventilation. With two New Zealand friends, Bruce Lynch (Cat Stevens' bass player at the time) and Graeme Myrhe, we drew plans and set about the work. After weeks of building a room within the room, for sound isolation, wiring through the walls and installing an industrial air conditioner with a ventilation shaft going up two storeys to dissipate air rumble noise, we were set to have all the lovely equipment I'd ordered, delivered. One evening I took Mary over to inspect the final building work and we sat quietly on the floor of the studio. We could faintly hear the television of our next-door neighbour; I looked at her in complete despair. So much for the soundproofing, I sat there almost sobbing, my head in my hands, while Mary comforted me. I even called the studio 'Visconti's folly'. We'd already lost a third of the volume of the space by constructing a room within a room, yet it was apparent that we needed another layer or two of something soft under something dense to cut the sound down even more. So Bruce and Graeme had to remove the hessian finish of the walls and shrink the room even more before the equipment could be installed. Nowadays one could hire one of many acousticians to build a home studio, but we had no such luxury in those days.

We finally conquered the leaking sound, but the former photography studio was now converted to a room larger than a cockpit but smaller than a bed-sit. Finally we were ready for the equipment to be installed: a 16-track MCI machine, a Trident console designed and built by my engineering mentor Malcolm Toft, monitor speakers by Klein & Hummel, signal processing gear by Urei and Valley People, and a lovely collection of condenser and dynamic microphones. The crowning glory was the latest digital delay processing unit from a new American company called Eventide. The words 'Eventide Digital Delay' would eventually be displayed on thousands of these popular units all over the world, but I had one of the first. Eventually bored tape operators in studios the world over would black out some of the letters so it said 'Even I Dig A Lay' – boys will be boys.

Shortly after the equipment arrived, Bowie called me in March '74.

'Tony, I'm producing my new album, it's got lots of guitar and keyboards, but I can't get a decent mix at any studio I've tried in London. Is there anywhere you can recommend, one that I might not know of?'

'Well you could always try my new studio.' I was only half joking. I went on to explain the set up and even before I had finished David said, 'I'll be over later with a 16-track tape and I'll try it out.'

What I hadn't told David was the fact that I had no studio furniture. I was just puttering around sitting on a carpenter's sawhorse. That night I pushed two sawhorses together and we sat there for hours mixing the opening track of what would become *Diamond Dogs*. I made a tape copy of the mix for David on a Revox reel-to-reel machine that I had set at the wrong speed. David left with the faulty copy but phoned at 2 a.m. to tell me to make a good copy and that someone would be right over to pick it up. At 5 a.m. I received another call from David saying that he loved the mix and wanted to continue in my studio.

Mary, Morgan and I were not living in our new house yet; we were still staying in the flat. The next morning I returned with a couple of kitchen chairs so that David and I could at least have chairs to sit on while we mixed. Late in the afternoon a huge Conran lorry arrived with a delivery; the delivery note said MainMan – Bowie's management company – had ordered furniture. There was a light pine dining room table, with four wicker chairs, a full set of dishes, bowls and cups, flatware, glasses (for wine and water) and two office chairs for the control room. David arrived soon afterwards wearing a big smile.

'That's kind of my studio warming present.'

'That's really lovely, but why a dining room set?'

'We are going to have our meals delivered Tony, that's why.'
We spent a delightful few weeks mixing the album, adding a
few overdubs, working the Eventide Digital Delay to the max
and taking longish dinner breaks for two. The food was prepared in fine restaurants and delivered to us, and we washed it
down with good claret; mixing had never been more civilized.

I witnessed a historical event in David's life during these sessions. David was growing disenchanted with his personal assistant, Cherry Vanilla (she had been christened the relatively
ordinary sounding Kathy Dorritie). David was within his rights
to have a very libertine lifestyle, unfortunately some of his staff
at MainMan also felt it was their right to make up their own
rules. Vanilla seemed to be absent whenever he needed her. One
day David called his office and told someone to fire Vanilla.
'Just send over someone efficient from the typing pool as a
temp.' A few hours later a very shy Corrine Schwab reported to
work at Melrose Terrace with a stenographer's pad and pencil
in her hands. She was wide-eyed and appeared to be almost
frightened. But there was more to her than met the eye and she
blossomed; so much so that she's David's personal assistant
even now – today she's known as Coco.

While I am credited as co-producer of *Diamond Dogs*, David
did extraordinary work in the studio before I got the tapes to
mix – the bulk of it, in fact – though my sonic fingerprints are
all over those mixes. I certainly think it's an extraordinary
album – one I still listen to regularly. It was interesting to see
David's honest approach to credits after Marc's less than generous ways. The album was released in May and the reviews were
very favourable; David Bowie had reinvented himself again.
Marc Bolan's *Zip Gun Boogie*, his first album without me,
failed to make a ripple; Marc still assumed 'the kids' did not
want him to reinvent himself.

*   *   *

In the summer David recorded his shows at the Philadelphia Tower Theater; I was not able to attend. It was reported at the time that my car broke down travelling from New York, but I don't recall that ever happening. David just took it upon himself to record the show for posterity, and then liked what he heard and decided to mix it into his first live album. There was one problem with this idea in that it was recorded very poorly, not that the performances were anything less than excellent on most of the songs.

David and I went to Electric Ladyland to mix the album, where the resident engineer, Eddie Kramer, intercepted us.

'I'm the only one who knows how to operate the complicated console in the studio.'

Having met Kramer, when I first arrived in London, I was suspicious. He was an engineer that Denny Cordell never wanted to work with, so consequently I didn't either. Kramer's work with Jimi Hendrix was considered classic even by 1973, but having had the pleasure of hearing Hendrix live several times I never liked the way he had been recorded. I know I won't get a lot of agreement, but I felt that a much heavier sound was available but not represented. What Kramer did well was to teach Hendrix about panning, reverbs and tape delays, the sonic flavours of that period, and he used them very creatively. Since the console and the studio were alien to me, I felt Kramer should play an active role.

First we had to fix a few backing vocals and the backing singers were brought in to re-sing their parts; poor stage monitoring was the cause of this as the singers had a great deal of difficulty hearing themselves and the other performers. This took a day. Kramer proceeded to engineer the mixes the next day. This was a tough album to mix and Kramer's habit of throwing back his head as he 'played' the mixing console like a concert pianist was a little overdone.

The '70s was a crazy decade, and 'Cocaine is a hell of a drug', as funkmaster Rick James said. One day during the mixing of *David Live*, David and I stood side by side at urinals having a pee. The men's room was crowded with a Latin American band recording in the next studio, taking a break. They were a really friendly bunch of guys, and recognized David instantly. As we were peeing two band members held a spoon of cocaine under our noses and insisted that we each have a toot before we finished peeing. Very decadent . . . very '70s.

I never liked the sound of *David Live* and was really gratified to get a chance to remix it in 2004 for a Surround Sound re-release. In all fairness to Eddie Kramer, the show was not recorded well and tools didn't exist in 1974 to fix some of the badly recorded tracks – there were big problems. In 2004 engineer Mario McNulty and I microscopically scanned through the sound files and corrected every abrupt change of volume and sound that the recording engineer made back in 1974. The new sonic quality makes it sound as if it was recorded today. Whatever my feeling was at the time about *David Live*, it entered the UK charts at No 2 and remained in the charts for twelve weeks.

I was amazed when David decided he wanted to make a soul album and called me in August '74 to tell me the news.

'We're going to make it in Philadelphia, using the musicians from MFSB and we're going to record it in Sigma Sound.' The studio was legendary and he got no argument from me. Having been a soul and R&B fan since he was a young teenager I knew David had it in him.

'The thing is Tony, we've started making demos already so you'll need to be on a plane tomorrow.'

As soon as I arrived I rushed straight to the studio to be greeted by a very skinny David and introduced to the band –

none of which were members of MFSB. They were Ziggy Stardust keyboard player Mike Garson, drummer Andy Newmark (Sly and The Family Stone), bassist Willy Weeks (Donny Hathaway) and saxophonist David Sanborn. Shortly after I arrived David's new guitarist, Carlos Alomar, arrived, his Gibson 355 in one hand and his small Fender amp in the other; with Carlos was his wife, Robin Clark, and their friend from the Bronx, Luther Vandross. The idea was for them to try out as backing singers, although Ava Cherry of the Astronettes was also onboard. I was shown into the control room and asked, 'Who's the engineer?'

The studio's chief engineer, Carl Paruolo, said, 'You are', with a very dejected look on his face. David had already decided he wasn't very happy with the sound they were getting, but it was nothing to do with Carl. In England David was used to hearing processed sounds at the session. I would do a fair amount of EQ (equalizing) and compression on all the instruments, the traditional British recording philosophy, which harkens back to mono, to 4-track days when you were recording, say, four instruments locked on one track. Long after we got the luxury of 8- and 16-track tape, we continued to record as if it were the 1960s. In America they recorded 'flat' with no processing even after they got 16-track tape, believing that it could be 'fixed in the mix'. Musicians in the USA had to suspend their judgement of sound, leaving the final sonic solutions to engineers at the mixing stage. David would have none of this, so I rolled up my sleeves and started engineering British style.

On my very first day, suffering from acute jet lag, we were still able to get a final version of 'Young Americans' on tape. From then on the sessions were great, due to the wonderfully talented and professional players. Unfortunately David was showing up later and later to the sessions; he had got into the habit of recording very late and sometimes propped himself up with a couple of 'toots', as someone always had some cocaine in the studio. I had already been taking charlie off and on for several years but I found myself taking more and more to try and deal with jet lag and David's late arrivals; I also liked it very much. The only time this became a strain on me was when I had to start going into the studio early to do overdubs with Garson, Alomar and Sanborn. We'd work all day and then David would appear at 11 p.m. and listen to the day's work, usually approving of what we'd done. Sometimes he decided that he needed the musicians for another couple of hours to do something else.

On one such day I was really suffering from sleep deprivation when David arrived at 1 a.m.

'I want to do some vocals now.'

Of course I complied, but around 10 a.m. cocaine was no longer an option for me. I had run out of every ounce of energy I had left. After yet another vocal take I said, 'David I can't stay awake any longer.'

'I'll finish up with Carl; you can take my limo back to the hotel,' he said with some disappointment in his voice.

It was a beautiful warm October morning and the limo slowly made its way through the busy traffic towards the Hotel Barclay in Rittenhouse Square. As I watched the faces of the cheerful Philadelphians cross at the lights, I realized that I was about to have a heart attack. My chest was pounding as if it was going to explode. I lay as still as possible, looking at the faces in the crowd behind my smoked glass windows thinking, This is the last thing I'm going to see, I am about to die. I was afraid that if I asked the driver to take me to a hospital I would be arrested and there would be a raid on the studio, implicating Bowie. I remembered that I had a bottle of Mogadon sleeping pills in my hotel. I thought if I could only reach them in time and take some, my heart would slow down. That was just what I did when I arrived at the hotel several minutes later. I took the elevator to my room, opened the bottle and swallowed 12 pills at once with a glass of water – and I waited. My pulse began to slow down within minutes and my chest stopped pounding. After about 10 minutes I started to slip into unconsciousness and I wasn't quite sure if I took an overdose, but somehow I wasn't bothered anymore. I woke up many hours later, and realized I had barely survived with the use of my 'street smarts'.

On a lighter side I instigated a visit of one of David's idols to the studio. One day before going to work I was listening to WMMR rock radio and the DJ, Ed Sciaky, announced that Bruce Springsteen had just visited his studio with a cassette of his latest songs. David loved Springsteen's music and played his first album to me. We had just recorded a cover of Springsteen's 'It's Hard To Be A Saint In The City'. I called the station and spoke to Sciaky off air and told him that he had to get Springsteen to our studio to meet David and hear the song.

'That's cool but the problem is Springsteen lives in a caravan and he could be parked along the highway anywhere in the Tri-State area,' said Sciaky. Undaunted he went in search of him and brought him to the studio that evening. Springsteen was very shy and seemed to be bewildered as to why anyone would want to record one of his songs. After a while he warmed up to his surroundings and he and David ended up having a really long and in-depth conversation.

Everyday there was a crowd of ardent Bowie fans outside the studio; they named themselves the Sigma Kids and knew the songs because the studio's soundproofing left a lot to be desired. On our final night David invited the Sigma Kids into the studio for a playback of the rough mixes – a lovely gesture. Afterwards we went to New York City to do further work on the album at the Hit Factory with Harry Maslin as the engineer. David had written two new songs, an alternative lyric to a Luther Vandross song, which became 'Fascination', and one of his own called '(All You've Got To Do Is) Win'. Willy Weeks and Andy Newmark were no longer available. I think it was Carlos Alomar who recommended Dennis Davis on drums and David found Emir Kassan to play bass. Davis came off immediately as a fantastically talented, left-field drummer, but it was apparent that he had never heard of David Bowie and never played anything but jazz. But he made himself invaluable and he remained Bowie's drummer for the next six albums.

One day while we were working at the Hit Factory, David phoned me.

'John Lennon's coming to my suite at the hotel tonight and it would be great if you could be there and buffer the meeting between us.' As we spoke David seemed to be very nervous. I, on the other hand, couldn't wait to meet Lennon. I arrived about 11 p.m. and having knocked on the door; there was no reply for a few minutes. I heard a lot of shuffling going on before a voice I didn't recognize said, 'Who is it?'

When I identified myself, Neil Aspinall, the former Beatles roadie and now an Apple executive, opened the door. As I walked in I looked to my left to see John Lennon emerging from the bathroom with a young Asian girl; I later found out she was May Pang. The four of us walked into the huge living room and there was David sitting on the floor next to a pretty Hispanic girl. Lennon and Pang were hiding in the bathroom as they thought I might have been the police; there was coke around and John didn't want to be implicated. Within minutes everything was mellow and we were all partaking in the twin pillars of rock 'n' roll camaraderie – Cognac and coke. David was shy and avoiding Lennon, he just sat on the floor drawing on a large sketchpad. The Hispanic girl never said a word and she was never introduced.

I turned to Lennon and said, 'If you don't mind, John, I have about a hundred questions I'd like to ask you.'

He turned out to be very charming and replied, 'I don't mind, mate, if I have the answers.'

I asked him, with technical curiosity, lots of questions about Beatles' recordings, including the fingering of the opening chord of 'A Hard Day's Night'. He was gracious and answered everything. When I told him how disappointed I was with Paul not crediting me with arranging the orchestral parts for *Band On The Run*, he surprised me with his answer.

'You know what, thanks for telling me that. Even if I whistled a part to an arranger, and it was my idea, I would still give the arranger a credit as "orchestrator". I was about to call Paul tomorrow and get together with him, but you just reminded me of what a fucking cunt he is.'

I was later relieved to find out that I had not been the cause of John and Paul not getting together, because May Pang assured me she and John had got together with the McCartneys at a later date.

After John and I had talked for hours he decided to break the ice with David, 'Hey David, do you have another one of those sketch pads?'

'Certainly.' David separated the leaves in half and gave John a bunch of pages and a pencil. They then entered into a fun sketching contest, each drawing rapid caricatures of each other. This finally drew them into conversation. I noticed that May Pang visibly disapproved of John's drinking and coke taking – her stern expression never changed. She was sitting next to me and hadn't said a single word all night, so I decided to make some small talk. I didn't know what to say at first, and clumsily asked her, despite knowing the answer, 'Are you Chinese or Japanese?'

'Chinese,' was her curt reply.

'Oh. Er, does your father know kung fu?' This elicited a dirty look from Pang and I had no choice but to turn to Apsinall for a conversation; luckily it went somewhat better.

Eventually everyone in the room finally got into a dismally dark conversation about 'what does it all mean', 'it' being life, which left us all staring dejectedly at the floor; we were not helped by the dwindling effects of the Cognac and coke. Finally at around 10 a.m. Lennon felt it was safe to leave. His reason being that if he left in broad daylight he would not be targeted by the cops. He feared he'd be arrested, the police would plant drugs on him and he'd be deported before he could get his US Green Card. I left shortly afterwards and returned to David's suite around 4 p.m. that afternoon to pick him up and go to the studio.

David was still sitting in the same spot by the coffee table with the Hispanic lady still sat beside him.

'Are you coming to the studio with me?'

'No, I think I'm going to bed now,' said David

When every possible overdub was completed in New York, David said, 'You can go back to London and mix it in your studio as I liked the sound we got on *Diamond Dogs*.'

I flew home as soon as I could, eager to see Mary and Morgan. At JFK, when I stopped to buy chewing gum, I put the master tapes on the floor beside me and paid for the gum. Standing in the queue to board the plane I realized I didn't have the tapes. I was back at the cash register within 20 seconds; the tapes were where I had left them and had been sitting there for at least 10 minutes. These days, parcels of that size would be destroyed immediately if left unattended. Hugely relieved I boarded the flight and eased into my first class seat, where I found myself next to David Bailey. He immediately engaged me in a conversation about his disastrous affair with Faye Dunaway. They had apparently had a massive fight earlier in the day. As I tried to commiserate with him he suddenly said, 'I have to call her right now.' With that he leapt up and dashed out of the plane with a stewardess yelling at him, 'You can't do that sir, we are taking off soon.'

Bailey just made it back in time and related the entire phone call to me. He told me that he didn't manage to patch it up with her over the phone, so we spent the rest of the flight complaining about women, how much they expected of us – or something like that. I suspect the amount we both drank had something to do with it.

I began mixing in London, aided by an 18-page telegram that David sent me from New York with his ideas. Before I did, I added string parts to three of the songs at Air Studios. When I had finished I sent the mixes to David in New York via courier service. A few days later I received a phone call from David – which deflated me.

'I've seen Lennon to let him hear my new version of "Across The Universe" and now John's added acoustic guitar.' Years later May Pang told me that Lennon shared my opinion and that he was not impressed with David's decision to cover this, of all of Lennon's songs. It was the second part of the phone call that really hurt the most.

'Then we wrote a new song based on a riff that Carlos Alomar has been doodling with; we've called it "Fame".'

'I would've happily paid to fly over on Concorde just to be at that session,' I told him.

David genuinely felt bad for me. He said he'd also had some afterthoughts and that he'd continue to overdub some last-minute things on our tracks with engineer Harry Maslin. In the end I think the album is largely my work; the Maslin remixes are so close to mine, with the backing voices and synthesizers that David added. I have to go down on record as saying that I love 'Fame' and would've liked to be a part of the team that made it. Maybe this was my karma for refusing to record 'Space Oddity' (I jest).

In 2005, I was able to have another chance at remixing *Young Americans* when I was asked to make 5.1-Surround Sound mix of the album. When I worked on 'Across The Universe' and 'Fame' I got goose bumps hearing John Lennon talking at the end of his rhythm guitar and vocal track. Revisiting David's vocals on this album was a treat, as a lot of the album's vocals are sung live with the band. It was difficult to record with the band blasting away in the same room. I set up two vocal mics electronically out of phase with each other. The out-of-phase microphones rendered the band very thin, it almost cancelled it out, but David's voice was full sounding because he only sang into one mic. I was thrilled to hear his voice soloed in a modern studio. David loved the mixes and the new depth that revealed a lot of lost detail in the performances.

During the making of *Young Americans* David embarked upon a most bizarre side project. He had the idea of turning *Diamond Dogs* into a future shock film. Instead of submitting a written treatment he decided to make a demo video in his hotel suite. Domestic camcorders didn't exist at the time, nor did easy editing on a computer – in fact there were no personal computers either (maybe just a gleam in the eyes of teenager Steve Jobs). Instead David sent out for various materials and constructed a 2-D small-scale set of a post-nuclear city. He rented professional video equipment, a professional video camera, two video recorders and a video-mixing console. He videoed his set for thirty minutes against a black cloth backdrop. Afterwards he played back the tape and he walked against the black cloth background and narrated his story treatment.

We combined the pre-recorded tape and live David, many times reduced, onto a second machine via the console, and it appeared as if he was actually in the city. I could see the combination on the monitor and I directed him to stand in a certain spot and point at what he was describing. The Lilliputian-sized David was at the right scale for the set and it all looked very convincing. I have never seen that video since, but it would be a hit just as it is.

When Mary and Morgan moved into Melrose Terrace the soundproofing within the house was still not as good as we thought. When I recorded my first rock band (Carmen, we made their second album, *Dancing On A Cold Wind*, here) Mary complained that the music was too loud in the living room just above the studio. Graeme had to remove the carpet and put five layers of plywood and plasterboard on the floor before Mary was completely happy. The intense sound pressure slowly caused the plaster in the dining-room ceiling to loosen. We had just finished our first Christmas meal at the house, cleared the table and taken Morgan out of his high chair when the ceiling collapsed and huge chunks of plaster crashed onto the dining-room table. We could have been seriously injured, or worse, had we still been sitting there.

Despite all the setbacks, the initial recordings coming out of my home studio sounded great, mainly because I had all the time in the world to finesse my work. If I couldn't sleep I'd go downstairs, power up and work on some detail that was nagging me. Home studios are commonplace nowadays but there were only a handful in 1974. It also allowed stay-at-home mum Mary to begin working on an album. Gerry Conway and Bruce Lynch (Cat Stevens' drummer and bass player) made regular visits to our studio. Mary recorded her own compositions, played guitar and the keyboard parts. We bought a

Minimoog synthesizer; we took it up to our bedroom on the first day we had it and played with it for hours in bed.

All in all life at 9 Melrose Terrace for Mary, Morgan and me was very cosy. We had a happy home life in our three-storied house, although we would occasionally be stressed from literally 'living over the shop'. Morgan would sometimes open the door of the living room and walk down to the studio. One day during the recording of a string overdub the players were taking a break in the studio lounge. I discovered Morgan, aged two-and-a-half, sitting in a t-shirt and underpants having a deep conversation with the cellist. Until we moved he would always spend a lot of time in the studio watching how records were made and often offering advice. One day Ron Mael of Sparks casually asked Morgan what he thought of the recording we were making. Morgan gave it a thought and wisely said, 'You have to put more sound between the speakers', stretching his arms wide. Ron turned to me with a surprised expression on his face and said, 'Wow.' Morgan's suggestion made us widen the stereo soundscape of that mix. Another time Morgan described a Moog synthesizer sound patch as 'Smee-you', an onomatopoeic word he'd invented to describe the envelope filter setting. We referred to that sound as 'Smee-you' thereafter.

chapter 8
the low down

When Bowie's *Young Americans* album was released in March 1975 it became a huge hit – it also confounded critics. Because of my involvement with it I had a call from Tommy Mottola to ask me if I would produce a group he managed.

'Tony, you're an expert in blue-eyed soul and Hall and Oates would benefit from your experience.'

Daryl Hall and John Oates had had a very minor hit at this point and while it is always flattering to be told you are perfect for a band I had already committed to record in London with Sparks. I had been a fan of theirs since hearing 'This Town Ain't Big Enough For The Both Of Us'; along with Queen's 'Bohemian Rhapsody' it was the most original single I had heard in years. Island's legendary A&R man Muff Winwood had approached me to produce them; they are typical of the kind of band I've always been attracted to. Unfortunately Art Rock had been an obscure dead-end for me; my failures with Gentle Giant and Carmen both bear witness to that. Whereas Carmen and Gentle Giant (who I have to admit were somewhat over complicated) didn't have the managerial muscle to give them the boost that groups like Yes and Emerson, Lake and Palmer had, Sparks was Art Pop! I could do lots of clever stuff, it would get on the radio – and might even become a hit.

Ron and Russell, the Mael brothers, were originally from Los Angeles and had made England their home just as I did. We had a lot in common. They turned me on to the Egon Ronay Hotel and Restaurant guide, which Mary and I considered to be an epicurean bible. Sparks was still a five-member rock band when they made 'This Town Ain't Big Enough For The Both Of Us', but the brothers were clearly in charge, and a very different breed from their British drummer, guitarist and bass player. They felt that the band's format held them back creatively and they wanted this album to be more experimental. I was ecstatic; any time a band said 'experimental' I was immediately on board. Working mainly in my home studio we created an atmosphere in which every song had its own universe, and its own specific character. Most important of all, there was a budget to achieve what we wanted.

On one of the tracks, 'Looks, Looks, Looks', it had to sound like the Count Basie band, something beyond the skills of the Sparks rhythm section. So we hired a Basie-size band and I wrote the arrangement. Ron and Russell were the only members of the group to play on the track, which precipitated grumbles and resentment from the others, especially Dinky Diamond, the band's drummer. Dinky would complain to Muff Winwood behind my back that the rest of the band wasn't featured enough. There weren't many tracks that did not feature the entire band, but this was definitely a new Sparks sound; the album was *Indiscreet* (years later I found out that it was a favourite of a young Steven Morrissey).

As fellow epicureans Mary and I recommended a favourite Chinese restaurant in Earl's Court to Ron and Russell, who adored Chinese food, especially the new Szechwan style that had recently been introduced to Londoners. Halfway through the meal Russell phoned me and asked if my face ever became paralysed during a meal at that restaurant; I immediately knew what had happened. I explained that the restaurant must have used far too much monosodium glutamate in the preparation of the food. I told them that feeling would eventually go away. Both of them were in a state of panic and were considering going to an emergency ward, but decided to call us first, since we had eaten there before. None of us ever ate there again.

My business partner Roger Myers had become the manager of Argent, a band that centred on the former keyboard player with the Zombies, Rod Argent. Soon after working with Sparks, Roger asked me to record Argent in my home studio, in order to cut costs. I was right back into Art Rock, but the experience was thoroughly enjoyable. At the beginning of the album, drummer Bob Henrit went down with Hepatitis B and was hospitalized. At the last minute an out-of-work Phil Collins stepped in to play drums. Roger, who had been totally against me building a home studio, became a convert, 'This was the best idea you ever had.'

This was the quietest year work-wise that I had had in five years and it was a welcome respite. Mary continued to write some really great songs; we had more than an album's worth of material and it had the added bonus of making Mary feel empowered. She was a wife and a mother, but she was making the music she'd always wanted to, with a freedom denied to her during her Apple days. Home recording continued all year and on into the next.

With a lot of activity in the home studio we begin to realize that it could be a dangerous place for a small child. Somehow Morgan managed to push a stool near the studio control box that had small holes for ventilation. Morgan stuck his hand inside one hole and was knocked back to the wall from a strong, 30-ampere shock. He was semi-conscious when we found him lying on the floor. It was the sound of him hitting the wall that got our attention. Another very bad experience was when I came back from a spell in New York and left my brief-case open on the floor of our living room. I only put it down briefly to show something to Mary. Morgan was in the brief-case in seconds, when we weren't looking, and managed to open a jar of Mogadon sleeping pills; there were only six left but he ate every one of them. We were completely oblivious to this until he started acting drunk and we noticed a white coating around his mouth. The three of us rushed to Hammersmith Hospital as fast as possible during late-afternoon rush hour traffic: we'd called an ambulance but they suggested it would be quicker for us to drive. Mary and I waited in the emergency ward as they pumped Morgan's stomach. Of course he survived, but he had to spend the night there under observation. That night Mary and I decided that it was not such a good idea to have a commercial home studio. We decided to look for a new home outside London. We decided that Berkshire would be a good idea – the capital was still accessible and it was on the way to Wales and Mary's parents. It was only after we moved there that we found out it was known as the 'Divorce Belt'.

The house we found was in Wargrave-on-Thames; the Old Vicarage was more a mansion than a house. It was a monstrous Georgian house with the date 1752 carved in a beam in the wine cellar. The house was set in four and a half acres of walled and gated land, with an arable field and an orchard of apple and pear trees. Separating our immense lawn from the arable field was a haha, a sunken trench-like wall meant to keep cattle in the field and stop them straying onto the garden area. The house had seven bedrooms, a huge reception area, a smaller reception area, a big kitchen and a coach house with a stable and small flat combined. At the local pub, The Bull, they called me 'Squire' and I was soon into quaffing pints of Brakspear (real) Ale. My mother had told Mary that I was a city boy and

I would never like living in the country. After spending one night, having the best sleep of my life and waking up to the sound of only birds, I decided she was wrong. In the garden was an out building called The Meeting Hall; it was a small, sturdy stone building with stained glass windows. One day I found Morgan systematically knocking out the small panes of glass with a hammer he had found; he got the first wallops on his bottom of his life.

The house had belonged to local MP Peter Emery, who had obsessively spent night after night sanding the banisters and woodwork for years; it eventually led to his divorce. We paid £75,000 for the house; it was the most expensive thing I had ever bought in my life. While I really enjoyed living in the Berkshire countryside there was a downside. For the first time since my career had taken off I felt I had to work because we needed the money; I didn't like the feeling.

We moved to the Old Vicarage in January 1976 when Mary was three months pregnant. Our daughter, Jessica, was born on 16 June. Whereas Morgan's birth had been fairly straightforward, Jessica's head never engaged and she was born in breach position, feet first. The midwives could not persuade her to move around. I was told that this wasn't uncommon, but I paled when I saw a big white paper parcel delivered to the delivery room, with 'Abnormal Delivery' emblazoned on it. The nurse opened the parcel and neatly placed all manners of scalpels and callipers, and even two types of saws for cutting through bone. But Jessica didn't need such extraction. Mary went into labour and out came Jessica into the world, feet first and peeing.

With a seven-bedroom Georgian mansion and two small children in our lives it was clear we would need help. Through an agency we found a lovely woman, Gloria Arroya, who came to us from the Philippines. Jessica spent most of her days with

Gloria and learned to speak English with a strong Filipino accent, pronouncing the number five as 'pive'. Gloria took care of all of us really well; she introduced us to Philippine cuisine and, most important of all, our children were well taken care of. Gloria sent almost all of her money back home to her children, to pay for their education.

Having a big new home meant that we often played host to the Hopkin family, who seemed to live even closer now that the M4 motorway was built; my parents would visit about once a year from Brooklyn. Part of the stable was converted to a large home studio, because while we still retained the house in Hammersmith as a studio it was often booked by other producers. Eventually Jake Riviera bought the Melrose Terrace house and ran Stiff Records from it; recording many of his artists in my home-built studio.

I had bought a brand new BMW motorcycle to make it quicker and easier to commute to London when I needed to record there. One afternoon I had it out in the courtyard trying to figure out how to dismantle and clean the air filter when I heard car tyres on the gravel behind me; I looked round and out of an Aston Martin stepped George Harrison. He lived in Henley-on-Thames and had had a chance meeting with Mary on the High Street. When she told him about my motorcycle he said he had to see it. So there I was kneeling in the gravel talking the finer points of BMW motorcycles with a Beatle.

Both Roger Myers and I were anxious to have a hit on Good Earth. Carmen's lack of success was a great disappointment to me and so as a favour I asked Mary to release at least a single for us. We found 'If You Love Me', a beautiful old Edith Piaf song, which I arranged for a traditional French pop orchestra with strings and accordion. The B-side was a song written by Mary called 'Tell Me Now', the first in her career. Unfortunately we faced pregnancy prejudice from the BBC when Mary went to sing the song on *Top Of The Pops*; they wouldn't show her on camera from her bodice down.

In an interview at the time of the record's release Mary remarked that she was not a good housewife and that we often fought because I didn't have clean clothes to wear in the morning. This was so true, but I wasn't necessarily looking for a housewife in Mary as much as I wanted her to be an active and creative partner. Mary was sleeping on average twelve hours a day and becoming more withdrawn from the marriage – long after the children were born. Making the single annoyed her and she made it perfectly clear that she was doing it for me and that she would not do any promotion other than *Top Of The Pops* and one other television show in Paris, where she had been asked to perform because it was a Piaf song. Strangely Mary had willingly sung back ups for whomever I was recording – Tom Paxton, Ralph McTell, Sparks and, later in this year, David Bowie. On the one hand I was fortunate to have one of the greatest voices in the world for a back-up singer, but on the other, what a waste of talent.

In the same interview Mary talked about the album tracks that we had been steadily recording and even said that it was to be called *With You Or Without You*, after a song penned by Liz Thorsen, who wrote both 'Earth Song' and 'Ocean Song' from the first album I'd recorded with her. It's an absolute tragedy that the album has never been released, nor the subsequent fifty songs we had finished; about half are Mary's own compositions.

Resentment from me had started to enter the marriage. It seemed like all our plans to be a great creative team had to take a back seat because, in Mary's eyes, raising a family took precedence over every thing. I argued that Mary's contemporaries had families and simultaneous careers, but she would have none of it.

'What's the point of having children if you're not going to raise them yourself?'

'Then why do you often spend twelve hours a day in bed and let Gloria and me take care of them?'

It was a circular, no win argument. Her long spells in bed continued long after Jessica was born. I put it down to a deep fear and resentment of the 'cruel' world out there, a music business world that chewed her up and spat her out, leaving Mary with a feeling of futility and frustration. I thought I could protect her from the business side of things, but the harm was done and she was emotionally scarred as a result. Not for one minute did I doubt that she loved the children and our life in the countryside, but at the same time I felt it was an excuse never to work again in an industry she'd grown to despise. A few years later when we were very close to releasing an album of this material, no company would sign her because of her refusal to promote the album with live gigs; once again raising the children was her excuse.

Despite Mary's single Good Earth was not having any real success as a label. Artists I wanted to sign, the really hot ones, went to bigger labels that could give them more of a cash advance. I had found four genuine sisters from Blackburn, Lancashire who were called The Surprise Sisters. We began recording in John Kongo's home studio in Barnes, London; I thought I had found Britain's answer to Patti LaBelle. Although they possessed great enthusiasm and were great live performers the truth was that they were good in the studio, not great, and I was no Nile Rodgers either.

I was lucky that just when I needed to I heard from David. It was during the long hot summer of 1976 and he called me from his home in Switzerland; he had been silent for quite a while. David had befriended and was working with the wonderfully named Brian Peter St John Le Baptiste de la Salle Eno.

'Tony, Brian is on the extension phone listening in and I have to tell you we've been experimenting with some ideas. We're thinking of going into a studio in September for a month. We don't have any actual songs yet but we're trying to combine Brian's ambient music techniques into writing rock songs. What do you think you would bring to the table?' It was the first time I'd heard the expression. I quickly thought and said, 'I have a new piece of equipment, only the second unit in Britain; it's called a Harmonizer. I've been experimenting with it everyday, I'm coming up with sounds that I've never heard before.'

'Yeah, but what kind of sounds?' asked David.

'Well, it fucks with the fabric of time.'

If ever I pulled one out of the hat that was it. They 'oo-ed' and 'ah-ed' and said that they loved that description.

'I can now change pitch without changing the speed of the tape, and vice versa. I can also use a feedback control to produce unearthly sounds, not like a synthesizer, but transform real organic sounds into magic.'

Essentially a Harmonizer is a sort of instant recording device but it can simultaneously play back the sound at a chosen pitch. In other words a piano can play a D, but the Harmonizer can almost instantly turn it into a lower D flat or a higher D sharp. It was initially invented to correct the pitch of singers or instruments that were out of tune, but in my hands I abused its purpose and came up with wonderful space-age sounds, sometimes horror-movie sounds.

'Look Tony, before we start recording I have to say this is strictly experimental, and nothing might come of it in the end. Are you prepared to maybe waste a month of your time?'

'Wasting a month of my time with David Bowie and Brian Eno is NOT wasting a month of my time.' It was my second bull's eye of the conversation.

Within a week I was off to Paris to catch a limo ride, again, to the Château d'Hérouville. I had waited for my well-packed Harmonizer at the fragile items pick up but it failed to show. I eventually found it on the normal baggage carousel; fortunately it worked perfectly.

David has been known to change guitarists frequently and he had long since parted with Mick Ronson. He wanted me to recommend one. I had been working with Ricky Gardiner with whom I made a single for my Good Earth label. He was one of the most original and evocative guitarists I'd ever worked with. He had all the right guitar effects pedals and he knew how to combine them to produce amazing sounds; his playing had a touch of Hendrix about it. By now David had settled with Carlos Alomar, George Murray and Dennis Davis as his reliable rhythm section, all Americans of colour. To augment the band we now had Ricky Gardiner, every inch a tall, lanky Glaswegian, and Roy Young, a London rock 'n' roll pianist who had been living in Hamburg since before the Beatles arrived there. Added to which there was the very cerebral Brian Eno with his briefcase EMS Synthi synthesizer.

The sessions began with a bang. Instead of starting with the ambient experiment we jumped into a rock band situation and great backing tracks started to emerge on the very first day. True to form there were no melodies or lyrics, just grooves and chord changes. David called them 'demos' but I recorded them carefully, knowing full well that these could end up as masters, and they did.

Before we recorded the first piece, I had to get sounds from each instrument, and in the case of the drums, one for each drum. I immediately set up my Harmonizer and decided to use one of the coolest tricks I'd discovered before I'd left London. (One of the first things I did with my Harmonizer was to record my four-year-old son Morgan saying, 'Daddy, can I have the car keys.' With a twist of the knob on the Harmonizer I converted him into a sixteen-year-old. It was eerie.) I sent a feed from the snare drum mic to the Harmonizer, I dropped the pitch by a semi-tone, and then I added feedback of this sound to itself. In simple terms it means a very deep snare sound that keeps cascading downwards in pitch; the initial impact had the 'crack' but then the 'thud' never seemed to stop, and, not only did it go on at length, but it got deeper and deeper in pitch, kind of like the sound a man makes when he gets punched in the stomach – 'ugh'. Everyone was amazed.

David scratched his head and said, 'I agree it's an amazing effect, but I'm dubious whether we'll use it.' I decided to leave it on and fed the effect only to Dennis Davis's headphones. He quickly realized that how loud he played influenced the reaction of the Harmonizer. Soon he was playing it like an instrument, creating drop offs of different character. During playbacks I sometimes lifted the volume on the return of the Harmonizer as we grew more familiar with it – we eventually loved it. Of course, it made the final cut and it has since been regarded as one of the most revolutionary drum sounds ever created. I am honoured on Eventide's website for creating this sound.

The album was made in a relaxed atmosphere and the company made for interesting and stimulating conversation over meals, and especially some long dinners. Dennis Davis amazed us with a story about when he was in the US Air Force. He accidentally walked through a restricted hangar and saw a crashed-up alien spacecraft. He was ordered to leave immediately and not to say a word about it. He hadn't to anybody but us, and who would believe a bunch of musos?

After two weeks of recording backing tracks and guitar overdubs, the band left and David, Brian and I continued to work on our own. Brian added wonderful sounds to the rock tracks by using his briefcase synth. David had been writing lyrics and started to try them out. Mary came over to Paris during the vocal period and added her 'Doo-doo-doos' to the intro of 'Sound And Vision', while Morgan played on the verdant grounds of the château with Zowie Bowie, who is almost a year older.

The ambient B-side of *Low* was created in the last two weeks in September. Often we would leave Brian alone, 'I've bored many an engineer to death laying down one note at time making ambient music "beds".' I showed him how to change over the tracks to record on and we just left him to it. The over-dubs were a different story, but very creative and highly inter-esting. We would lay down a click track of, say, forty beats per minute. I would record my voice on a second track counting for five minutes, so every beat had a specific number. Because the music on top was so dreamy, it was often not apparent that there was a pulse under each composition on side two. Not much was planned; the two composers were writing on the spot. In the spirit of Zen Impressionism, Brian overheard my son Morgan repeatedly playing A-B-C on the piano in the studio; Brian gently lifted Morgan down off the piano bench and continued the melody from A-B-C. These notes are the opening notes of 'Warzawa'.

Two things marred this fantastic month. One was food poi-soning that David and I both suffered after eating cheese that had been left out of the fridge all night. It was a Sunday morning when we called the French doctor, and he was very pissed off; he would only see David and refused to see me. I had to share David's medicine. The other was the fact that in the midst of recording David frequently had to leave and drive to Paris to have meetings with his lawyers because he was break-ing a management contract with his soon-to-be former manager Michael Lippman. Some days David would return in a foul mood. During these last two weeks Brian and I would get on with things until David rejoined us.

An unexpected vibe during the making of *Low* was the added frisson of the château's ghosts. George Sands, the female poet, and Frederick Chopin had lived and loved there centuries earlier; they were known to roam the hallways. David could not sleep in the master bedroom, the same room Marc Bolan had wanted two years earlier, as there was a dark corner in the room that never seemed to brighten up, no matter how many lights you turned on. I took the room, but never felt anything that frightened me – nothing leapt out of the dark corner. Brian, however, would be woken every morning by a tap on his shoulder; when he opened his eyes there was never anyone there. The only time I felt a little creepy was going back to my room alone, after everyone had retired. The 'Honky Chateau' could've been a set for a Dracula film.

A very welcome resident was Iggy Pop, who hovered in the background for the entire month. He was a very positive influence, feeding the project with creative energy. Iggy was present at most of the sessions and even sings a bit on 'What In The World'. One night David decided to start a spoken word album; David loved Iggy's stories about his days with The Stooges. For a few nights in a row, David, and I sat in the darkened studio asking Iggy questions with the tape rolling. The stories were both decadent and hilarious. I have never heard these tapes since; they would make perfect Podcasts.

Eventually we had to leave the château, as the equipment was increasingly unreliable. Added to which we were infiltrated by a member of the French music press who posed as some kind of minder; on top of all that the food was getting worse. David, along with Coco and Iggy decided to drive to Berlin. I met them there later and we mixed the album at Hansa studios in Berlin.

The mixing of *Low* and the mixing of *The Idiot* are a kind of Berlin blur; I think I mixed *Low* and was asked to come back in a month to sort out the tracks for Iggy's album. David brought back his *Low* rhythm section along with Ricky Gardiner; David was the producer and keyboard player. When I came to mix the tracks I found they were a mess, it was because of a cry for help that I was back in Berlin. There was a sonic struggle, a clash of clean German engineering and British grit. Iggy often started a song singing very quietly and then gradually built up to a scream (as in 'China Girl'), distorting the microphone preamplifier. This was one of those 'happy accidents' again, because the vocal wouldn't be the same if it were any other way now. Usually there was no take two to correct the over-modulation. I love this album!

When *Low* came out in February 1977 the critics were dumb-founded. The sound went against everything currently on the market. RCA executives and Tony Defries (who was still entitled to a percentage of future Bowie earnings) tried to prevent the album being released. 'I'll buy him a house in Philadelphia,' grumbled one RCA exec, expecting Young Americans II. It's what makes David brilliant – always expect the unexpected.

As the complete antithesis to working with David and Brian (and Iggy) I recorded an album with Peter Sarstedt and his two brothers, Clive and Richard (Richard had recorded, and had some big hits in the '60s, as Eden Kane). In 1976 the Sarstedt Brothers album, *World's Apart Together*, came out on Good Earth. It was autobiographical, about their youth growing up in India before coming to live in London. Peter had written a smash hit in the late 1960s entitled 'Where Do You Go To My Lovely?' It was a waltz and it had an accordion on it, which I can't stand – even in the hands of an expert. But the words were very trippy-hippy and Peter was a gorgeous man in those days, looking very much the dashing gypsy.

A lot of blood, sweat and tears went into making their album; the songs were wonderful and I was working with three lead singers, a real treat. When they blended in harmony it was

Above Steve Peregrine Took and Marc Bolan recording vocal overdubs on *Unicorn*, their third album as Tyrannosaurus Rex. Trident Studios, St. Anne's Court, Soho, London, 1969.

Above Marc Bolan, Howard Kaylan and Mark Volman recording backing vocals for 'Get It On', for the *Electric Warrior* album. Wally Heider Studios, Los Angeles, 1971.

Above My girlfriend Liz Hartley, Angie Bowie (née Barnett) and David Bowie. This was taken on the first night we spent at Haddon Hall, 1969.

Above Angie Bowie posing in front of the magnificent stained glass window on the half-landing leading to the upper gallery, Haddon Hall, 1970.

Above Taken in the garden of Haddon Hall, with other residents and friends, 1970. On the bottom row are: John Cambridge (drummer), Angie Bowie, David Bowie and Nita Bowes (now Nita Clarke of 10 Downing St, union advisor to Tony Blair).

Left John Cambridge getting a haircut at a party in Beckenham, 1970. Mick Ronson looks on with Roger the Roadie behind him. David Bowie (with his *Space Oddity* perm) and Angie Bowie are on the settee.

Right David Bowie painting the kitchen wall in Haddon Hall, 1970.

Above On the back porch of Haddon Hall, 1970.

Above Learning songs for the album *The Man Who Sold The World* in the front
room of Haddon Hall. (*Left to right*): David Bowie (turned away from the
camera), Mick Ronson and John Cambridge (turned away).

Above (*Left to right*): Bill Legend (drummer) Mick O'Halloran (road manager),
Marc Bolan and Steve Currie (bassist) of T.Rex. They were waiting to board a
plane to Los Angeles for gigging and recording. Taken at the TWA terminal at
JFK International Airport, New York, 1971.

Above When they visited, my mother prepared a special dinner for T.Rex with Italian specialities aubergine parmigiana, stuffed mushrooms, stuffed artichokes and meatballs (Marc, a vegetarian, refrained from the meatballs*). (Left to right),* Marc Bolan, Bill Legend, Mickey Finn, Josephine Visconti, Liz Hartley and Steve Currie. Brooklyn, New York, 1971.

Above Marc Bolan looking at a chocolate cake that my mother made in celebration of T.Rex's 'Hot Love' reaching number one in the charts. The letters were made with sliced almonds.

Above At Air Studios in Oxford Circus, London. The photo was taken by my wife, Mary Hopkin, in 1972.

Left Taken in 1971, when I was first dating Mary Hopkin. She is in costume, backstage, before singing a period piece for the summer season in Margate, Kent. Lonnie Donegan was co-starring with Mary.

Below Mary, taking time off from the summer season, with me in an apple orchard, Margate, 1971.

the tight, glistening sound that could only be created by musical siblings. One late evening, at the now defunct Marquee Studios behind London's Wardour Street, Peter was desperately trying to get a vocal finished on a very sensitive song. His brothers and I were feeling more and more depressed as Peter seemingly sank deeper and deeper into despair. He just couldn't get the feel right, or sing in tune – it was just all wrong. Peter even tried a spliff but that only made things worse.

Finally Peter said, very dramatically,

'I just can't go on. I'm going to go off in the corner of the studio to try and get my head together. Please don't bother me.'

Back in the control room the five of us, the engineer, assistant engineer, the two brothers and I, were completely bummed out by Peter's black mood. We just sat in the semi-dark and tried to console one another.

'Oh, he gets in these moods sometimes. It'll be all right,' said Richard.

'Yeah, but maybe something is wrong with the backing track, maybe we'll have to re-record it,' countered Clive.

'No, we can't do that, it will be too expensive,' said I. 'Let's just hope he can pull out of this.'

Just then we were interrupted. Peter was back on microphone, saying, 'Okay you guys, I'm ready. Let's take it.' We were not prepared for what we saw. There was Peter Sarstedt standing in front of the microphone stark naked. Somehow his beard preserved his dignity, but only just. He had a devilish grin on his face and said that he was ready to 'bare' his soul (with the addition of his hairy chest and manhood).

Peter's vocal finally went great. He obviously knew what he was doing. Suddenly I got a cheeky idea. I told all the guys in the control room to strip. It would be a perfect end to a bad evening. We simply had to one-up Peter. But to ask a room full of reserved Englishmen to strip at a moment's notice is a nigh-on impossible task and no one volunteered to be first. I had to lead the way, as always. Most of us stripped before Peter got back to the control room, with one or two others still in the process. We got him! When he walked in on this sight he collapsed in a heap laughing himself silly.

Although we lived in Wargrave, Mary was at the Melrose Terrace studio/house the day that Phil Lynott and Scott Gorham pulled up in a black limo and stumbled to our front door waving large cans of Fosters lager. Mary and I looked at each other; we knew it was going to be a tough meeting and an even a tougher album if I took it on. With all the T.Rex and David Bowie successes behind me I was in demand and I could pick and choose whom I worked with. So why would I choose Thin Lizzy?

I had already been introduced to Phil during a live recording at Capital Radio's studios in London. Although he was quite drunk he was very charming and explained to me, with Mary sitting in, how they wanted to expand their sound and have me do what I had done for Bolan and Bowie's music. I loved 'The Boys Are Back In Town' and for that reason alone, and the fact that they were charming, I said yes. Because Phil and Brian Downey were Irish citizens and Scott Gorham was American, they were free to record outside the UK and not declare overseas earnings. As an American I found this perfectly acceptable and we agreed to find a studio not in France or Germany, but in Toronto, Canada.

In late spring I flew to Toronto eager to get started. My first problem was getting through Immigration. I made the mistake of saying I was going to work in Canada. The problem was as an American I needed a work permit and when I told the officials that I was a freelance record producer hired specifically for recording Thin Lizzy, they argued that I was putting Canadian producers out of work. I was told to wait in a holding room, where I sat for three hours, not even permitted to make a phone call. It was an extremely demoralizing experience and the others I was penned in with had the bleakest look on their faces; most likely some of them would be deported, and I could be too. When I finally saw an Immigration official I was flabbergasted to hear that they didn't even have the profession of 'Record Producer' on their list of professions; it exactly replicated my experience in London 10 years earlier. I was let into Canada without further hassle, but I was rattled to the core and very angry.

I didn't work the first day, but the next day I was picked up by Phil's personal roadie, Charlie, and taken to the studio and greeted by head engineer Jon Bojic. It was a lovely studio, albeit with a very strange monitor speaker area. Huge pieces of clear Plexiglas stretched from the bottom of the monitor speakers to the top of the recording console, like a kind of children's slide. I was told it was to correct the sound and focus the high end; I never got used to it.

I had only met Scott and Phil before I arrived in Toronto and was pleased to find that Brian Downey, the drummer, was very polite; I could hear from his warm ups that he was going to be a joy to work with. Guitarist Brian Robertson was a different story. He was in a foul mood when I first met him and remained in one throughout making the album. After a few days' work I noticed that once the band became comfortable the drugs started to appear. I'm no prude, but when some band members got stoned they were only able to perform for about two and a half hours a day. Downey did not use drugs or drink, so I had no problems in the drum department. But the other three stone heads would simply get sloppy. After a week things almost ground to a halt because of their sloppiness and the growing surliness of Robertson.

When it came time to overdub his solos I would record him, encourage him and then say, 'Would you like to come into the control room for a listen?'

'If you like it it's okay with me,' was his mumbled reply. He never once came in for a playback. He'd take another swig of Courvoisier and stagger to the lounge room after each solo.

I asked Phil, 'What's going on with Brian?'

He smiled and said, 'Don't worry about him, he's a moody sort.' For my part I couldn't work that way.

Amidst all the difficulties, the people that ran the studio did their level best to lighten the mood. There was a lovely Asian lady receptionist who prepared several pounds of cooked shrimp with spicy sauce for us every night after she quit work at 6 p.m. On several occasions the staff prepared a barbecue for us.

After a week Mary, Morgan, Jessica and nanny Gloria came to join me. The hotel made the mistake of putting them next to 21-year-old Brian Robertson's room. He would play his boom box as loud as possible for most of the night, into the early hours of the morning. Eventually I called Thin Lizzy's managers, Chris O'Donnell and Phil Morrison, back in London.

'I'm going to walk off the album if you don't sort out the work ethic and the morale problem within the group.' I couldn't have been more blunt.

'I'll call Phil immediately and get it sorted out,' said O'Donnell. Robertson was moved to another floor and Chris O'Donnell arrived in Toronto a day later to smooth things over. Sometimes being a producer takes you into areas that have nothing specifically to do with the music. I was employed to deliver a great album but the circumstances at the start of *Bad Reputation* were not going to get us anywhere. The band was a bunch of boys and their behaviour was not what I needed to get the job done. My yardstick was Iggy. He was far wilder than anyone in Thin Lizzy, yet he managed to get his act together in the studio; I expected nothing less from them.

The next day a very sheepish Phil Lynott tried to pacify me.

'I know that drugs and alcohol are a problem with Scott and Robbo, but my mother turned me on to smoking spliffs when I was thirteen. I can handle it but they can't. I'll have a word with them.'

I told Phil that he was as much to blame for the collapse of the sessions and he was a little taken aback that he would be called on it. 'Look Tony I promise I'll cut down but it's impossible to cut it out completely.'

The chemical abuse didn't stop completely but the band behaved better, even Robbo; in fact the bulk of this album was recorded after this incident. My issue was not the drugs; it was with drugs while we were trying to work.

We stayed at a four-star hotel called the Plaza II and every night after we'd finished in the studio we went to the lounge bar to unwind with a nightcap. The very straight-looking bartender took a liking to us and kept the bar open after hours. One night he shocked us when he asked if we'd like a line of coke. Of course we said yes. Out came a glass chopping board and the bartender took a gram of cocaine out of his pocket and chopped it out for us. On another evening a lone drunk was being abusive towards Phil, mumbling racial slurs at him. The bartender leapt over the bar like Bruce Lee and punched the drunk several times in the face. Then he dragged him out the front door and told the doorman to get rid of him. Rock 'n' roll comes in many forms.

Putting to one side the difficulties with the band, I was very happy that Mary and the kids had come to Toronto. I was working so hard since we got married that we needed more contact. Toronto was gorgeous in the late spring. We took the kids to Ontario Park one morning. It was crowded with hundreds of happy Canadian kids. There were all sorts of colourful recreational things like swings, slides, rope bridges, etc. Three-year-old Morgan went berserk when he saw this place. He pulled free of my hand and ran into the crowd disappearing for over an hour. Gloria held on to baby Jessica whilst Mary and I went in two directions to find Morgan, but he was short then and we only caught glimpses of his blond locks. When we did get his attention he'd have a maniacal smile on his face and run away from us again; he must have thought the whole thing was a game.

Mary was asked by Phil to add some back-up vocals, so she came to the studio and sang on 'Dear Lord'. I wrote heavenly Celtic choir parts for her and she overdubbed her voice sixteen times to sing the glorious intro and outro. It was enough to make a rock band dewy-eyed. After finishing our backing tracks and overdubs, I knew it would be a struggle for me to mix in this studio; I still couldn't get used to the Plexiglas. We found another studio in the city for the mix and a few more overdubs. Scott's brother-in-law was the drummer for Supertramp and we all went to see them play a concert of theirs in Toronto. We asked John Helliwell, their sax player, to come and play something on 'Dancing In The Moonlight'. Amazingly, after all the drama, the album was actually delivered on time.

One of rock's greatest myths is the creative effect of drugs on the making of great music. I have tried recording music with and without chemical substances and I can put my hand on my heart and say that chemicals and the studio don't mix. I have stayed awake all night, propped up by lines of charlie and worked on music that, more often than not, sounded like a load of rubbish the following day. Booze and doobies are just as bad. As I said, I'm not a moralist, although drugs seem more potentially lethal in the 'noughties' – kids, I would avoid them. The smartest rock stars I've worked with have been relatively sober in the studio, simply because it's hard, precision work. They'd do whatever floated their boat when the sessions were over – and that was none of my business.

chapter 9
ich bin ein berliner

While I was in Toronto I had a call from David's PA, Coco Schwab, saying that he needed me in Berlin to begin work on his next album. Because of last-minute hitches with the Thin Lizzy album I was a week late getting there; Coco seemed upset with me. I was told that David had little regard for Thin Lizzy and couldn't see why I would even want to work with them. It's one of the perils of being a producer; guilt through association with an artist whom another performer does not respect or – put another way – hates their music, can sometimes put a job and a relationship in jeopardy. Many of the artists I have worked with, and especially Marc, saw things from the perspective of loyalty.

Brian Eno was also in Berlin and rather than working in the smaller studio at Hansa we were in their flagship studio located extremely close to the Berlin wall. The band and myself were staying in the Schloss Hotel Gerhus; nowadays it's called the Schlosshotel Vier Jahreszeiten. Whereas *Low* was recorded in a manner akin to a pilot 'flying blind', we now had a basic strategy and I could see very early on that we were going to make an improved album along the same lines. The band was, again, Dennis Davis, George Murray and Carlos Alomar along with David, who was by this time a more confident keyboard player and played on piano for lots of the songs. Brian and Bowie had started to write songs, but only came to the studio with basic chord progressions and relied on the rhythm section to 'funkify' and 'rock' them. Dennis Davis, the most original drummer I've ever worked with, spotted some conga drums in the corner of the studio and set them up next to his floor tom-tom. He managed to play patterns on the congas while playing normal rock drums; it was a staggering effect.

The band, having set a standard with *Low* was anxious to reach for a higher creative level. Recording in the efficiently run Hansa studio in a walled city surrounded by a Communist country provided an alchemy that created a more positive atmosphere than during the making of *Low*. The wonderful house engineer, Edu Meyer, who maintained a very stable environment for us to work in, helped this. There was one conspicuous absentee – a lead guitarist. It had been decided that we would wait until we felt the time was right to call Robert Fripp of King Crimson to come in and add his finishing touches. Fripp and Eno had already recorded two albums together and they had worked out great new ways to record an electric guitar.

The backing tracks were a dream to record and for me they were over much too soon. We recorded a song without a title one afternoon; it would become 'Heroes'. David played keyboards live on the track that was over seven minutes long; very little was left off the album cut. After the rhythm section went home, Brian spent about a week on overdubs using his 'magic' suitcase. Fripp was finally called and arrived with only a guitar; no amplifier was needed. He plugged his guitar into several guitar effects pedals and gave Brian his output from the last effect. After that Brian 'treated' the guitar through envelope filters which constantly mutated the sound. Three tracks were recorded in this way for *Heroes* because it was so difficult to perform simultaneously with the effects. It was really a two-man performance as Eno constantly mutated Fripp's sound.

After they were finished we knew we had some great ideas on tape, but we realized a great deal of non-linear editing would be needed to make a composite guitar track. This was a challenge in the days before computer-based recording; the concept of cut-and-paste didn't exist. The whole process involved a huge amount of trial and error; we often had to start the two machines at exactly the right moment and freely 'fly' a part from one tape machine to another.

When it came to adding in Robert's guitar, I casually played the three guitar takes together and it had a jaw-dropping effect on all of us. The constant mutation of the three sounds was entirely complimentary and we had the intro of 'Heroes' without doing anything more. It's now instantly recognizable as sound in our collective psyche. Fripp overdubbed all his guitar parts in less than two days. What seems like a synth on most of the rock tracks of the album are actually Fripp's guitar being treated through the 'magic' briefcase. Fripp also punctuated his glorious playing with very dry West Country humour, which kept us in stitches. 'P'raps, Oi'll wave the "sword of union" with some Berlin lass tonight?' he'd mumble through a crack in the doorway several times during that weekend.

Another two weeks were spent on recording an ambient music Side B, of which 'Moss Garden' is my favourite. The last track of the ambient side broke from the pattern of *Low* by ending with a rock track with a vocal. After Brian left Berlin we added some percussion to some tracks; all this was typical of how David worked. His ideas were spontaneous and he liked them executed quickly to see how the notion played out. In David's mind *Heroes* cried out for a cowbell, but it was too late to order a box of percussion from a rental company. We couldn't find a cowbell anywhere in the studio but we found an empty tape platter (in those days it was a German recording preference to put a tightly wound reel of tape on an open platter with the top of the tape exposed). Because we had a limited number of tracks David and I overdubbed the percussion elements of 'tape platter' and tambourine standing side by side.

If I've given the impression that this was the album finished, nothing could have been further from the truth. Not a single vocal had been recorded, or a melody and lyric written until just David and I remained at Hansa. This was no easy task and there were long lulls when David had to concentrate on writing. He'd arrive at the studio with a partial lyric, and we'd start recording his vocal with what little he'd have. I would record the first two lines, then he would hold up his hand for me to stop, listen to the playback, and then he'd write another scribbled couplet on his pad atop the studio piano. I could hear him off mic mumbling a few alternates then walk up to the mic with something to sing. When he had something he'd ask me to 'drop-in' his voice immediately after his first couplet. As tedious as this might sound he'd usually finish writing the song and performing the final vocal in under two hours. This would also include double tracking some lines and a chorus, if need be.

'Heroes' was just about the only lyric that was recorded in the traditional manner. But the writing of the song was difficult. I had met a Berlin jazz singer, Antonia Maass, a few nights earlier in a nightclub; I was very impressed with her singing, especially her vocal agility and extended high range, and we had a brief affair in Berlin (Mary found out). She was visiting the studio that day and we went for a walk after David asked us to leave him for a couple of hours so he could finish the lyrics. As we walked in front of the Berlin wall, which was very close to Hansa, we stopped and kissed. At that moment, a lyrically frustrated Bowie was looking out of the studio's control room studio. I can't tell you where he pulled the other images in his song, but we were the couple that inspired:

I can remember
Standing
By the wall
And the guns
Shot above our heads
And we kissed
As though nothing could fall

Antonia also contributed excellent backing vocals on 'Beauty and the Beast' and she was the translator for the German lyrics of *Heroes*, called *Helden*.

Berlin was an amazing city and, with Iggy Pop there as well, we spent a delightful two months making *Heroes*. Some evenings we would go to a club and have a meal or we would visit Berlin artists and musicians; we spent one evening at the home of Edgar Fröse of Tangerine Dream. We even ventured into East Berlin. As we passed through passport control an East German guard stared at David's and Iggy's passports in disbelief before yelling to a comrade, '*Hey Fritz, komm hier!*' A small group of armed guards came over and broke out laughing at the sight of David's *Space Oddity*-era photo of his permed hair, they laughed even harder at Iggy's platinum Beatles cut. We nervously grinned, took our passports back and drove into a very drab East Berlin, where we had dinner with a British diplomat, Anthony, whose girlfriend insisted on calling him Ants. In Communist Germany they didn't have many brand names, if any at all, so the rare billboard was emblazoned with a picture of a fish and the words '*Esst Fisch*', or a picture with a milk bottle and the words '*Trink Milch*'. In the streets were the ubiquitous Trebant and a few Warburgs; the cars looked like they were 25 years old, but were in fact the latest models, fresh off the assembly lines. Even the women had a 1950s look about them, with long tight skirts, high heels and beehive hairdos. At the Apollo restaurant we had a splendid lunch, served by stiffly mannered waiters and waitresses; one of them reminded me of Frau Blucher in *Young Frankenstein*. The servers wore black clothes, stiffly starched shirts and long white aprons from the chest to the shoes. Next to the restaurant was the Bertolt Brecht theatre and after lunch we had a tour; we imagined the premieres of *The Threepenny Opera*, and *Mahagony*. Afterwards we drove back to Checkpoint Charlie and just before the bridge into the west we noticed desperate-looking East Germans who longed to be smuggled into the western sector. I imagined how some of these people had been cut off from their families literally overnight when the wall went up.

The nightlife in Berlin gave us culture of a very different kind. We visited two very different drag clubs, Romy Haag's and the Lutzower Lampe. Romy Haag's was a high tech place, all very shiny and glittery. Attractive (real) females served drinks manoeuvring on roller skates through the dense crowd, never spilling a drop. Romy, a gorgeous six-foot-plus transvestite often lip-synched to Bowie's 'Port Of Amsterdam' played at double speed. Often there were as many as eight performers frantically lip-synching at the same time on a very small stage, maybe ten feet wide. Strobe lights were also going off, which made the performances even more frenetic.

The other club, the Lutzower Lampe, was in a derelict, bombed-out part of the city; the interior hadn't changed since the 1920s. A knock on a door would be answered by a small peep-hole opening and a deep voice bellowing, '*Ja?*' We had to give a 'code', speakeasy-style, to gain entry. The door-person was Daisy, a transvestite who made no attempt to conceal her *basso pro-fundo*. Inside it was dark and yellowish and the booths were upholstered in maroon velvet. Against the wall was a huge gilded mirror that reflected the backs of the performers. There was no stage; it was literally a floorshow. There was a German 'hostess' and a French 'chanteuse' but the star was Viola Scotti. 'She' had been until a few years earlier a civil servant before deciding to come out and sing as a woman in this club. She was a fragile, petite thing, thin, with a long pointed nose and piercing brown eyes, who could easily pass for a woman in her forties. In fact, all the transvestites were 'of a certain age'. When Viola wasn't performing she would sit shyly off to the side, wearing a cashmere cardigan to stay warm. She was so different from the other performers who would boldly sit in our laps and attempt to 'tongue' us when we politely kissed them goodnight. But Viola's specialty was *Carmen* and its famous aria, which was performed in almost the same key as a female would sing. She would spring to life as a mad, aggressive gypsy woman and sing directly into one's face unflinchingly – being the recipient of all her attention was difficult as her eyes were crossed. As she left to sing to another man she would bash you on the head with her tambourine, emphasizing the high note of each descending chromatic line. David and I both had our heads bashed a couple of times.

Drag clubs were not the haunts of transvestites and gays particularly. The entertainment was provided by the cross-dressing performers but the clientele were mostly very straight. Romy Haag's catered to young, hip heterosexuals, while the Lutzower Lampe catered to older middle-class couples; we even saw a family with a teenage son and daughter laughing it up at the double entendres. All of it went right over our heads since we didn't speak German and, anyway, we were there for Viola Scotti.

In the final stages of making the album we settled into an intimate studio family. Coco Schwab, David's assistant, had a separate apartment in the same building and Iggy had his own bedroom in David's flat. We spent some nights eating home-cooked food. I prepared a Tibetan meal as taught to me by our mutual Buddhist teacher, Chime Rinpoche (David had mentioned him to me when we'd first met, and I'd pestered David until eventually I got to meet him. To me it was a dream fulfilled, to finally meet a reincarnated lama from Tibet – Rinpoche means that the lama is reincarnated. Chime belongs to the Kargyu sect of Buddhism, the second oldest of the four major sects. I became a student of meditation, and eventually took the vow of the Three Precepts and became a Buddhist. I studied intensely for a while and made great progress in meditation, but I got so busy I was unable to study with Chime on a regular basis. He was always gracious and understanding and his nickname for me was 'Tony *Top-Of-The-Pops*'.)

One evening I gave David and Iggy haircuts. Iggy wanted a buzz cut but I only had scissors and instead gave him a botched up Mohican. Sometimes David and Iggy would don cloth-caps, wrap scarves around their necks and we'd all drink lager at the corner bar, unmolested. Berlin seemed to be a haven for everyone to be as anonymous as they wished to be.

When Mary appeared on *Top of the Pops* to promote 'If You Love Me' in March 1976, the show where they wouldn't reveal her pregnancy, Marc Bolan was also appearing. At the very moment that we came out of Mary's dressing room Marc and Gloria Jones, by now his common-law wife, walked out of theirs. We froze for a second, and then Marc and I walked towards each other and hugged. Nothing was mentioned about our break up, despite this being the first time I'd seen or spoken to him since I'd sent my letter of resignation. He and Gloria had a young son, Rolan, and we chatted briefly about having boys to bring up; we promised to stay in touch. We didn't.

I also worked with a heavy rock band called Dirty Tricks and made an album called *Night Man*. My business partner Roger Myers signed them to a management deal and persuaded me to work with them. I don't remember much about this project because I was drunk for the entire month. (I felt a burden to accept work to keep my company afloat. I got to this point in my life by making creative and innovative records. Now the sole purpose of my life seemed to be about financially supporting my business and family.) We worked in a very basic studio in Dean Street in Soho called Zodiac that was run by a pair of Indian businessmen who couldn't make a profitable go of it. I was their last client, they said, and they were going to sell the lease. I instantly bought it and got Graeme Myrhe, the studio manager in my Hammersmith home studio, to gut most of the place and build my Good Earth studios. This is where I met Colin Thurston; he was the engineer for Dirty Tricks. He became the new chief engineer in Dean Street (he eventually worked with Duran Duran on many of their hits, as well as Iggy Pop's *Lust For Life*).

Marc had managed to get his own series on TV, and David had agreed to appear performing 'Heroes' as part of the album promotion. David and Marc wrote a song together to end the show, but immediately after the intro Marc slipped and fell off the stage. The union technicians refused to shoot a retake and that was the last the public ever saw of Marc – him falling off the stage as David Bowie, trying to look cool in shades, cracked up. After the show Colin Thurston had dinner with Marc and David in Soho. He took them to see my new studio at 59 Dean Street; Marc loved what he saw and told Colin that he'd like to work there. Three days later, in the early hours of 16 September 1977, Marc was in a purple Mini that was being driven by Gloria Jones when it left the road and hit a tree in Barnes, west London. Marc, who was two weeks away from his thirtieth birthday, was killed instantly.

Mary and I went to the funeral service in Golders Green. His coffin had been draped with white flowers in the shape of a swan, although these had been removed when it came time for it to enter the cremation room. As the robotic arm glided up from a thin crevice and moved the coffin into the inferno, Marc's mother screamed, 'My boy!' and everyone at the service completely lost it. June Bolan did not attend, but told me that she'd gone to the hospital the night he died and was allowed to be with his body for a bit. She kissed him and said her final goodbye.

'Apart from a small bruise on his forehead there was nothing that indicated he'd been in an accident; he looked beautiful,' she told me. Gloria Jones did not attend the ceremony because she was still in hospital in a semi-conscious daze with a wired-up broken jaw.

There was definitely an A list and B list of celebrities. Rod Stewart sat next to Bowie who sat next to Elton John; just along from them was Steve Harley. Mary and I were upstairs with the rest of T.Rex. After the service I was standing outside when a kid came up to me, I assumed he was going to ask for an autograph or something; many fans had been doing that to the A-listers. He actually just wanted to thank me for producing Marc; I was very touched. After the service we were driven in limos to EMI Records for a small party with canapés and sandwiches; I had a few stiff shots of whisky. I chatted with Steve Currie, Marc's former bass player in T.Rex, who was not speaking too kindly about Marc, commenting on how abusive he was as a bandleader – even more bad blood must've taken place after I left. Steve also died in a motoring accident, in Portugal, where he was living, in 1981. He was killed in a head-on collision with a truck that didn't have its headlights on early one morning.

Midway through the summer of this busy year an album came out that I had worked on during the spring. I still had a soft spot for Art Rock, which is where Caravan fitted in. They were amongst the finest musicians I've worked with. Pye Hastings their guitarist had a 'thing' for Vicki Brown, the beautiful vocalist who was married to Skiffle legend Joe Brown. He specifically wanted her to sing on 'Give Me More' and have her whisper, 'would you like to touch', which rendered him nearly orgasmic in the control room. We recorded this album at a short-lived studio in North London called Unique.

I was still trying to get something to happen with my Good Earth label – all I needed was that elusive 'big one'. I signed a band called Omaha Sheriff, not just because it was a brilliant name. They had a singer, Paul Muggleton, who is one of the greatest vocalists I've ever worked with; likewise Bob Noble their keyboard player. Together they wrote amazing, complex pop songs. Chris Birkett, their guitarist, was also very talented and he went on to be a producer in his own right, working with Sinead O'Connor amongst others. Michael Spence was just starting to spread his wings as a drummer (he excelled himself on the second Omaha Sheriff album); I was the bass player for the album, although I relinquished the role to my mate Bruce Lynch for one track, and then he officially joined the group. I regret never having a hit with this group. By now I had learned a very humbling lesson – I was not a great record label person and from that point on I should just stick to production. However, I regard this as one of the best albums I've ever produced, and the unreleased follow-up was even better. Years later Paul Muggleton would leave his wife for Judy Tzuke, another artist I had signed.

It was hard spending so much time away from Mary and the kids – a successful rock 'n' roll career and marriage is always a tricky combination. With good projects we were in a position to buy the things that made our home even more beautiful. With her own money Mary bought a house and twelve acres in Llandeilo, South Wales; despite making frequent trips there we never spent a single night in it. We talked about growing organic vegetables but neither of us could ever bring ourselves to become farmers. Eventually Mary asked Ricky and Virginia Gardiner (Ricky had played guitar on *Low*) to manage it and they lived there for years, turning it into a profitable market garden.

Despite seeming to attract the rock stars with tax schemes, which took me abroad to work too often, when I was at home I embraced the good life in the country. At The Bull, my local pub, I learned to enjoy darts and was even invited to join the pub's dongola team. A dongola is a sort of gondola for eight one-oared rowers and a steering person at the rear. A child sits at the helm and calls the strokes. Our team was very competitive, under the supervision of an Alpha-Type advertising executive by the name of John French. Wargrave and Shiplake are neighbouring villages and have their own annual regatta, although it's not as prestigious as the famous Henley Regatta just down the river. We trained hard, we drank together and for two weeks leading up to the race I would eat 'muscle food', fried eggs and steak for breakfast. French was a hard taskmaster.

The landlord, Richard Wilson, was a resting actor with a very pronounced stammer, although when he recited something he'd memorized, a soliloquy for instance, he didn't stammer. My love for real ale enticed me to join CAMRA (the Campaign For Real Ale) and I begged Richard to let me work behind the bar several times (I was rehearsing for a time when I would buy a pub – a fantasy). It was a difficult job, adding the sum of the ordered drinks (the trick is to add during the pulling of the pint) and making sure that when a labourer extended his pint glass and asked for a 'half' you went at least an inch over the half line. There was no tipping in the public bar, only a stern, judgemental nod when you get the amount right. When you told drinkers the price of a round, they would as often as not open their hand with the correct amount sitting in their palm, ready and waiting. The 'Toffs', on the other hand, would never count their change. The Bull was a fun pub. Richard, with his theatrical flair, would throw theme evenings, especially on St George's Day. We would dress up as lords and ladies, often wearing the clothes of the opposite sex; another, rather risqué night involved the obligatory Vicars and Tarts.

Like all rural places our land was overrun with rabbits. The local farm workers freely killed the rabbits on our land and took them to Richard for free pints. For a few days there would be Rabbit Curry, Rabbit Fricassee, Rabbit Stew, and many other exotic rabbit dishes on the menu; no matter how it is disguised rabbit is my least favourite food.

Our house was so big there was room for everything. A couple of bedrooms were never even used. I had my own photographic darkroom and an 8-track studio in the stable. The kids had a playroom off the kitchen where they were allowed to draw all over the walls in crayon. On one side of the kitchen was a hatch that opened into the spacious dining room. When our families stayed with us, which was often, the hatch was used every evening with Gloria passing dishes through the wall. At Christmas 1977 we watched a particularly scary Christmas horror made-for-TV film. The story was about a witch who was killed and buried in a tree. Spiders nested in her body and crawled out at night to kill descendants of her murderers. That night the branch of a large tree outside our bedroom window kept scratching the window making the same sound as when the spiders attacked in the drama. Mary and I were up most of the night, too terrified to sleep. The next morning I cut off the branch.

This was about the busiest working period of my life – I'm surprised I didn't kill myself, looking back at it. Mary called me a workaholic – I thought it was normal for a man to work as much as possible and for his wife to rule the family home. That's what

I observed in my household; my Dad had up to three jobs at once and would work most weekends. Mary and I started drifting apart. I would come back home and look at my beautiful wife and kids and home and I couldn't believe I was a part of it for a few days. As soon as I'd get used to domestic bliss, and Mary and I would get into sync (which wasn't easy since my brain was still preoccupied with my last album), I'd be off to another album in another country.

My first project of 1978 was the Steve Gibbons Band; Steve himself came from Birmingham and should've been a big star. He wrote and sang what I've always described as thinking man's rockabilly. In making this album I was reunited with Trevor Burton, the bass player of The Move, who was now in Steve's band. I thought there were at least four hit singles on it but the best any of them did was No 56. I guess the times were not right for rockabilly, no matter how cerebral and psychedelic we dressed it up. Bill Curbishly and Peter Meaden, who also managed The Who, managed them. A tragedy marred the merry making of this album, when Peter committed suicide shortly after it was finished.

A nightly ritual during the recording was to go to a pub across the road from Shaftsbury Avenue in the very short Macclesfield Street. It was called De Hems, a Dutch name, and was run by a wise arse Australian landlord called Ron. He loved musicians and we were always invited to drink after hours. The clientele was a strange mixture of musicians, tourists and Chinese restaurant workers and gamblers. Directly across the street was the restaurant of my kung fu teacher's father. We would pile in there on many an evening and have special dishes made for us, ones that were not on the menu. Soho was a magic place back then, not the sterile movie set it is today. It was dangerous and seedy, perfect inspiration for my low down musicians.

From rockabilly I went straight to hard rock and Thin Lizzy; I must have been a glutton for punishment. *Bad Reputation* had been a hit and Thin Lizzy wanted me to work on the next studio album. This time David Bowie made sure I was booked to start work with him on a specific date. Phil Lynott gave me a choice: to start a studio album, stop after a month to work with Bowie, and then resume working with them afterwards. Plan B was to release a live album that we felt could easily be finished in a month – we opted for the live album.

I should have realized as soon as the tapes arrived that I was going to be in trouble. The band had recorded several shows in America and Europe, which in itself may not have been a problem. The difficulties started when I found the tape formats were different; some were recorded at the new fashionable 30 ips (inches per second) and the rest at 15 ips. Some used the Dolby A system, some didn't; some with the AES frequency curve and some with the European CCIR curve. Without getting too technical, this was a nightmare.

When we listened to the tapes they were definitely a little too rough to do straightforward mixing as originally planned. Phil begged to be able to fix a few vocals by dropping in a few lines in each song. It proved almost impossible to match the microphone characteristics on each track. The vocal tracks also had a lot of drums and guitar leakage, noticeably missing when Phil re-sang a line in an acoustically dry studio. Rather than endless hours of trying to match the sound we found it easier to have Phil simply re-sing everything. Things then got even more complicated.

'The trouble is Tony that my bass playing really suffers when I'm singing live and playing at the same time.' He was right, he missed a lot of notes. Once again we couldn't match the sound from the different cities, so we set his stage gear up in the studio and he replayed every bass part. Good Earth had a three-tiered control room. Phil stood on the top tier towering over me sitting on the middle tier as I recorded his bass. Interestingly Phil used his radio transmitter for his bass so that he could move around like he did on stage; I was also getting a visual performance, which made the whole thing more entertaining. Phil also wanted me to blast the volume so that he could feel the sound rumble in his feet the way he did on stage.

Having sorted all Phil's mistakes the guitarists, Scott Gorham and Brian Robertson, began to notice that the guitar sounds could have been better. I have no idea who they used as the engineer but they were absolutely right. Fortunately, instead of replacing their guitars they merely added an extra guitar each to fatten the sound of the original ones.

We had started out working in my studio but decamped to Paris for a weekend to finish it off. Mary came with me, and Phil brought his new wife Caroline and the four of us had a wonderful and hilarious dinner at La Coupole one night. At first the waiters refused to serve Phil because he seemed drunk (and Black, apparently). Undeterred he used his suave Dublin charm to order yet another 'Gin d'Orange' in restaurant French. They then also refused to serve Phil with eighteen raw oysters, saying that the mixture of Gin and oysters would make him sick. Phil poured on even more charm and was served the oysters. He downed every one of them – and they stayed down.

Lynott was the last of a dying (literally) breed. He wanted the world to know that he rocked hard, lived hard and played hard. For the inner sleeve of the double album he insisted that I photograph a line of coke and a straw on a silver record; he used the photo.

Doing an 'in concert' album this way was cheating, slightly (everyone does it), but the album is about 55 per cent live and the overdubs gave the poorly recorded performances a more uniform sound. This took a lot more time than we planned, which meant I was again late for Bowie's album. On the plus side, *Live and Dangerous* became a big hit and remains a primer for 'How To Be A Rock Band', inspiring thousands of younger rock bands; even U2 claim it as an early influence.

I had committed to David that I would be in America during April and May to oversee and engineer the recording of his live shows; he wasn't about to delay his tour for me to take more time to finish Thin Lizzy. In the end it got so tight that they flew me to New York on Concorde at the end of April. Flying on Concorde was a great experience. Although the fare was more than a first class fare the seats were hardly luxurious – in fact they were closer to economy-sized seats. Supersonic flight exacts a lower weight and lighter construction. Every one of the four times I flew on Concorde I sat next to a wealthy portly person who spilled over into my seat. To compensate for the cramped seat the food and wine were expensive; Dom Perignon flowed throughout the flight and filet mignon and lobster were the choices for the main course. The stewardesses, trained specially for Concorde flights, were abnormally cheerful, like Stepford Wives. Still, New York was a mere 3 hours and 15 minutes away, well worth the 'inconvenience'. You actually landed in New York two hours before you took off from London.

I was more impressed with the technology; turbulence was only felt before we broke the sound barrier. We had to fly subsonic over land but once we were over the Atlantic the engines would roar (breaking the sound barrier created a sonic boom and we weren't allowed to frighten the Irish or English cows). Once we elevated to an altitude of 11 miles the interior cabin was very quiet because we were flying faster than our own engine noise. We were on the edge of Earth's atmosphere, and at this altitude you could see the separation between the blue sky and dark outer space with a purplish thin band between them; you could also see the curvature of the earth. On a panel just behind the cockpit was a large LED readout with gave our speed in MACH, the speed of sound. As we accelerated after take off the readout would start with a decimal point then a number, like .82, which was still slower than the sound barrier. Once we hit the sound barrier we'd see a read out like 1.35 and upwards, usually maintaining a speed of MACH 1.98, just under twice the speed of sound. At some points we'd hit MACH 2.0 and slightly above and the passengers would break out into spontaneous applause. The captain announced that we were flying faster than a bullet shot from a rifle – if someone shot a bullet ahead of us, we'd see it appear as if it were hovering in the sky next to us, then we'd pass it. This was mind-blowing for me.

We taped two shows in Philadelphia, before taping a show in Providence, Rhode Island and another in Boston; these shows were done properly, unlike the Thin Lizzy or *David Live* tapes – this time I was the engineer. The North American section of the shows finished up in New York on 7, 8 and 9 May. We had originally planned to record at Madison Square Garden, but we learned that they charged massive fees for recording there, including an obligatory royalty.

At Madison Square Garden I stood next to David's guests, Andy Warhol and Yoko Ono, for about an hour just off to the side of the stage; there were no seats left, even for them. Our standing room gave us a great view with David 30 feet from us, backed by a band that was one of the best he ever assembled. The guitarist Adrian Belew was so close he often turned and smiled at us after a blistering solo. If this wasn't magical enough something even more surreal was about to happen. As I stood there I noticed a smell in the air, a nostalgic whiff of something earthy, yet not unpleasant. It reminded me of the few times I visited a farm as a little city boy, but this was something more exotic. As I turned around I saw, through a large passage-way leading from the side of the stage to the dressing rooms, an elephant – a real one. I then saw the beginnings of another elephant and it had its trunk wrapped around the tail of the previous elephant; they moved slowly from one end of the passageway to the other. This being Madison Square Garden, the circus was in town; I'd been there as a child to see The Ringling Brothers, Barnum and Bailey Circus.

For the recording at the Spectrum Arena in Philadelphia, the New Boston Garden Arena in Boston and Civic Center in Providence, we used a mobile studio belonging to RCA, David's label. It operated from a huge truck and I found myself in the capable hands of their best engineers as my assistants. My plan was to record the performances very carefully, as if it were a studio album. I supervised the microphone placements includ-ing those placed over the audience. I had to make sure that the band was close mic'd for maximum separation between their sounds to ensure more control during mixing. I wanted the audience to sound big and real and I wanted the natural reverb in the concert halls to enhance the sound of the record. I used four microphones for the audience, not the more common two that are usually placed left and right in the house. Quadraphonic recording was still viable in the late 1970s and I wanted to cover the possibility; years later my Surround Sound mix recreated the spatial feeling of being in the audience.

This is a truly live album, not at all like *Live and Dangerous*. Fans adore bootlegs and cherish any perceived 'mistakes' as very vibey things; *Stage* is 100 per cent live. There wasn't time during the tight touring schedule to fix anything. The perform-ances were selected from the four nights. It's almost impossible to perceive the different sound of each venue. When the mixes were finished I tracked David and the band down in Munich on 20 May and played them the album. They were thrilled.

The only 'cheating' I am guilty of was cutting into the middle of 'Station To Station' with a section from another night and city. The beginning and end are from Boston but the middle is from Providence. The possibility of making such edits was planned from the time I set up the sound for the first show. After I made an initial band set up, complete with equalization, dynamic processing and track assignment, I instructed the crew never to change anything on the console from show to show, and to always to use the same exact microphones. After each show a big X was made across the console in white tape, with a written warning that anyone who touched it would be, at the very least, castrated. Enormous credit goes to drummer Dennis Davis for consistently playing the same tempo from night to night, making such an edit possible. Top honours go to David for delivering some his best ever live vocals.

We made a drastic decision to put the album into a very different running order than the live performances. We assembled the tracks in a sort of chronological order, as to the date they were originally recorded, from 'Ziggy Stardust' to 'Heroes'; David loved the idea. The Brian Eno ambient compositions took up one of the four sides of the double vinyl LP. In 2004 I got to work with the tapes again to remix it in Surround Sound. Remixing David in his 1977 incarnation in 2004, I can barely perceive any evidence of aging in his voice. If a Dorian Gray-type portrait of his vocal cords exists, he keeps it well hidden. He is one of the most amazing performers of our time, and these performances seem timeless to me.

When the European tour was over and everyone had had a month off, David brought his touring band into the studio to record his next album. Brian Eno was on hand once again to add his creativity. He and David had already begun writing songs prior to my arrival at Mountain Studios, in Montreux, Switzerland (David had moved there and lived in nearby

Vevey). The two of them once again showed up with just chord changes and vague ideas for rhythm backing for what was to be the third album in Bowie's so called 'Berlin Trilogy'. It was the same rhythm section as for *Low* and *Heroes*, but with the addition of keyboard players Sean Mayes and Roger Powell, Simon House on electric violin and the latest guitarist in Bowie's guitar hero lineage – Adrian Belew.

While the studio was very cramped it is the best in the area. It wasn't really a studio for recording a band at all but was used to record live concerts in the huge auditorium that was below us. It was small and really an overdub studio but the main auditorium was booked for the whole summer. Later on Queen was able to rent the auditorium and got far better sounds than we managed to achieve. We crammed all eight musicians in that room for two weeks. It was a constant battle with the air conditioner, which usually won; the musicians often recorded shirtless in stifling heat.

This band was one of the best Bowie bands I ever worked with; the combination of Simon House's violin and Adrian Belew was a logical progression from the lead work that Fripp had established on *Heroes*. There was even more experimentation – Eno and Bowie were great at that – including a session at which everyone swapped instruments to record 'Boys Keep Swinging'. Another day Eno asked for a blackboard and wrote his eight favourite chords in big block letters. He then said to the rhythm section of Carlos, Dennis and George, 'Okay, I'd like you to play a funky groove', and he held a teacher's pointer in his hand with a demeanour not unlike a professor from Oxford.

'I will point to a chord and you will change over to that chord after four beats.'

This was not on the face of it Brian's finest idea and I could see the rhythm section exchanging irritable looks as if to say 'what an asshole'.

This fruitless jam took up two hours of 24-track tape. David wasn't so sure about it but instructed me to fool around with the jam and edit the best pieces together. 'Tony just try and construct a backing track.' With that everyone left for the day and I eventually got something vaguely usable but not spectacular enough to work with.

Not every experiment was a waste of time and Brian had great ideas that flew. We recorded three separate songs that had the exact same chord structure and the same key; two were definitely brilliant – 'Boys Keep Swinging' and 'Fantastic Voyage'. We almost ventured into recording the entire album with these chord changes. The song 'African Nightlife' was based on a jam of the Dale Hawkins classic 'Susie Q'. 'Move On' was inspired by playing the recording of 'All The Young Dudes' backwards and then everyone learning to play it that way. David and I flipped the new version's tape over and played it backwards, and sang the melody of 'All The Young Dudes' (forwards – I know I've lost most of you) and that became 'Move On'. We decided to fuse Turkish music and Reggae together, but as the rhythm section was American they were none too familiar with Reggae. David and I coached Dennis in the art of putting the kick drum on the back beat, where the snare usually goes, and I played a Jamaican 'up-chop' rhythm guitar live with the band to keep the feel going. Simon House overdubbed a fantastic Arabic violin part and there we had it – 'Yasassin'. 'Red Money' was the only track not recorded by the band; it was 'Sister Midnight' originally recorded by Iggy Pop, but slowed down and with a new melody and lyric.

After a seven-month hiatus David called me and said we would finish *The Lodger* at the Hit Factory in New York with just David, Adrian Belew and myself. We recorded some new jams with Belew on drums, myself on bass and David on guitar, but nothing came of it. Instead we settled for some Belew guitar overdubs and I replaced the bass on 'Boys Keep Swinging', the experimental track where the band switched instruments. Carlos Alomar played the drums quite well, but Dennis Davis, who is left-handed, never played a satisfactory bass part on George Murray's right-handed bass. I played an over-the-top bass part on the song, in the spirit of 'The Man Who Sold The World'.

We were relegated to studio D because we booked at the last minute. 'D' implies the quality of the studio. It had very little gear and without the now ubiquitous equipment hire companies, we had to make do with what there was. Kiss was in one of the bigger rooms at the Hit Factory and one day Gene Simmons and Paul Stanley came in to pay homage to David. Honestly, they were unrecognizable without their makeup but we took their word that they were Kiss. They humbly told David that if it hadn't been for his pioneering music, clothes and stage presentations during the Ziggy period, then they wouldn't be Kiss. With an icy gaze David gave them a conservative thanks; he circumvented their request to play them our new music. He made it obvious that he wanted to get on with work and they made a hasty retreat. As soon as they left David said, 'Well, it's about fucking time they admitted it!'

Another time Mick Jagger dropped by. I had met him before during the final stages of *Young Americans*. Jagger spent an evening with David and me, jamming and singing old rock and roll songs to the accompaniment of an acoustic guitar. I impressed Jagger by knowing the right chords to Del Shannon's 'Runaway'. We shared a bunch of Italian stuffed artichokes my mother had sent over to fatten David up – she was worried about his health. Now Jagger managed to criticize everything we played from *Lodger*. David looked over to me for support and I had to chime in with, 'We like it that way', and David would add, 'I wouldn't dream of changing it.' What could've been a fun evening was spoiled because Jagger seemed to have some other agenda. Finally Jagger, in a frustrated tone, said, 'Okay, I'm leaving. I'm going to Joni Mitchell's session and see if I can sabotage that.'

On another night David and I were having dinner in a classy restaurant in NYC. We noticed that there seemed to be a lot of people arriving altogether, at least a dozen men, all dressed in black. David said, 'Look it's John Belushi.'

The five-foot-seven comedian was surrounded by twelve security guards. David went over to greet Belushi, I joined him and we were introduced. Belushi explained the large number of guards around him: 'I have six bodyguards for protection and the other six are to stop me from acquiring drugs. When I walk into a room I can tell who is carrying and I will get it from them.'

It was a situation that was well known to us. We didn't go to clubs much when we were working, but a couple of times we did after we finished work. The most exclusive clubs were open to us when David appeared at the velvet rope. The club life in the 1970s was fuelled on cocaine; snorting coke in the men's and women's toilet stalls was rife and unisex. One night I had had enough and I told David I wanted to go; this was 10 a.m. and the club was still crowded.

'I think I'll stay,' said David. Outside I told Tony Mascia, David's chauffeur, that David was okay and I grabbed a taxi in the bright morning Manhattan sun. That night David told me he stayed until midday. All I could think of was, poor Tony Mascia.

During mixing we were asked if two groupies could come in for a visit. We were up for a laugh so we told them to wait for a few minutes. With a white grease pencil we drew four white lines on the black Formica panel of the recording console and put a newspaper over the lines. When the girls came in we took an instant dislike to them, but we were still eager to play our little trick on them. When we offered them a couple of 'lines' they were extremely enthusiastic. We carefully lifted the newspaper and gave the first girl a rolled-up dollar bill. She lowered her head to the lines, took a deep snort and couldn't believe nothing went up her nose. She complained that she'd been overdoing cocaine recently but enthusiastically continued her attempts at getting a pencil line up her nose. We finally had to call it off because she just didn't get it. After we explained the joke they left quickly.

Between *The Lodger* sessions I had been back in the studio with Thin Lizzy to work on our second studio album together; yet again for tax reasons it had to be recorded abroad. This time we chose Pathé Marconi studios at Boulogne Billancourt on the outskirts of Paris. We chose it because the Rolling Stones had recorded their *Some Girls* album there the previous year. The studio's main function was for recording film scores; it was in a bleak neighbourhood, and the atmosphere inside was not helped by drab fluorescent tubes and dreary off-white walls.

Gary Moore had officially replaced Brian 'Robbo' Robertson and his presence and artistry were extremely uplifting; the mood of the other members was perceptibly lighter. Phil Lynott had outdone himself with writing a true Celtic Rock opus, the seven-minute long 'Roison Dubh' (Black Rose). It was a grand work, which required intense concentration, and even though Moore could've played all the guitar parts himself it was touching to see him painstakingly teach Scott Gorham the second harmony parts. Even so it didn't take very long to record the album, as the rest of the tracks were more traditional Thin Lizzy rock. On the off time we went to a huge nightclub in a former cinema called La Palace. The name Thin Lizzy could also push aside any velvet rope, and we were escorted directly to the manager's inner sanctum, where copious amounts of cocaine were chopped out for the band – we never paid for drinks either. A last-minute addition to the album was the very sweet 'My Sarah', inspired by Phil's new baby daughter. In fact it was recorded in London after we finished the other tracks in Paris and I think it was meant for a Phil Lynott solo album but he decided to add it to *Black Rose*; it's only Phil and Gary Moore, with drums supplied by a Roland beat box machine.

Phil's health was an issue during this album. After a few nights of heavy partying, he could not get out of bed one day. He was physically drained. He would see no one but his personal roadie, Charlie, who came to me worried and frustrated because Phil refused to see a doctor. He wouldn't even see me. I told Charlie to have plenty of chicken soup on hand and feed Phil with a spoon if necessary. I had a bottle of Bach Rescue Remedy (a homeopathic elixir designed to suppress panic and fear in emergencies) and told Charlie to lace his drink with it (only four drops per 8 oz. glass). It was three days before we saw Phil again, but I always felt that this was a turning point and the beginning of the end. Phil tragically died in 1986, from a multitude of health problems, drugs not being the least.

I was reunited with Rick Wakeman professionally. I always enjoyed his company and loved his playing and so when he asked me to produce a solo album I accepted without hesitation; it was also good to keep my hand in with a bit of Art Rock. In reality what was originally a cool concept turned out to be a logistical nightmare, which marred the recording. We were to record at Rick's home, high in the Swiss Alps. The British crew could not drive the mobile recording truck, a 16-wheeler articulated lorry, up the narrow hairpin turns. For a week we would drive down to the first hairpin turn everyday and muse about how we would get it up the hill. Then we go to the pub and have lunch. We called the Swiss Army to see if they could lift the truck with one of two massive helicopters that they owned, but the cost was too prohibitive. Finally Rick's wife called a firm of Swiss transport experts and they sent two Swiss drivers who got the damn thing up the hill. At one point they stopped and built a small platform of plywood and two-by-fours that helped them drive off the road, over the precipice, and allowed them make what seemed to be an eight-point turn. The British drivers were agape at some of these stunts. This was accomplished when Rick spent the day in Geneva, not believing that this would ever happen. When he got home and saw the truck in his courtyard, he shook his head and said, 'I'm going to bed.'

Despite being as busy as ever I spent as much time as I could at home in Wargrave with Mary and the kids. Mary and I were still working on more tracks, especially as her writing was getting better and better. We even started to 'shop' her around to labels and at every one we got the same reaction: 'We'd love to release the album but only if Mary consents to tour in support of it.' She adamantly refused to do so and her recording career remained in limbo. On reflection she was before her time. Nowadays artists with her dislike for live performance enjoy a career on the Internet.

Any frustrations associated with Mary's career were nothing compared to my continued dislike of the low pressure in British water supplies. My morning shower was more a trickle than a shower and so I was relieved to find a company that installed a great American shower in Britain that hit you with high pressure from eight sides (it needed electric pumps hidden in the loft). In a 'no expense spared' moment I had it installed. For me this was the year I became really clean.

chapter 10
all change

The end of the 1970s, a decade in which I had made my reputation and then consolidated it in a way that I could never have
imagined, brought change in all kinds of ways. When I arrived
in London in the middle of the Summer of Love I had been all
wide-eyed and keen to learn the alchemy of production. I had
not only learned it, but I had created alchemy of my own.
Almost 13 years later with all the success, my marriage to Mary
and our two lovely kids, we were – to many who looked at us
– the perfect musical couple. However, from the successes of the
'70s it all went badly wrong in 1980, a year that was one of the
unhappiest of my life. It would usher in a decade that would
prove to be frustrating, disheartening and, while it had some
real highs, it was ultimately downright awful for my career.

Professionally the year had started out fine, if in rather low-
key fashion with the release of an album called *Bright As Fire* by
Mike Westbrook's Orchestra. My good friend, and drummer,
Andy Duncan had asked me to mix this jazz record. It was
something I had never done before and I accepted and was interested to find that Mike was not writing for bass at the time, so
it was very definitely a challenge. I thoroughly enjoyed working
with Mike and Kate Westbrook, consummate jazz pros.

I had also started work on David's new album: as always it
was a joy to start a new Bowie album. It was our eighth studio

album together and we began working in New York City in February, where David was now spending much of his time. However, there was one problem. I was burnt out. I had been working too hard ever since the day I got my first hit single with T.Rex. I had been spending too much of my time abroad and even if I was working in the UK I all too often stayed overnight in London. Even as I was preparing for the trip to New York, Mary and I were discussing separation. I didn't want to pass up working with David, and at the same time I didn't want to leave Mary and the kids for another long project. It was a dilemma and as usual it was work that won.

We had booked the Power Station, a studio that had not been open very long but already had a reputation for being the finest in the world. It was designed and owned by Tony Bongiovi, a cousin of Jon Bon Jovi, a wiz-kid who figured out the exact dimensions of Motown Studios' echo chamber just from listening to their records. He had done this by calculating the amount of reverb decay on their recordings. He sent a letter to Motown describing his findings and asked for a job. He was hired – they could use a smart kid like him. Once he worked at their studios he realized that they had many more secrets; they had a Pultec tube (valve) equalizer permanently installed in each input and each output of their 24-track machines, a total of 48 Pultecs in each control room. The sound of a microphone or tape track passing through a Pultec is very sweet, full and pleasing. Most really well-equipped studios might have as many as six Pultecs, and you have to choose carefully what six elements you are going to use them for: vocals, drums, bass, guitars. Plus they're very expensive, and there is only a limited supply in the world. This studio had 48 Pultecs! Every track of the tape had a Pultec to pass through – the analogue sound of wet dreams. When Tony built the Power Station on the west side of Manhattan he copied Motown's concept. We were assigned a fabulous engineer named

Larry Alexander; I was happy to turn over this responsibility in such a maverick studio because he knew what made it tick.

Before beginning work on every Bowie album we had joked about making this one our *Sgt. Pepper*; I think the only time we were 100 per cent serious was at the beginning of making *The Man Who Sold The World*. The day after I arrived in NYC I went to the Power Station and loved what I saw; David was waiting with the musicians, his usual rhythm section of Carlos, Dennis and George, showing them his new device. They were fascinated with the little box with headphones attached. As I walked in he was putting the headphones on Carlos. After a few seconds Carlos shouted at the top his lungs (a phenomenon we'd all too soon get accustomed to), 'Shit this thing is LOUD! It sounds great!' David had the first Sony Walkman any of us had seen. We all had a listen and were equally amazed by this audio marvel; of course we all wanted one. Despite having listened to music before on headphones, before this we would have to be attached to a huge amplifier and remain stationary. Listening to music on a pocket-sized player was an altogether different and novel experience. How quaint it all seems now that we live in a world of iPods.

After the novelty of the Walkman had worn off I asked David what his new music was like. I had been asked to rush to New York, which gave me reason to believe I was going to hear something really special.

'I haven't really finished a song yet. I've just got some chord changes. You know what I'm like Tony.' Normally I would've said, okay, let's just roll up our sleeves and start the slow process of creating something from nothing. But this time I was incensed – I was almost furious.

'I could have come over in a week or so's time after you and the band had worked some things out.' There was nastiness in my voice, which was out of character for me, and particularly for me towards David whom I loved working with. The east to west jet lag made me feel even worse than usual.

David looked at me hesitantly and said, 'Tony, why don't you just go back to the hotel and rest until tomorrow. I'll come and see you later if we finish up early enough.'

Back in my room I thought he was surely going to ask me to leave. I thought it wouldn't be a bad thing. Maybe it was time he worked on his own or with someone else. I had a marriage that was very shaky and two little kids that I hardly saw anymore. As I lay there feeling sorry for myself there was a knock at the door; it was David.

'Are you all right Tony?'

'Yeah, I'm fine,' I lied. 'I'm just a little upset that things are so un-together.' Before I could say another word David walked over to me, put his hands on my shoulders, looked directly at me and asked, 'What's wrong, Tony?'

I completely lost it. I shuddered in his arms and sobbed until I could stop.

'My marriage is over, David.'

It was a strange choice of words. It was as if I had made my decision. I told him about how distant Mary and I were and how I didn't think it was going to work anymore. I told him how much I was afraid to lose my children. He listened in silence and told me to take another day off and decide whether I wanted to stay or go back home. He said he knew what I was going through (David's own problems had been well publicized). I looked at David Bowie in that moment and saw my old friend. I under-estimated how much he cared for me. He hadn't come to fire me; he was genuinely concerned about me.

I phoned Mary in the morning and told her how devastated I'd felt the night before. I had thought our situation over and offered her a solution:

'David gave me the choice to come home but maybe we should use this time apart to see if we really miss each other and want to stay together.' She agreed that I should stay in New York. That afternoon I went to the studio and worked for the next three to four weeks.

My mood changed dramatically. Much of this team had been together since *Low* and I could hear magic taking place as the band ran through some ideas with David. Larry Alexander and I started to shape the sound, the combined experience of a very solid-sounding American engineer and myself, British trained and full of sonically and musically diverse suggestions. I immersed myself in the music with David and the band whipping the 'head arrangements' together. Lo and behold David admitted to having one finished song, something he'd started when he was 16 years old. He had not played it to me in all the time I'd known him; it was to become 'It's No Game', the opener and closer of the album.

Soon great tracks were emerging. As before we were getting visitations from New York musicians; Jimmy Destry of Blondie and Tom Verlaine of Television each left a little bit of themselves in the overdubs. It really was starting to shape up as a kind of *Sgt. Pepper* with each track developing its own persona. Initially they were all wordless songs, with the exception of 'It's No Game'. For weeks one song had the working title of 'People Are Turning To Gold' until David wrote the lyric for 'Ashes To Ashes' over the backing track. Another we called 'Jamaica' was based on a jam that David and the band had had in Jamaica when they were on tour. For purposes of delineating choruses when the band was recording David would sing, 'Woo, oh, Ja-mai-ca', over the funky beat. Months later, at the eleventh hour David came up with, 'Ooh, oh, Fashion'. That track was going to be thrown away because David was frustrated with not being able to find a lyric.

The Power Station was a multi-storied studio complex. We shared the lounge with Bruce Springsteen and his E street band, as they were recording in the other studio on our floor. This was a nice reunion with Springsteen, having first met him five years earlier during the making of *Young Americans*. The shyness had gone; now he was a somebody. We would often find ourselves taking meal breaks together in the lounge. On one break Dennis Davis sat next to Bruce Springsteen whose food had arrived earlier than ours. Dennis, the hard-hitting drummer, appeared to be starving. Springsteen caught him longingly staring at his order of spare ribs and offered him some. Bowie was on the other side of Springsteen and heard Dennis ask him a question that had David stifling a laugh. He scribbled something on a piece of paper and passed it to me. 'Dennis just asked Springsteen what band he was in!' After five years with Bowie, Dennis still hardly knew who was who in Rock; he was ever the jazz funk master drummer from Harlem.

We had no real keyboard player at these sessions, which made it very convenient having the E Street Band next door. David desperately wanted a Wurlitzer stereo electric piano on the track that would develop into 'Ashes To Ashes' – he also needed someone to play it. We had a stereo Wurlitzer delivered and David popped into Springsteen's session and came back with their keyboardist Roy Bittan. David explained to him the concept of the now famous piano intro to the song and then the light chording he wanted for the verses. Unfortunately when we powered up the Wurlitzer we discovered only one side worked and even then not very well. We were impatient to use the talented Bitten and it was too late in the evening to order a replacement so I suggested that we use a normal piano and I would attempt to make it sound like a stereo Wurlitzer. Back in London I had recently acquired a new piece of gear called the Instant Flanger; luckily the Power Station had one too. I soon got a decent moving stereo image to emulate a Wurlitzer but I couldn't resist playing with it further and then got a ridiculous shaking sound – which everyone in the studio instantly loved. That's the piano sound in the intro and outro of 'Ashes To Ashes', a grand piano played by Roy Bitten going through an Instant Flanger in a way it was never meant to be used.

This is the sheer pleasure of working with David Bowie. He always let me do my thing and I always felt I couldn't let him down. I don't exactly know how we were introduced to Chuck Hammer, but he came to our sessions with the first guitar synthesizer we'd every seen or heard. He gave us a quick demonstration of how he would pick a note and out of his amplifier would come a symphonic string session. Naturally we had to have this instrument on our 'Sgt. Pepper', but I also had to do 'my thing' to it. Instead of putting a microphone on the amp, I had been told that there was great reverberation in the back staircase of the studio, a continuous four storeys. I asked Larry to put a microphone on the bottom landing and another on the top landing and we put Chuck's amp just outside the door of our second-floor control room. The sound was glorious. It's the warm string choir you hear on the part that goes 'I've never done good things. I've never done bad things . . .'

After two and a half weeks of backing tracks and about a week of overdubs, we had wonderful tracks but only 'It's No Game' as a finished song with a real title. David asked if I wouldn't mind waiting a couple of months to give him time to write lyrics. We made tentative plans to reconvene in June, in London. David was a man of his word. He actually wrote songs in the interim, real songs! When I heard him sing the lyrics to 'Ashes To Ashes' I got goose bumps. It was the character of Major Tom from 'Space Oddity' brought up to the present. Back on my own familiar turf we got up to tricks that were truly amazing.

*　　*　　*

I am always asked what it is like to produce David Bowie, espe-cially his vocals. Lots of fans assume that he suddenly appears in the studio in a puff of smoke, wearing a cape. They assume that he arrives with cleverly crafted lyrics, the band knows the music and we record an entire song in ten minutes flat. As most people know that is the furthest from the way records are made. We would often spend from seven weeks to four months making an album, and most of it is tedious work making maybe a hundred creative and technical decisions a day. Most of that is my job. David's job is to be a creative genius – a hard thing to do 24 hours a day. With him it's a lot of experimentation, a lot of stuff isn't used in the final cut. Every step of the way he asks my opinion, asks for suggestions and I would likewise offer both without solicitation; I'm a record producer and I'm responsible for everything that happens in the studio.

David Bowie is a great singer; there is no doubt about it. He sings from a deep internal well of experience and he's got a natural talent for expressing anything he feels when he sings. I can't say that for everyone I've worked with. But even David Bowie needs to be directed when he sings, albeit minimally, but he depends on feedback. However it's important to know that when you ask David to sing something again you'd better have a good reason why. He doesn't want to hear, '. . . just for the hell of it', or '. . . just to be safe, we'll do another take'. He wants to know that you've been really listening to him and he expects a reaction – sometimes I am the sole member of his audience in the studio. Having said that, there are many times I would just say via the talkback microphone, 'That was great, David, just great. Come on in and have a listen.'

Here is a breakdown of some of the work that went into the making of each song on *Scary Monsters*.

'It's No Game (Part One)' – What is that sound? I must've been asked what the sounds are at the beginning of this track and opening of the album a hundred times. I thought it would sound great if the album started with the sound of tape rolling. I mic'd my Lyrec 24-track tape deck in stereo and recorded the sound of me rewinding the tape briefly, then pressing the play button. It directly cuts in to Dennis Davis waving a soccer fan's ratchet over his head and his count-in. The 910 Harmonizer is back with a vengeance on this track, as is evident on the ratchet and the first snare drum beat. David had the lyric translated into Japanese by a professor friend in Tokyo but couldn't seem to make the syllables fit. We needed a native speaker to coach David, and my PA Diane Wagg found a Japanese actress who was playing a part in *The King and I* at the London Palladium (starring Yul Brynner). The ebullient young lady, Michi Hirota, quickly surmised that the translation was literal and not poetic. It had too many syllables to fit the melody. Therefore David could not sing it in Japanese but had the brilliant idea of getting Ms Hirota to recite the lyrics as a narrative over the music. She was somewhat taken aback by this idea, but soon got into it with coaxing and coaching from both David and me. She was quite a stunning looker as well, which turned this into a delightful afternoon's work. David's vocal following the narrative was delivered with blood-curdling passion. Immediately afterwards we sang the back-up vocals together, my voice is the higher one. Robert Fripp spent a day or two adding his amazing guitar to this song and several others, this time without the addition of Brian Eno's briefcase.

'Up The Hill Backwards' – I love the intro because it's in 7/4, a signature often associated with Greek music. We asked a casual friend, Lynn Maitland, to join David and I singing a group vocal for this song, another big departure for David since he doesn't sing solo on this. The ending is a glorious 'jam' back in the time signature of 7/4 with Fripp playing magnificently. I'm playing acoustic rhythm guitar in 7/4, something one can only aspire to really, as I'm clenching my teeth during the performance, consciously counting all the time: it didn't come naturally.

'Scary Monsters (and Super Freaks)' – I adore this track. The 'barking dog' in the intro, the solo and the ending come from a little flat plastic keyboard that was made by EMS, the same manufacturer as Brian Eno's SYNTHI briefcase keyboard. It was called The Wasp. I programmed a descending bass line and fed the snare drum into the trigger circuit of the keyboard. Sometimes the kick drum and tom-toms that bled into the snare drum track also triggered the sequence. George Murray played a conventional bass part back in New York, but we made it pulsate by putting it into a Kepex gate and we had Dennis Davis's steady eighth-note kick drum pattern trigger the bass. David sang all the backing vocals on this track.

'Ashes To Ashes' – This track is glorious. Roy Bittan played the piano as described earlier. In London we brought in Andy Clark, a session keyboardist introduced to me by Andy Duncan. He provided the symphonic sounds at the end of this track. I played percussion. The video, a surreal masterpiece, was directed by David Mallet and featured members of London's New Romantic movement, including Steve Strange.

'Fashion' – This track almost missed making the album. David couldn't get beyond the working title, 'Jamaica', for months. The day before he wrote the lyric he told me he'd probably drop the song. I implored him to write a lyric because this was probably the most modern and commercial-sounding track on the album. He returned to the studio early the next day announcing, 'I've got it!' This was the last vocal we recorded for the album and mixing commenced that evening. The 'whoop' intro sound is Andy Clark's sequencer's oddly chosen sound for a 'click', to follow when one programmes a part. It ended up as a kind of Reggae upstroke for most of the song. For the first time Dennis Davis played to a drum machine pattern. The original plan was to leave the machine out of the mix, playing Dennis's drums only, but he was so tight with it we left it in for parts of the song. I treated it with digital effects to make it more techno. Again, David is the only backing singer on this song: May Pang appeared in the video. She's one of the people who says 'Beep-beep' in a close up. This was made during a period when she and David were dating.

'Teenage Wildlife' – This is a peculiar anthem-type song. It took me a long time to warm to this track, but I adore it years later. There's a little bit of 'Heroes' in this, along with a Ronettes-type vocal backing supplied by myself, my assistant engineer Chris Porter and Lynn Maitland. David directed us from the control room and the parts were made up on 'the fly'. Chuck Hammer's synthesizer guitar is back in this one but it is not as obvious as it was on 'Ashes To Ashes'.

'Scream Like A Baby' – This evolved from a song originally written for the Astronettes, 'I Am A Laser'. I was involved as an arranger back then, so I knew the song quite well. At the Power Station this was recorded as 'I Am A Laser' but David had rewritten the lyrics in the interim. We got up to some cool percussion tricks on this one using digital effects. I love the chord changes of this song, David's forte. In the song's bridge (at 2:39) David speaks the same words in the left and right speakers. But on one overdub I constantly slowed down the track whilst he was speaking. On the other track I constantly sped up the track as he spoke. The result is very mind twisting. David was no stranger to changing tape speeds, as he had to do that whilst recording 'Fame' to get the extreme high and low vocals.

'Kingdom Come' – This is the album's cover song. Tom Verlaine, who came to the overdub sessions in New York, wrote it. We asked Verlaine if he would like to overdub some guitar and he agreed. He asked if it would be okay to rent some guitar amps.

It looked as though Verlaine was a little down on his luck and lugubrious in those days – and maybe he didn't own a guitar amp. The next day David and I were met with the sight of Tom Verlaine auditioning every guitar amp in New York City. No exaggeration – there were about 30 guitar amps in the studio. He would play the same phrase in one, unplug his guitar and move to the next amp. We talked to him about the part and he said he had some ideas, but he was searching for a good sound. Hours drifted, we had lunch, watched some afternoon television and left Verlaine still auditioning amps at 7 p.m. I don't think we ever used a note of his playing, if we even recorded him. We never saw him after that day. Again the backing vocals pulled the track into some kind of psycho-Ronettes area.

'Because You're Young' – 'Townshend is coming to the studio today,' announced David apprehensively. I had read how much Pete Townshend had been drinking and he was still busting up hotel rooms so I was apprehensive too. When he arrived he seemed to be in a foul, laconic mood. David asked if there was anything we could get for him and he asked for a bottle of wine. I asked if he wanted red or white and he snarled back, 'There's no such thing as white wine!' Whoops. I was hoping he wouldn't hurl the empty bottle through my studio window. He sort of settled in and asked what we wanted him to do on this track. David looked at me kind of puzzled and asked, 'Chords?' Townshend asked, 'What kind of chords?' I think both David and I were a little afraid to state the obvious, but I finally offered, 'Er, Pete Townshend chords.' Townshend shrugged, 'Oh, windmills', and did a perfect windmill on his guitar, traditionally grazing his right-hand knuckles. Within 30 minutes the chords were laid on the track, the bottle of red wine was drained and Townshend exited onto Dean Street.

'It's No Game (Part Two)' – I don't know how intentional it was at this point, but like *Sgt. Pepper* we reprised the opening song at the end of the album. This was actually the same exact backing track and a great example of how mixing and different overdubs can change the nature of a track completely. The opener version was a fiery affair, but as a closer it was now gentle and let the listener down easy. This version was completely in English, as it was originally conceived. As the album opened with a recording of my 24-track machine starting up, the album closes with the sound of the tape running out and the reel slowing down to a complete stop.

There are obvious sudden sonic changes in the mixes of this album. This was deliberate and achieved long before the days of automated consoles and computer editing. The way we did it was to make sure we had a superb main mix that we were happy with. Then we'd go back to specific sections, sometimes something as short as a two-second tom-tom fill, rearrange the faders, add special effects and equalization changes. Then I would edit all the smaller, special pieces back into the main mix with razor blade cuts and splicing tape. There is a limit to how many times an edit can be undone, about two to three times, then the backing comes off the tape, so I had to be very careful. I would sit at the stereo tape machine with a strong light on the tape heads, a grease pencil behind my ear and a microphone boom adjusted like a letter T and have the various pieces to be edited in hanging from a wire, like fish drying in the sun. I would often send everyone out of the control room so I could concentrate. A song like 'Scary Monsters' would have as much as ten edited sections.

Before beginning work on *Scary Monsters* I met a charming man named Zaine Griff and we began working together. I'd been approached by Ziggy clones before but he looked absolutely amazing and acceptable and I would not have worked with someone who slavishly copied a musical style, but Zaine's music was different and very good. He was a New Zealander, but he was no provincial country boy, quite the opposite – he was very sophisticated and urbane. He was a sharp dresser – tall and androgynously handsome. Zaine had studied mime with David's teacher, Lindsay Kemp; one of his contemporaries was the then unknown Kate Bush. Zaine was an accomplished bass player and a great songwriter; it was the vocals that were always a struggle for him. For his album we used friends of Zaine's, including a very clever programmer/ keyboard player named Hans Zimmer (who has since become one of the most important film score composers in Hollywood; it's amazing that I worked so closely with him and also with another film score icon, Michael Kamen, with David Bowie years before).

During the making of Zaine's album I was asked by Bowie to put together a band to record some songs for an appearance on the *Kenny Everett* TV show. As I was working with Zaine at the time I decided to use him on bass to play along with my friend Andy Duncan on drums. I should have predicted that Zaine would dress to the nines for the studio recording, while Bowie was just having an ordinary day in his civvies. His initial reaction to Zaine was not favourable and he looked upon my use of Zaine as some kind of an insensitive joke. I must admit I found it humorous. It wasn't my fault Bowie had started a trend and there were countless young men and women walking around London as Ziggy clones. One of the songs was a very sparse version of 'Space Oddity' and another, an electronic re-recording of 'Panic In Detroit'; my voice is the talking computer on this recording. Both recordings have been available as bonus tracks on Bowie reissues.

Things with Mary at home, though, reached rock bottom.

Midway through 1980, following a particularly bad row, our marriage ended. We'd been discussing separation for some months now but this was something else. It was on Saturday, 7 June and it was so bad that Mary took the children to a friend's house in the middle of the night. I had fallen asleep earlier after a bout of heavy drinking; I'd also taken some sleeping pills. She didn't leave a note and Gloria didn't know where she'd gone. Two days later I received a letter from Mary's lawyer demanding that I leave the 'matrimonial home'. I didn't know how to get out of this downward spiral, I felt that our marriage was beyond saving and I was largely to blame. By Monday evening the entire village knew what had happened; I felt nothing but shame and disgrace. Through Mary's lawyer I asked to see Jessica on her fourth birthday, which was a week later, and Mary agreed. I had been staying elsewhere and returned to the house on the Saturday to find Mary had a neighbour present for the meeting. I was warned not to molest her or the children; this shocked me, as I did not remotely begin to see myself as a molester of either women or children. It's so often the atmosphere that divorces start out in and from then on it's difficult to keep a sense of perspective on it all. I spent an hour or so with Jessica and left before her party began. The following day I packed a small bag and took a trip to Ibiza; I needed to get away.

When I returned from Spain my personal assistant, Diane Wagg, had found a house for me to rent in Sumner Place Mews SW7. The converted coach house was a kind of safe haven in a busy area of London; it was small but it was on two floors. The ground floor had only a bedroom and a bathroom. The top floor had a large sitting room with a kitchenette off to the side. It was reasonably furnished with a comfortable bed, couch, coffee table, dining-room table and writing desk. I spent my time there confused, disoriented and drinking heavily. Sometimes I had the kids for the weekends. Mary and I, both shy people by nature, never spoke about reconciliation, in fact we rarely spoke at all. I made sure they had enough money to live comfortably.

I followed up my earlier endeavours in the year by starting to work with Hazel O'Connor; *Breaking Glass* was both an album and a movie. My involvement started from an invitation by Davina Belling, the movie's producer, to meet Brian Gibson, the director they'd hired to make a movie of *Rock Follies*, a TV series about three girl singers who create a band. When I met Brian they'd found one girl to star in the movie and I met her at Davina's home in Notting Hill Gate. At the start of the evening Hazel O'Connor was quiet and I was aware that Gibson was carefully watching how she and I interacted when we were speaking. He told me that after Hazel had passed the audition he became more interested in her personal story than in the *Rock Follies* idea, and so they had decided to tailor the script for just her. Hazel was the genuine article, a true member of the Punk generation; she was also writing her own songs for the film, which I thought was a courageous thing for them to do. I listened to the first song with great trepidation; it was 'Calls The Tune', a kind of Bacharach-type waltz – very unusual for a punk. But I liked it and even before it was finished I began to think about what I would do with it.

Gibson quoted me verbatim in the relative art-follows-life scene in the film, when the producer says, 'I like it, it's off-the-wall. I hear strings.' Gibson needed a model for the film's record producer character played by Jon Finch (as Bob Wood) and he looked no further than me. I was slightly taken aback to see that the 'Wood' character dressed like me, had a haircut like me and said what I said – albeit with an English accent. When Brian Gibson had asked Hazel who she wanted to produce her music she said, 'There's only one producer – Tony Visconti.' In the film, when 'Kate' is asked who she wants to produce her music she responds, 'There's only one producer – Bob Wood.' Jon Finch was sent to a couple of our sessions to observe me although I didn't know it at the time. Gibson wanted him to learn as many of my mannerisms as he could. He even made the Bob Wood character a martial arts expert (not that I am or was – just keen) and I was asked to help write the scene when Kate's manager, played by Phil Daniels, threatens Wood with a bottle.

When I found out that I was going to be portrayed in the film I said to Gibson, 'Why can't I play the role?'

'Tony, people have great difficulty playing themselves,' he replied.

Instead, I got a small part in the film as a keyboard player in Kate's band during the performance of 'Eighth Day'. Even though I was positioned on a high tier way in the back of the stage Gibson reprimanded me for overacting.

On one occasion I was asked to meet Gibson for a script discussion over lunch at the BBC Television Centre. When I arrived at the table there was a woman already sitting with Gibson. 'I hope you don't mind Helen Mirren joining us.' I was a big fan of hers and my first British girlfriend, Sheila Cane, was always being taken for her, as there was more than a passing resemblance; it felt a bit freaky.

This was an exciting project to work on between the Power Station recordings and the completion of Bowie's *Scary Monsters*. It was very challenging. Not only was Hazel rewriting the script, rehearsing and shooting scenes with the actors during the day, her assignment was sometimes to come back in the morning with a new song to fit a scene. Hazel complied with Gibson's every suggestion. A very punky song was needed for the opening of the film. I was on standby in the studio with session musicians waiting for Hazel to show up; when she did we immediately learned and recorded 'Writing On The Wall'. We finished the song by mid afternoon and rushed a mix of it to Brian Gibson so they could shoot the scene that day. Sometimes I'd meet Hazel at her small flat and work out the arrangements with her as she was writing a song. Next morning I would teach it to the band, giving her a break to have a lie in.

This was a truly challenging album because it had to be a musical chronicle of the early Punk days of Hazel's character (Kate) to her zenith as a female Ziggy Stardust-type. I had to achieve this with the same session musicians, trusted friends who were versatile and able to work under these testing conditions. Hazel was a joy to work with; in real life she was very similar to the character she was portraying. 'Breaking Glass' is also the title of a David Bowie song from *Low*. During the overdubs and mixing of *Scary Monsters* I told David about the film and the female Ziggy that Hazel becomes at the end. Coincidentally he needed a haircut and I commented that Hazel had been cutting my hair since the filming began. He asked to meet Hazel and I made sure that she brought her pair of scissors that night. Hazel couldn't believe it was happening to her, but she did a very professional job on David's locks and invited him to a shoot for the film. David showed up for the shooting of the song 'Give Me An Inch' and Hazel suddenly became aware of him in the middle of filming a scene as he was watching her from the side of the stage.

Thin Lizzy very definitely started another trend for me. Whereas artists talk of their blue period, or whatever, I had my Irish period. It was one that went on sporadically for a number of years. People who have some knowledge of my career would probably say The Boomtown Rats were the second Irish band I worked with, but that honour goes to The Radiators. Making their album *Ghostown* turned out to be a very enjoyable experience; despite having been introduced to me by Thin Lizzy they were a lot less troublesome to work with. I met them while

I was mixing *Black Rose* and as soon as I heard some of Phil Chevron's Brecht-like writing I was interested in working with them. The group gave me free rein over the arrangements and we came up with what I think was a truly great album, but maybe too clever for it's own good. It had great Punk sensibilities but it seemed to fall between the cracks of the current genres at the time.

The Boomtown Rats also paid a visit during the mixing of *Black Rose*; I ended up working with them in slightly more unusual circumstances. After Mary and I broke up I took a spontaneous trip to Ibiza by invitation of an employee friend in my studio, Louise de Ville Morel. She knew I needed to get away and told me to go to Ibiza to be met by her friends Peter and Kirsten, who were staying in another friend's *finca,* a small farm in the middle of the island. The couple were very kind to me when I arrived a few days ahead of Louise. Ibiza made me feel alive again, which is very easy under the warm Mediterranean sun. When Louise arrived we travelled around as two couples, although Louise and I never had a romantic inclination towards each other. One day Kirsten announced that we were going to the beach. When we got there I immediately knew I was heading into uncharted territory; no one had any clothes on. My three friends knew about it, but I wasn't in on the secret. The other three were out of their brief clothes in seconds and as my trunks dropped to my ankles I thought, this is it; I'm officially a nudist! I had never seen my housemates in the nude, but I soon got over it. It was delightful to swim in the nude; we spent hours there and much of it in the water. I never expected such severe sunburn, which was mainly on my behind as it had been sticking out of the water for most of the time. Even my penis was a little sunburned.

One of the highlights of that trip was discovering a wonderful state-of-the-art recording studio smack in the middle of the island; an eccentric German named Fritz owned it, a tall blond handsome man in his thirties. He was so proud of his gem; it was not only a great studio but he also provided room and board for up to a dozen people. There was plenty of room for indoor recreation and the crowning glory, besides the studio, was the large swimming pool. I spent a day there with Kirsten and company sunbathing in the nude, only to be interrupted by Fritz giving a guided tour to a top New York record company executive, Dick Wingate. Even though I was used to being nude on Ibiza I was a little embarrassed to meet someone in the record industry – under-dressed as I was.

While I was in Ibiza Bob Geldof had enquired whether I'd like to produce the next Boomtown Rats album. I liked the band and 'I Don't Like Mondays' was one of my favourite singles and so when I got back and Bob called me I told him that I would love to produce them. I recommended Ibiza Sound very highly. Bob had already spent a year in Spain, as an English teacher (can you imagine all the Spaniards he taught speaking with his pronounced Dublin accent?) and knew that Ibiza would be a glorious and exotic place to make the record. The studio was booked immediately and we made our way to Ibiza; the band took a plane and I started out three days earlier on my Suzuki 350cc motorcycle.

One thing that was kept from me when I first visited the studio was that there was no electrical power or telephone lines to that part of the island. Fritz powered the studio with a 1200 horsepower diesel generator, with a 600 hp backup generator. They were located behind one of the outbuildings and running inconspicuously while I was at the studio. Now, it had to run constantly to power the recording studio and, more importantly, the huge central air conditioning; it would've reached the temperature of an oven without it. We felt a little guilty at night after work. If we wanted to watch some British videotapes, the only means of entertainment, the 1200 hp would have to be kept running. On two occasions we went to a nightclub, but the band was on a tight budget and considered this sheer luxury. Most of the time we had no other choice but to make a record. One of the best things about Ibiza Sound was dinnertime, as Fritz hired a chef who had cooked for the royal family of Monaco. We had gourmet cuisine every night and it was usually prepared from locally grown products and fresh fish from the sea. Once a week they would get out the enormous paella pan, about five feet in diameter, and make the best paella I've ever eaten.

The sessions went really well and the entire band was really happy to be there, although there are difficulties in producing a band of six. Simon Crowe, the drummer, was the easiest to work with; he knew the songs thoroughly as he could also play other instruments. He also proved to be an excellent backing singer and would also step in when the other musicians were proving to be difficult to work with – he seemed to know what would make my job easier. Johnnie Fingers was also easy to work with but I could never get really close to him. He didn't say much and he had an eccentric habit of never getting out of his pyjamas; he wore them 24-hours a day and even performed on stage in them. My biggest challenge was working with the guitarists, Gerry Cott and Gerry Roberts; it certainly seemed like the age of the amazing guitar heroes was over. A lot of time was spent coaxing great performances and sounds from them. Peter Briquette, the bass player, warned me up front that he took a long time overdubbing his parts, so at least working with him didn't come as a surprise; it did take a long time. Geldof was the most undisciplined artist. Without doubt he is a born leader, he's very intelligent and writes great songs. It's just that singing isn't his forte. I developed a prison mentality during this album, despite there being that beautiful pool right outside the studio. I was stuck inside the studio. The rest of the band would lounge at the pool or nap as I was working with others, one at a time.

The studio had, in common with most studios built in the 1970s, 'dead' acoustics. It also had one unique feature. A wealthy dog, cat and parrot-loving woman had formerly owned the property. To stop the dogs from making a mess within the grounds, she had a tunnel dug under the main road, this was fortified and paved to allow her dogs, which she'd specially trained, to run through the tunnel to reach the adjoining field to do their 'business'. We put Simon Crowe in the disused tunnel for a snare drum overdub. We had a microphone on each end of the tunnel; it's the one of the best reverbs I've ever heard. The tunnel was also used for some guitar and vocal effects.

When we had finished all the basic recording it was back to London to work at Good Earth studios. We added some over-dubs and mixed the album, which went well apart from the fact that Geldof would always return the next day to say that he wanted more top, more treble frequencies added on all the instruments. His yardstick was to compare a cassette copy he'd taken home with him to commercially released records, which always sound brighter than a pre-mastered studio mix. He wouldn't give me the benefit of the doubt when I said a master-ing engineer could and should make the mixes very, very bright. When we brought the album to a mastering engineer we could never get it bright enough to please Bob; to me the mastered vinyl sounded too brittle and tinny. Simon Crowe, ever the diplomat, said, 'Bob even listens to his record collection at home with the treble full on to 10. I can't bear to listen to music at his house.'

My professional life was business as usual, with work taking up a lot of the time, the only difference being I wasn't living with

Mary and the kids. At my new bachelor digs in South Kensington I was drinking most of the time, so much so that I don't have much of a memory of the first six months living without Mary. I spent New Year's Eve in a drunken state with Gordon Fordyce, the chief engineer at the studio. I'm sure he was there out of sympathy and perhaps to stop me trying to do something stupid. I was devastated. I felt sorry for myself. I wondered how it came to be that I was not with my wife and children on New Year's Eve. I felt like a ghost.

In the early part of 1981 Gordon Fordyce was the only friend who hung out with me at my flat. We would drink, play records and go to the local pub. I had very little contact with the opposite sex, but one night I successfully chatted up a stripper I'd met in my local; I regretted it almost immediately. I even contacted someone through the personal ads in *Time Out* magazine, but couldn't go through with the actual meeting – it felt too desperate. I would be sober for the regular weekend visits of the children, which would often be fun, although Jessica was only four years old and often cried that she wanted to go home. Mary and I never talked much, and especially not about reuniting or divorcing; our separation remained static.

One night Gordon phoned his ex-girlfriend Tiffany from my house; he asked her over and she arrived with a girlfriend, Lynn. For me, female company was a much-needed diversion from these two-man bachelor parties. It proved to be better than I expected, as Lynn was great looking, as well as being very funny and feisty. The girls arrived in an advanced state of inebriation and somehow Lynn and I migrated to the bedroom. When we woke up in the afternoon Gordon and Tiffany were gone. Lynn stayed for the day and we found that we also enjoyed each other's company sober; she was 18 and I was 36.

Shortly after we began seeing each other regularly I went down with a terrible dose of flu; Lynn came to the flat and fed me chicken soup, orange juice and doses of LemSip at regular intervals. I fell in love with her during my illness and it was reciprocated. Shortly after that she moved in, and while we partied together we were sober most of the time. We did the usual couple things, going to films, watching videos, long drives, long walks and laughing – all the kind of things stated in a *Time Out* personal ad. My kids liked Lynn and she was very accommodating when they stayed over. This was so important to me as I needed their presence and my home life needed stability.

Nine months after I split with Mary I had finally stopped beating myself up and trying to drown my sorrows. If I couldn't make it through by sheer willpower, I now had the support of a good woman and the responsibilities of raising children from a distance and supporting them; and of managing the recording careers of those I worked for. The external realities were stronger than my internal demons – for the time being.

chapter 11
modern life

One night in June 1981 Lynn and I spent the evening drinking, and I continued long after she'd gone to bed. In my maudlin state I thought about how I'd lost my children and Mary; I even told myself I didn't enjoy producing records any more. It was strange, because I'd been in a fairly positive space since I'd been living with Lynn; in fact I was quite happy. Somehow in my depressing drunken stupor I became desperately morose; I even lost consciousness. How long I'd been in that state I've no idea, but the next thing I knew was lying in Lynn's arms.

'I heard you moaning and gurgling; it woke me up. Tony you look dreadful.'

Later she told me I was worse than that – I had looked deathly ill. I'll never forget the date; it was 14 June, two days before Jessica's fifth birthday. Lynn put me to bed, where I stayed for most of the following day. The day after Mary delivered the kids to me, and later, as I sat in McDonald's on the corner of Dean Street, I saw in Jessica's eyes every reason I needed to pull myself out of the downward spiral in which I'd found myself. Although it wasn't a cataclysmic moment when everything suddenly changed, the incident did have a profound effect on me.

I did go back to drinking and using a little charlie, only less frequently and in moderation; Lynn made sure I never overdid it. Confidence in myself was still an issue; I was slowly regaining the faith I needed in myself to be a producer. The fact was, I had been turning down work in the year since Mary and I had split up. I felt able to work with Hazel O'Connor again, because we had a previously good relationship, and she was easy to work with.

After *Breaking Glass* was a big success for Hazel she had become more in control of her life. She had relinquished all her rights in *Breaking Glass* to the film's producers and so when it came time for a follow-up she got herself a proper record deal with an advance and a royalty. She had more confidence for this record; sometimes this bordered on arrogance. She had had a stormy real life affair with Jon Finch, the actor who played her producer in the film, and many times I comforted Hazel during phone conversations; she'd cry and pour her heart out to me. Hazel's brother Neil was a really good guitarist and she brought him in to join the new band. Despite the album being an excellent follow up to *Breaking Glass* I think the press and public perceived Hazel to be a one-hit wonder, due mainly to her being the star of a movie. *Cover Plus* made a very poor showing in the charts.

The idea of working with new artists was still difficult for me to contemplate and yet I needed to get back into the studio. I got a call offering me the job of mixing the Stranglers album; I thought it would be the perfect way to ease my way back into work.

It was anything but. The Stranglers were a dark band and the mixing proved to be no walk in the park. From the first day I was tested. Bass player J.J. Burnell came across as very arrogant, bragging about the fact that he had been kicked out of the Shotokan Karate Centre in Japan for bullying. After I showed him my little kung fu workout room in the studio he kicked the Wing Chun wooden dummy repeatedly with his Doc Martens until it was barely hanging off the wall. I was upset by that and sidelined him for quite a while; ironically we somehow grew to be the closest of all the group members. I loved the sound of Hugh Cornwell's voice; I found him charismatic, but very distant. Dave Greenfield, a nervous smiler who sweated a lot, carried a huge black leather holdall, which he kept beside him at all times, even when he went to the men's room. When I asked what he kept inside it he nervously replied, 'Oh, books.' Jet Black was equally unfathomable; although he was a great drummer to work with, I never saw him smile once and I could never get a conversation going with him. God only knows what he did in his spare time. They were very proficient musicians, however some overdubs were needed before I mixed the album. They were strongly opinionated but I managed to make everyone happy. The album produced their first No 1 – 'Golden Brown', a love song. I don't usually ask about the meaning of lyrics, but I was so struck by this track that I did; Hugh told me it was about Chinese heroin, so I said to myself a very slow, 'Ooooooo-kay.'

While it was a jump in at the deep end for a fragile me, it toughened me up enough to get back into the studio again. The following year I had a call from Hugh Cornwell, which was quickly followed by a ticket to Brussels where the group was finishing the album that became *Feline*. I was a little surprised and gratified that they wanted to work with me again. They might have been a solemn group, but surprisingly these sessions were quite enjoyable. Our days would start with Hugh and me getting up before noon and going for a run through the streets of Brussels.

After working with the Stranglers in 1981 I decided to take a motorcycling vacation through France and Spain with the intention of ending up in Ibiza; I had an open invitation from Fritz, the owner of Ibiza Sound, to stay anytime. I didn't bother to phone ahead because they rarely answered their phone calls; they relied on an answering machine at their small office in Ibiza town. With Lynn behind me on my Suzuki we arrived in Ibiza six days after leaving London; we had taken the Hovercraft from Dover to Calais, and then the French national route 20 all the way to the foothills of the Pyrenees. We never booked a hotel ahead of time but always found a delightful place to stay every night. The weather was great and we enjoyed ourselves, although Lynn complained of boredom riding pillion; sometimes she would nod off while I was driving at 70 mph. We took an overnight ferry from Barcelona to Ibiza.

When we arrived at Ibiza Sound I was shocked to find the Boomtown Rats recording an album with Kevin Godley and Lol Crème as producers. They were equally surprised to see Lynn and me. Fritz wouldn't allow us to go to a hotel and insisted that we stayed at the studio complex. From time to time we were invited into the studio to listen to the work in progress; Geldof, took me aside, 'It's fuckin' weird having you here with Kevin and Lol producing.'

'I agree. I think it's best if we left.'

'No, Tony, it's okay. I just needed to tell you, that's all. The trouble is, I'm not enjoying working with Kevin and Lol. They can't work on more than one fuckin' song at a time. I don't like having to start a track and then only leave it when it's finished four days later; it's not how I work best.'

I could do little but commiserate.

After about a week Lynn and I decided to leave, after all you can only have so many visits to a nude beach, nightclubs, restaurants and shopping trips. We rode slowly back to London but on the way stopped in the middle of France to see a London friend of Lynn's called Nikki, who was staying at a beautiful house with a pool. Nikki had a French friend staying with her but it soon became apparent that dropping in out of the blue was not to their liking – the open invitation was now closed.

No sooner had we got back to London than I got a call from Bob Geldof.

'Tony, we've fuckin' had enough of Kevin and Lol; seeing you again reminded us of how much we had enjoyed working with you.'

They brought the unfinished masters back to London where we proceeded to finish the overdubs and mix the album at Good Earth. The only issue was once again the amount of high end Bob wanted, but I think we were all happy with the outcome.

Having been practising different martial arts since I was 17 I studied the readily accessible Taekwando and Karate, but Bruce Lee films in the 1970s led me to seek out Chinese martial arts. Until then, Bruce Lee's films Chinese martial arts were hidden behind the 'Bamboo Curtain'. I managed to find Chinese teachers in London where I studied two styles, the little known Fung Sau and Wing Chun. I became increasingly fascinated by the stories I'd read about Tai Chi Chuan, which was described as an 'internal' martial art. As I was getting older and in need of staying fit, I wanted to study this low impact, mysterious martial art. Lynn and I found an advert for the British Tai Chi Chuan Association (BTTCA) in *Time Out* and began lessons with Grand Master John Kells in September 1981. I took to it immediately, and although Lynn lasted the initial 10 weeks she opted out to devote more time to gaining her degree in theatre at Mountview College in North London. The inner peace I gained during Tai Chi practice diminished my desire to get high as a solution to depression. I felt great naturally.

In late 1981 I received an invitation to go to my high school's twentieth reunion; having decided it would be fun I flew to

New York and stayed with my parents in Brooklyn. There were lots of my old classmates there, most of whom looked really healthy. It was fun to trade stories and meet their spouses, although I was there on my own. I was most surprised to see David Geffen who was by then a big music biz mogul; I couldn't help thinking that it was not up to his Hollywood social standards. Nevertheless we had a lovely chat and as we were leaving he offered me a lift in his limo back to Manhattan – I declined as I was staying a mere ten streets away with Mum and Dad.

'Here's my number Tony. Give me a call tomorrow, I have an artist I'd be interested in you working with.'

Two days later, having called David, I found myself sitting in a restaurant near the UN building talking to Geffen's head of A&R, John Kolodner. He was already a legend in the business as an A&R man who (almost) always picked the megastars.

'I only eat in this restaurant and only sit in this booth when I'm in New York,' said John.

'Why's that?' I asked.

'There's twelve feet of concrete in the wall between us and the street for the security of the diplomats that dine here, in case of an assassination attempt.'

'Oh, right,' said I thinking, Why do you need that kind of protection? He also discussed how much he loved women, lots of women, implying that he was a connoisseur of fine dames. This seemed odd for a small, slight man who wore his beard chest-length and shaggy. We finally got around to talking about me producing John Hiatt for Geffen Records. I hadn't heard about Hiatt but Kolodner filled me in on what a respected writer he was. Later I was sent some of Hiatt's recordings and I was very impressed with his voice and writing.

I returned to the Power Station in New York in early 1982 and spent a few weeks working with Haitt's band. I was fed up with working abroad so much, so I persuaded them into finishing the album at Good Earth. Chris Porter, my studio manger, had been installing a new monitoring system while I was in New York. On the phone from London Chris assured me things were going well, but when I arrived back at Good Earth to start the mixes I found the wall where the monitors were supposed to be installed just timber framework with the speaker cabinets still in boxes.

'I'm sorry Tony, there have been unforeseen delays, but I promise you the speakers will be installed and ready tomorrow.' When we returned the next day the speakers still weren't quite installed.

'Sorry Tony, I've been up all night fixing things up.'

'You look like it,' was all I could say.

In truth I was livid because I told Hiatt what a great studio I had and he hadn't stopped frowning since we arrived the day before. Although the new speaker system was technically superior to what we had before, we jumped straight into mixing without making critical tests. I owe the mediocre sound of this superb album to the monitor drama. Hiatt was a very serious and sombre man who rarely smiled even when things went well. Although he's never said it to me I know that I let him down.

With my year of rehabilitation nearing an end I had a call from Bowie asking me to go to Berlin once again; it would turn out to be the last time. David had acted in *Baal*, a BBC TV special of a musical by Bertolt Brecht in which he sang five songs to the accompaniment of a banjo. He was so taken by the songs that he decided to re-record them in Berlin with full arrangements for a pit band; the type of German musical theatre band that Brecht wrote them for originally. It had one of everything rather than sections of instruments – one violin, one cello, one trumpet, one trombone, etc. – about fifteen musicians in all.

Above Phil Collins had just left Genesis and was out of work so he played drums as a session player for Rod Argent's group, Argent, as their drummer was ill and couldn't play on the album. This was taken in my home studio in Shepherds Bush, London, 1975.

Above Russell and Ron Mael of Sparks. Taken at Air Studios, London, during the recording of 'Get In The Swing' for the album titled *Indiscreet*. London, 1975.

Right David Bowie in Sigma Sound Studios, Philadelphia, during the making of *Young Americans*.

Left Iggy Pop swimming in the buff during the recording of *Low*, Château D'Hérouville, France, 1976.

Below David Bowie composing the lyrics for *Heroes* in Hansa Studios (by the wall), Berlin, Germany, 1977.

Above David Bowie and Jimmy Destri (keyboardist for Blondie), during the making of the *Scary Monsters* album, Power Station, New York, 1979.

Above Brian Eno playing a 'treated' piano for the album *The Lodger* in Mountain Studios, Montreux, Switzerland, 1979.

Left With Phil Lynott at my Good Earth Studios party, 1979.

Right Phil Lynott and Siouxie Sioux, having a jocular moment in the hallway at Good Earth Studios.

Below Brian Robertson and Phil Lynott during the making *of Bad Reputation* at Toronto Sound, Canada, 1977.

Above Paula Yates and Bob Geldof at the same party.

Left Bob Geldof during the making of *Mondo Bongo* in Ibiza Sound, Ibiza, 1980.

Above Paul McCartney during the making of 'Only Love Remains' on the *Press To Play* album. This was taken in his personal studio on the Sussex coast, 1986.

Left Edge and Bono of U2 during the making of *A Sort Of Homecoming* at Good Earth Studios.

Right Elaine Paige and me on my motorcycle, riding to a recording session in London, 1984.

Left Adam Ant examining artwork for his new single 'Apollo 9' during the making of *Viva Le Rock* in Good Earth Studios, London, 1984.

Below With May Pang on our wedding day, New York City, 1989. Justin Hayward, from the Moody Blues, was best man.

Above Me with Rolan Bolan, son of Marc Bolan and Gloria Jones; during an interview for the *Born To Boogie* T.Rex DVD. London, 2005.

Left Master Ren Guang-Yi (Chen Style Taiji), Lou Reed & me during a *Tai Chi and Kung Fu* magazine photo shoot. New York City, 2005.

Above With Morrissey during the making of the album *Ringleader Of The Tormentors*, in Rome, Italy, 2005.

I arrived in a bitterly cold Berlin in early January. After a night out with David and Dominic Muldownney, a film composer who had arranged the five songs, we started about midday the following day. David was supposed to sing live with the orchestra but he arrived late. We had to start the recording without him because this wasn't rock and roll – this was a 'legitimate' session with union musicians. David was pleased to sit out the live vocals and listen to the complex arrangements being laid down; it gave him a chance to mentally rehearse. After the band had left, David sang all five vocals in a couple of hours without a hitch. The music was so strange and different it gave me goose bumps during the vocal session. The next day I mixed all five songs. It's a pity these recordings weren't made before the BBC TV production. David himself financed the project and wanted to record them in this fashion for posterity.

Later in the year David made a video of 'The Drowned Girl' and added 'Wild Is The Wind' from his *Station To Station* album for the shoot. David Mallet directed it at Good Earth studios and I was asked to act the part of an upright bass player in the video. Mel Gaynor from Simple Minds mimed as the drummer and Andy Hamilton, a friend of mine, was the sax player; in her only video appearance, Coco Schwab mimed as the guitarist. Mel, Andy and I dressed in Ivy League '60s suits with narrow lapels and narrow ties; it turned out to be the only Bowie video I've ever been in.

With my life steadily getting back on track I bought a house in White Hall Park Road in Chiswick; a lovely three-storey terraced house in a cul-de-sac with a small garden that my kids could play in. I had the loft converted into a home studio, but unfortunately the next-door neighbour on one side hated my musical efforts. Summer weekends were glorious with long walks along the Thames and sometimes to nearby Kew, across the bridge. Our neighbours on the other side were very cool;

Rod was a handsome advertising executive waiting for his divorce and Jacqui was a statuesque model who sunbathed topless with her model friends in their adjoining back garden. We were often over at each other's houses, dining and drinking together. My loft home studio was a source of creativity for my kids and they shared a bedroom. They would spend hours playing with the keyboard and drum machine and we would sometimes write and record songs together. Morgan got an original Sinclair computer – one of the first – for his birthday and spent many hours writing programs. It was the start of a passion for computers for Morgan, who today is a respected and well-known jingle writer, as well as my personal computer hotline source.

After the disappointment of the Haitt album I was hoping for something better when it came time to work with the delightfully named Hayzee Fantayzee; with hindsight was it me or was it just a slack year? I was called by Paul Caplin, an alumni of Animal Magnet, to produce his new band. When I met Kate Garner and Jeremiah Healy, who jointly fronted the band, I was convinced by their appearance alone that this was the most exciting thing I'd seen in a couple of years. Kate and Jeremiah were ragamuffin Glam rockers; she a model and he was a slim, strikingly good-looking club DJ. Maybe it was the fact that they were a decade younger than me and I thought my association with Hayzee Fantayzee would remedy my old geezer rock 'n' roll image.

As the Linn Drum was now all the rage, we too dispensed with using a live drummer and deferred to this marvellous and very expensive beat box that played back real samples of drums instead of synthesized drums. The songs were very whimsical and although Kate and Jeremiah couldn't sing very well, they could 'Rap'. I was very much a musical part of these productions as the guitarist and bassist. Paul Caplin programmed the Linn Drum, the sparse keyboards and the sound effects. 'John

Wayne Is Big Leggy', a covertly insulting tribute to what he represented in cowboy films, made it to No 11 in the singles charts
and gave them several appearances on *Top Of The Pops*. When
all is said and done they were little more than a novelty act,
without much substance. Their album's title, *Battle Hymns For
Children Singing*, was the best thing about it.

I was used to David Bowie using other producers. The first time
it happened was when I recommended Gus Dudgeon to
produce *Space Oddity*. The second time was after *The Man
Who Sold The World* when he used Ken Scott to record *Hunky
Dory*; I had introduced David to Ken on the earlier sessions.
The next time was after *Young Americans* when David continued to do post-production with Harry Maslin, the engineer
at the Hit Factory; Harry then went on to co-produce *Station
To Station*. In each situation there had been a respectable
amount of time involved for me to learn that he was going to
work with someone else.

In the autumn of 1982 I thought it must be about time I
heard about working with David on the new album at the
Power Station in New York; we had discussed it a month earlier
on the phone. I asked my PA, Diane Wagg, to phone Coco
Schwab for a recording schedule so we could book flights and
things. Diane was ashen-faced when she got off the phone.

'Coco said that David had met Chic's producer Nile Rodgers
in a nightclub a few days earlier and they were now holed up
at the Power Station and David was going to record the album
with him. David says he's sorry.'

It was my turn to be ashen-faced; I just couldn't believe such
a devastating cancellation at such short notice. It had always
been David's way to tell me any disturbing news directly, like
the time I was still mixing an earlier version of *Young
Americans* back in London and he recorded 'Fame' with John

Lennon without me. As I had put aside the next three months for David I had a huge gap in my schedule, it was almost Christmas and I was suddenly very depressed.

With a sudden dearth of creativity in my life I was lucky to get a call from Rob Dickins, who was the managing director of WEA in London.

'Tony, would you like to produce Modern Romance?' I was aware of them because their picture was all over the music press. I welcomed the challenge of making a pop record and I now had a lot of toys in my studios that I didn't have back in the T.Rex days and thought, this could be a fun project.

They were a happy lot, dressed well (especially when compared to my pleb taste in fashion) and had very carefully managed coifs, possibly the most important aspect of 1980s fashion. One thing I never expected was that they would party every bit as heavily as Thin Lizzy. Again coke dealers frequented my studio, and frequent runs to the off-licence on Old Compton Street kept the champagne flowing. Despite the party, the sessions were light hearted and initially resulted in a No 4 hit single, 'The Best Years Of Our Lives'. Even though their music was snubbed by the hipsters at the time, the production techniques were first class and the band was eager to do whatever it took to get results. The singles all did very well in the charts, although their fans weren't an album-buying group and *A Trick Of The Light* didn't even make the Top 50. One member was a budding film score writer, John Du Prez, who played brass in the group. John later scored many hit films, mainly for director Terry Gilliam, and also co-wrote the music for *Spamalot* with Eric Idle.

Still twiddling my thumbs, I was very surprised to get a call from Tim Rice, the lyricist partner on many of Andrew Lloyd Webber's early successes; he was instantly warm and informal.

'Hi Tony, I was wondering if you would be interested in producing Elaine Paige?'

'I would,' I told him. 'I think she has a great voice and I'd very much like to work with her, but I have no experience with musical theatre.'

'But that's why we want to work with you. I love the idea of David Bowie's producer, producing Elaine Paige. I know some will think it a bizarre idea, but I'm convinced it will work.'

I was very happy to work with the first lady of British musical theatre, if they were happy to take the chance. Three days later I went for a meeting, having been warned that Elaine could be a little tricky. The first thing that struck me when we met at her house in Barnes was that she was much shorter than I imagined; Tim was much taller. As anticipated, one of the first things she said to me in passing was, 'I don't suffer fools!' After a three-hour meeting I was even more convinced that it was a good idea.

They wanted to do an album based on show tunes, which were Elaine's forte, but they wanted me to give the songs a contemporary setting. They had drawn up a 'short' list of 200 'possibles'; after several more meetings we eventually whittled this down to just 12. To bridge the gap between contemporary music and classic show tunes we needed a very versatile musical director. I had been working with Robin Smith, an amazing keyboard player and top London session musician. He was fully involved in the selection, setting the songs and arranging the music; a great deal of credit must go to him for what turned out to be a wonderful album.

It was also fun to make, although there was frequently a creative tug-of-war with Elaine. Elaine felt uncomfortable with some of the hybrid musical setting ideas that Robin and I came up with. Eventually the music settled into a more familiar theatrical setting, but it was still Elaine Paige as she had never been heard before. At the time she was in the London production of

Chess, at the Prince Charles Theatre just three blocks away from Good Earth. Every night she'd be driven by limo to the studio and we'd record her vocals starting around 11:30 p.m.; she'd be all warmed up from her performance. Elaine was a perfectionist, like me, and we both strived for the same thing. She also craved direction and I enjoyed thinking up ways to bring new life to these time-honoured songs with such a well-trained, passionate and very versatile singer.

When we finished I thought that the album would be one of those slow steady sellers and not get much attention. But WEA gave it a big budget TV advertising campaign and with the public getting the Elaine Paige album they'd always wanted *Stage* went to No.2 in the album chart; Tim Rice's formula paid off big time. It certainly made a lot of record reviewers take notice and scratch their heads saying, 'Elaine Paige – Tony Visconti?' It might have been way down on the 'cool quotient' but I stand by this record.

The following year Elaine made another theme album, this time singing songs from the cinema. I really enjoyed working with Elaine again; the combination of her amazing voice and talents, plus great cinematic songs I would never get to record with a rock band was a joy. *Cinema* was not the hit that *Stage* was, but it was a hit nevertheless. For our third album together, in 1985, we took the song 'Love Hurts' as the theme. It's a good album. Like many third albums in my career, we stretched our wings even more and made sounds that were very compelling. Robin Smith was the keyboard player and musical director for the third time and outshone himself on this one.

In 1986 I did a Christmas album with Elaine; I guess it was the only thing left for us to do. I think every producer worth his salt has to produce at least one Christmas song – the wisdom being that a great Christmas album can be a perennial seller. We went out of our way to find unusual songs, not the perennial evergreens. One review said, 'Overall, this is not the commercialized-to-death Christmas album that gets piped over store speakers; it's a Christmas album that works for people who hate Christmas albums.' That works for me too.

Shortly after working with Elaine for the first time, I worked with another female singer who couldn't have been more different. Linda McCartney had remained in touch after we'd met on *Band On The Run*. She called from time to time for a chat, once asking me to recommend a good piano teacher. As a member of Wings she received a lot of criticism for getting such a coveted position, but at the same time she was very aware of her shortcomings and studied music with the teacher I recommended.

By 1983 she was also writing her own songs and asked if I would listen to something she had written. We met on the top floor of MPL (McCartney Productions Ltd) in Soho Square where she played me her strange, yet truly beautiful song. It was a love song, a ballad in three distinct sections.

'Why isn't Paul producing it?'

'Oh, he's busy recording music for his new film, *Give My Regards To Broad Street*.'

I was more than happy to work with Linda because I felt it was a great song that deserved recognition. We worked on the track for a week at Good Earth using the Linn Drum while I played bass (although I felt a little intimidated that Paul was going to hear it). Linda played basic keyboards and I programmed a midi string orchestral arrangement; Andy Hamilton played sax and I persuaded Mary (who'd babysat for the McCartneys before she was herself famous) and Linda Lovich to sing backing vocals. It turned out really well.

There was one difficult aspect of the recording in that Paul was half a mile down the road in AIR studios recording his soundtrack music; every couple of hours he'd phone Linda to see how she was doing. Virtually everyday, around 4 p.m. and sometimes earlier, he'd call and say he was finished for the day and wanted to go home; Linda was expected to drop everything and join him in the limo ride. I was okay with this as I was able to refine the production without her being there. Linda regretted that she wasn't able stay for Mary and Lovich's backing vocal session, and gave vent to her resentment. On the last day of the production Linda phoned and asked me to take the master tape to AIR studios where Paul, George Martin and Geoff Emerick were working.

When I arrived only Paul and Geoff Emerick were in the control room; Paul and I drifted into a conversation about the psychological nature of the different keys. I was telling him that the key of D was always regarded as 'pastoral' and the key of F, for instance, was considered a key for martial music. From behind me, 'No it's not!' boomed the voice of George Martin, who was just returning from the men's room. In a state of what I perceived as indignation he challenged my statement in front of Paul. I could see in that moment that George had been Paul's mentor in all things classical and he would have no one usurp his position. I backed off because the subject of keys was one of conjecture anyway; the classical composers and early Greek philosophers who came up with these theories were almost always in conflict. If they couldn't agree, then neither would George and I.

We then got around to talking about Linda's record, which was called 'Love's Full Glory'; Paul said it sounded so good there might be a place in the film for it. Linda later told me that Paul had suggested that if the single did come out she should release it under a pseudonym; he argued it would be too easy to get a hit with the McCartney surname (in Linda's case, Eastman would do quite nicely). Ultimately it never made the cut for the movie but a stripped-down, revamped version was released on her album *Wild Prairie* in 1998, the year of her death. You can tell that Linda worked very hard on this 'pocket symphony' and wanted it to turn out great. The only thing that dates it is the use of the Linn Drum, the sophisticated drum machine of the '80s that temporarily put drummers on the dole. I would love to do a remix of this song and add a real drummer.

Following Modern Romance with Elaine and then Linda highlighted the juxtaposition in my career at this point. As the year ended I was fully aware that times had changed. It was more than a decade since I had had my first hit record and I was now considered to be of an earlier generation by the industry. Engineers, tape operators and just about everyone else I'd worked with in a studio were by this time famous producers: Martin Rushent, Roy Thomas Baker, Ken Scott, Steve Churchyard, Chris Thomas, to name just a few. It was a notion that came home very forcibly during the making of *Bite* by Altered Images; it was a turning point in my career. For the first time it really hit home to me that the bands I was working with were a lot younger than me (I was only two years older than Marc Bolan and David Bowie). The best thing about the group was working with the elfin-like Claire Grogan. They were almost a one-hit-wonder band with 'Happy Birthday' and Claire was already a well-known actress on television and in films. The advances in studio techniques and equipment were breeding mediocre musicians who needed the 'fix-in-the-mix' treatment. I was so frustrated during the recording that I wanted to take the bass and guitar out of the group's hands and play them myself. I had worked with some brilliant musicians in the '70s and while there were some good bands in the '80s I certainly wasn't working with them.

*   *   *

In June 1983, shortly after the Altered Images album came out, I heard from Bowie's camp. He was in the middle of The Serious Moonlight tour to promote his *Let's Dance* album. I hadn't heard from him since he had gone into the studio with Nile Rodgers. I received a call from David's business manager, Pat Gibbons, asking me to fly to Scotland on David's request to analyse his live sound; the reviews were saying the sound wasn't good. I thought that if this was the only way to get an audience with Bowie, who had been avoiding me to date, then so be it. When I arrived I was taken to a hotel where Bowie and the band had day rooms, and David and I came face-to-face in his suite. The first thing he did was to apologize for making his last-minute decision to switch producers. I was instantly taken with his openness and said it was okay. I did tell him I was hurt by the lateness of the decision and then we dropped the subject.

David was using a line up augmented with extra backing singers and brass players. As I walked around Murrayfield Stadium in Edinburgh all I could really hear was an enormous kick drum, a thick snare drum and a very bassy vocal sound, with hardly any high frequencies present for diction. The electric guitars and bass were one muddy mess, too. The horns and backing vocalists were virtually inaudible. This wasn't the sound company that David had wanted to hire because they were already doing sound for Bob Dylan. It was apparent that the front-of-house mixer didn't really know Bowie's material or sound at all.

After the concert I found myself flying from Edinburgh to Luton airport in a luxury private jet with David and the band. Instead of customary airline seats it was fitted with couches and armchairs with seat belts. The floor was carpeted with thick plush carpets. There was a bar with attractive stewardesses offering drinks and food. It was like a Hugh Hefner event on a plane. I wasn't ready for what happened next. David asked me to join him and Carlos Alomar in the 'bedroom' so we could have a private talk about the sound problem. Sure enough, there was a double bed in the back of the plane and there we sat to discuss the sound. I read my notes to both of them and David asked me to attend a concert in Brixton the following night to tell the mixing engineer what to do. When we approached Luton the captain told us to fasten our seat belts and I got up to return to go to the main cabin. David said we didn't have to; we'd use the 'bed belt'. I was astonished when he asked me to lie down along with Carlos and he strapped the three of us on the bed. I felt like I was in a Marx Brothers film.

I went to the sound check at Brixton and sorted out the sound to Bowie's delight. The Texan sound engineer drawled, 'If I made a mix like that my boss would fire me', to which I responded, 'If you don't make a mix like that David Bowie's going to fire you!' David offered me the job to do live sound for the rest of the tour on the spot. I was pleased by this compliment but I couldn't do it anyway, as I was to leave the next day for a two-week holiday with my young kids to Jersey, in the Channel Islands.

My frustration at working with newer artists boiled over when I went to Hilversum Studios in Holland to work with Orchestral Manoeuvres in the Dark. The studio was huge, having been designed for movie soundtracks, and was not very conducive to great recording. OMD were nice people, but after three days of playing with drum machines and watching the band painstakingly program some very simple things, I knew I wasn't going to last very long. I had hit a wall of prejudice towards musicians who couldn't play very well – or programme very well, in this case. If we were in London, perhaps I could have left the band for a few hours to work through the tedium of programming. But we were on a peninsula surrounded by a hostile sea in early spring; there was nowhere to go. I ended up arranging some brass parts for one of their songs and I left the album. It was the first time in my career I'd ever done that.

Squeeze, however, was one of my favourite bands and Chris Difford and Glen Tillbrook wrote some great songs, so I was looking forward to working on their album as a duo. It all started out well but ended up as being the first album of my career to be taken away from me to be mixed by someone else. I felt hostile having this done to me, and especially so after I heard the deplorable mixes. Most annoying of all was the fact that the engineer triggered the live snare drum with a sample that often misfired and sounded late; I was convinced people thought it was my fault. I've seen Chris since but we've never discussed why it was taken away from me – it's water under the bridge now.

My frustrations at the way the industry was going, allied to my irritation at what I was having to do as a producer, were slightly alleviated by the success of Good Earth Studios. It was a great facility and was solidly booked so I wasn't in any financial straits. I parted company with Roger Myers because I felt his interests were by this time outside the music business. Had we remained together I would've been a partner in the Peppermint Lounge, a bar and restaurant he opened in Cambridge Circus. Now, without a business partner I felt the onus was on me to become more of a boss, for want of a better word; I had a staff of half a dozen people. My PA, Diane Wagg, pretty much ran the day-to-day business of the studio. I felt I could build up the business further, if I only knew how.

I met a manager called Stephanie Gluck who was interested in me producing a band she managed; I didn't like the group's music but I was very impressed with her presentation. She had a positive can-do attitude and her communication was very direct. At the end of the meeting I asked innocently, 'Have you taken some kind of training?'

'Yes, I have.' She beamed. She told me that her small management company was part of a much larger company called Programmes. She invited me to come and see the company in Queens Park, north London.

I met Stephanie a few days later where I was introduced to several other people, among them a lady named Kim Coe. It was in a very large open plan building and Stephanie took me into the 'phone room' which was filled with about twenty round tables; there were about a dozen telemarketers at each table with a phone 'manager' coaching each team. Every few seconds a phoner would shout 'Order!' in a very stylised accent, like 'Awe-DUH!' The entire room of nearly 130 people would break into spontaneous applause. I was impressed by their team spirit, although the 'phone room' eerily reminded me of *SMERSH*, the underground headquarters in the comedy spy series *Get Smart*. In a smaller office, in which there were four or five people, I was shown Roar (a marketing and publicity company). One of the Roar team was Steve Budd, now a very successful manager of record producers (but who is no longer associated with Programmes). Another person who worked for Roar was a 24-year-old Carole Caplin, who has since found 'fame' as the life coach of Prime Minister Tony Blair's wife, Cherie. Carole did makeovers and was a physical trainer to artists that were signed to Roar. There was another company associated with Roar, The Exhibitionists – who organized business exhibitions and trained people to operate them. Carole trained attractive young girls to talk to the clients at these events. I found her to be a very sweet, kind and caring person, although she always seemed a little out of her depth at Roar; I introduced her to Robin Smith, my keyboard-playing friend who worked on Elaine Paige's albums, and they went out for a while.

I was told that they offered training to people outside their company. That night I went to an introduction meeting and signed up for the very next course. I felt that this was a kind of positive motivation that was missing, not only in my life, but in the music business in general.

I wouldn't exactly call the Exegesis Seminar 'fun' but I ran the gamut of emotions sitting in the seminar room, keeping 'The Agreements' and learning much about myself. But, there was a no alcohol rule during 10 days of the seminar; it was just one of 'The Agreements' I had to keep. Failure to keep one was a potentially terrifying experience, involving getting called to the front of the room and told that you had no 'Integrity' in front of the group. About 70 of us trainees sat in a tight forma- tion of seats with an aisle down the middle. Portions of the seminar were in the control of various 'Group Leaders' and each portion had a theme.

If this sounds familiar to those who looked for 'enlighten- ment in a weekend' during the 1970s, it's because this was the British version of EST (Eberhard's Seminar Training) – almost word for word. A very charismatic and enterprising man, Robert D'Aubigney, had taken EST in the USA and studied other disciplines such as Gurdieff's teachings and Sufism, which he adapted, along with the controversial, but American- accepted thing-to-do, training for the British public. He added some extra themes to the training and extended the EST three- day training to a further midweek evening and a second weekend. Originally D'Aubigney was the only group leader, but later many 'Graduates', mainly from Bristol, eventually became group leaders; Kim Coe was his gifted second in command.

The effectiveness and success of the seminar were dependent on a carefully constructed programme. Keeping 'The Agreements' coupled with never knowing what was to come next made the anticipation the hardest thing to deal with.

'Enlightenment' must come as an experience; you can't describe it, feel it, taste it or read about it in a book – this is how it was explained, akin to Zen principles. The EST and Exegesis Seminar training seemed the closest thing we had in the West to Zen. No flowery jargon was used; the course was expressed in the somewhat brutal language of the late twentieth century. For me, it worked; the process seemed to help me shed some of the emotional burden I had been carrying since childhood.

Even though it's impossible to remember every moment of the seminar I definitely came away with a spiritual swagger. I wasn't so obsessed with wanting to be a better 'boss': instead I wanted to share this gift with everyone I loved, which included my staff. At a meeting back at Good Earth I told them about my amazing weekends of self-discovery. I told them it wasn't mandatory, but I would love for them to take this seminar and I would pay for it, as I considered this business training: there was a virtual mutiny. Exegesis and Programmes had had a good deal of negative press and Diane had done some 'research' while I was in the training. She shared the tabloid view that one got 'brainwashed' if one took this seminar; of course I'd probably been 'brainwashed' too. Within a short period Diane and some members of my staff resigned. A smear campaign against me began to spread through the music business, though this was not Diane's doing. Its basic message was, 'Tony Visconti is part of a brainwashing cult.' The inevitable happened; all of my 'I'm all right Jack' staff left and I invited Roar Enterprises into my studio. Ironically my studio suffered very little. Even in a climate when studios were finding it hard to survive we were thriving.

In deference to public opinion of sinister goings on in their company (as fuelled by tabloid press), I never saw any evidence that Programmes behaved much differently from any other corporation that required their employees to be trained rigorously in teamwork, and encouraged its management and staff to socialize.

The working conditions at Programmes seemed mentally healthy and the support system was very caring. Programmes ceased to function as a company in the 1990s, and I haven't seen or had contact with Robert D'Aubigney since 1989. I've maintained some contact with ex-Programmes members, who seem to be leading healthy and successful lives and do not belong to a cult. I don't either.

Lynn and I called it quits in the middle of 1985. In a year she was to graduate from theatrical school and embark on a very successful career as a West End stage manager. I decided to move from Chiswick and found a great first-floor flat in a block called Harley House on Marylebone High Street. In 1966 Mick Jagger lived at 52 Harley House for about a year so it had an impeccable rock pedigree. When I moved there, Bill Curbishly, The Who's manager, had the front flat on the ground floor. Eric Clapton's manager had the back flat on the ground floor, directly underneath me. Roger Forrester, Clapton's manager was unusual for someone in the music business as he appeared to have no love of music whatsoever. No matter how quiet I played music during the daytime he would bang on his ceiling with a broom. One day I went downstairs to his flat and asked to see him. A muscular bodyguard escorted me into his office. As I sat down Forrester said,

'What are you going to do about this problem?'

'There's no problem. I can play music until 10 p.m., according to the rules in the lease.' I added, 'Besides, you're in the music business anyway.'

'I am not in the music business!' He almost spat it out. He went on to say he was a lawyer, as his face reddened, but to me being Clapton's manager made him a music businessperson by default.

'Anyway, I'm not going to stop playing music in the daytime.'

As this was barely out of my mouth he leapt out of his chair, and he lunged at me, trying to grapple. He had a hold of my shirt while actually saying, 'Grrrrrrrr!' which made me laugh. All this despite the fact that he was a good five inches shorter than me, and fifteen years older. I couldn't believe this was happening as we wrestled to the ground, but I was able to jam my forearm into his neck, which made him release my shirt. As I stood up I looked at him pathetically lying on the floor and all I could think of to say was, 'You're crazy!'

I started for the door just as his bodyguard appeared to block my exit. I've no idea what prompted me but I just yelled, 'Your employer is a crazy man. If you don't get out of my way I'll take you out as well.'

It made him move aside so I was able to make a hasty retreat (some body-guard), followed by a crazed Forrester into the ground floor lobby yelling quite loud and irrationally. He never bothered me again.

I was very definitely not at my busiest in 1985. I had met Adam Ant briefly at an awards show in 1981. We exchanged a few words, among them the wish to work with each other. I had great respect for him and thought that his singles and image where uniquely entertaining. When we hooked up to make an album at Good Earth I found his energy amazing; a real live wire in the studio with many great ideas. Marco Pirroni, who had a collection of guitars to die for, was a perfect stable foil to Ant's mercurial meanderings. He played a Gretsch White Falcon, the guitar I most covet, and owned not just one but several models manufactured in different years with different specifications. Pirroni's style was a murky mixture of Duane Eddy and Ennio Morriconi. The entire band played well and were all very versatile. You may be surprised to know that I stand by this album, *Vive Le Rock*, as one of my best. It's a

321

shame that by the time it was made Adam Ant's huge wave had crashed on the beach. I think it's every bit as good as his earlier albums.

When John Lodge and Justin Hayward walked into my kitchen at Harley House, my gaze immediately went to their hair. They were both blond – very blond. I had a recollection from earlier days of them with mousy brown hair worn in hippie fashion. Their teeth also gleamed; they were cosmetically perfect. They told me that the Moody Blues hadn't made a record in 10 years and they had a new batch of material that had chart potential. I had been a fan of the band since 'Go Now' had topped the charts in 1965, although John and Justin weren't in the group when it was recorded. They had joined in late 1966 and were the saving grace of the band with the wonderfully conceived *Days Of Future Past* album, which included 'Nights In White Satin', one of rock's great love anthems. I was very keen to work with this band, possibly because they were about my age, although when I met the other Moodies for dinner in a Vietnamese restaurant in Soho I thought that drummer Graeme Edge was the dad of one of the other members.

Good Earth was booked out for months by the band and Patrick Moraz's keyboards took up most of the studio; he played them remotely through a midi keyboard in the control room. Instead of recording the basic tracks in the conventional live group configuration, they wanted to make this album with the latest technology; they had pioneered the use of the Mellotron and wanted to maintain their groundbreaking reputation. We started every track with a programmed drum part on the Linn Drum, which Graeme Edge would later play along to, adding tasty fills and cymbal crashes. Whereas Patrick Moraz played with amazing virtuosity on most of the tracks, some songs, including 'Your Wildest Dreams' were played on programmed keyboards. Moraz started to programme but the new programme he'd just acquired seemed to take far too long to do something I was able to do relatively quickly. I had a simple Roland MC500 sequencer that I had been working with for a long time and was totally familiar with. I did a trial arrangement for the band one day and I got the job as programmer as well as producer.

We spent almost nine months on that album; 'Your Wildest Dreams' alone took a month to record, but became the band's first hit single in over 10 years and made quite a showing in America. Justin especially loved working in my Soho studio, which inspired his song and the title of their album – *The Other Side Of Life.*

If the Moody Blues represented something akin to the old guard even in the mid 1980s, Bono and U2 were the complete antithesis. One day I had a phone call from Bono.

'Brian Eno and Daniel Lanois have been trying to edit 'A Sort Of Homecoming' from our *Unforgettable Fire* album into a shortened single format, but can't quite get it. Besides which, we've been playing it on tour and now do a much more powerful version of it. Would you like to try another edit of the album version or, failing that, could you record us live in front of an audience?'

After I listened to the song several times I called Bono back.

'There's a strong chorus in the song that you use too infrequently and it's recorded with a too spacey backing to have impact on radio. Besides which the long instrumentals are superfluous for a single. I think it would be better to re-record it.'

We had a meeting in a London rehearsal studio to work on the ideas for a single format arrangement of the song I had written out; the band tried my suggestions. I had dissected the song and analysed what were the verses (V) and choruses (C) and converted them to a blatant V-C-V-C-MIDDLE-C-C, but with a steady beat throughout. After a couple of plays they agreed that they loved the new version.

A few days later I was on the tour bus with U2, catching their shows in Manchester and Birmingham. We recorded the shows every night with a mobile recording studio with their trusted engineer Kevin Killan. We didn't get a satisfactory, steadily played, version in Manchester or Birmingham and I was a little worried. I suggested that we record a backing track right on the stage at Wembley Arena prior to the show and then, if we didn't get a better version that night, we would take the backing track, plus the enormous reverb of the arena, into the studio and overdub from there. I had told them about the many overdubs on Thin Lizzy's *Live and Dangerous* album, which convinced them still further as they worshipped them. I was able to overdub the audience from that evening – the recording studio is a magical place. Bono thanked me and told me that I had given him a great lesson in song writing, which I found hard to believe, but he was sincere. I had hoped to work with them again, but it never happened. The EP *Wide Awake In America* that featured the single was a big seller. For years I would often bump into their manager Paul McGuiness, who would always comment, 'We made a lot of money for you.' Well, I thought we both did pretty well out of it – but it still wasn't enough to retire on.

chapter 12
back to basics

In 1986 I made a French connection when François Ravard, the manager of Les Rita Mitsouko, contacted me about working with his band. Having had a hit album and single on Virgin France they wanted to record in London. I adored their music, it was so fresh and left field, so I agreed to do it. Everything about Catherine Ringer and Fred Chichin was eccentric; the common-law husband and wife had a young daughter called Ginger Ringer, used retro electronic equipment, and they liked to play trashy guitars. Although they had made a good deal of money by the time I met them they insisted on wearing old clothes; chartreuse and bright pink cardigans made of synthetic material bought in a discount shop was the norm. In fact they wore the same cardies every day for five weeks.

I loved making this album. Catherine, a very original singer, was capable of just about anything; she could sound like Bolan or Bowie or Piaf. Added to that she was the most emotionally overboard singer I'd ever worked with. Fred was a 'funk master' and played his guitar and vintage synths with great élan. *The No Comprendo* was a big hit in France, promoted with outrageous videos made by Jean-Baptiste Modino. 'Andy' was remixed many times and was a big hit in New York discos.

The following year we made another album, *Marc & Robert*, much of it recorded in France. While I worked in Paris I had an apartment behind the Comédie Française theatre in Paris and would often catch the actors on a break having a cigarette by the stage door dressed in their period costumes. I commuted to work every day on my motorcycle, as did Fred. We would enter the studio via the freight door and we'd park our bikes in the middle of the studio. There was an added bonus for me while recording this album in that Sparks were invited to make a guest appearance on two songs: they had met Les Rita on a French TV show. With Russell and Ron Mael there it was good eating every night. I had no idea that Russell could speak fluent French; my French was also improving and for a while I considered living in Paris. I celebrated my 44th birthday by jogging past the Pere Lachaise cemetery and waving to Jim Morrison's tombstone. Fred and Catherine presented me with my birthday gift – two bottles of claret from my favourite vineyard, St Emilion, in the vintage of my birth year: 'It was a very hard year to find, Tony, because it was not a year that was great,' said Fred.

I wanted to share a bottle with Fred and Catherine but they insisted that I had the pleasure all to myself; it wasn't very good, but the gesture was wonderful.

In the early summer of 1985 I was pleased to hear Paul McCartney's voice on the phone. He was enquiring if I'd like to arrange a song for his new album. I drove down to his outrageously beautiful recording studio on the Sussex coast; it's in a circular, disused old mock windmill. Paul and I went upstairs to a lounge room that had many instruments strewn around. Paul proudly pulled his ageing Hofner violin bass off the wall and showed me a set list taped to the rib of the bass; the once clear adhesive tape was by then old and dark yellow. The set list included 'Twist And Shout', 'I Saw Her Standing There' and most of the songs recorded on the *Please Please Me* album. The hairs on the back of my neck stood on end.

Before we got down to business Paul confronted me: 'Why did you and Mary split up?' I was so taken aback by this and embarrassingly answered, 'Er, we grew apart.' Paul could see how choked I was in answering him and didn't pursue it further. After a little more small talk Paul played me 'Only Love Remains', a gorgeous ballad. He said he wanted to record it live with a small orchestra of strings, woodwind instruments and a rhythm section. 'I want to play piano and sing it live in the same room with the musicians.'

When the day came to record, Paul had the 30 or so musicians taken down to Sussex by coach. The plan was to try and record a rhythm track in the morning, to be safe, and overdub the orchestral instruments in the afternoon. Once that was achieved we had a go recording the entire ensemble with Paul singing and playing live. The musicians from the orchestra spent the morning and lunchtime in the local pub and were well lubricated by the time we sent for them around 2:30 p.m. We managed the overdub, then set up for the live performance. I stood next to him as he played piano and sang, while I conducted the orchestra; it was like having my own private McCartney concert. I would look over to Paul for a cue and he would smile and continue to sing to me. He never made a mistake and each take was a 'keeper'.

In 1987 my lease ran out in Harley House and the new rent was going to be ridiculous, so I rented a spacious house at 100 Chamberlayne Road, Kensal Rise. A bonus of living in the area was it was a nice area to jog in. One morning I was jogging through the Willesden Sports Centre grounds, it was very early and there was a lot of mist around. I heard a noise above me and looked up to see what could only be a UFO fly slowly overhead; I could see flashing lights and little windows on the spacecraft as it was just a few hundred feet over my head. When I got home I turned on the radio to hear that Richard Branson had converted a blimp to imitate a UFO for an advertising stunt. Because of the misty conditions his bogus UFO was more convincing than he'd intended as there had been hundreds of reported UFO sightings to the police.

Soon after moving to Kensal Rise I began working on the Moody Blues' follow-up to *The Other Side Of Life*. It was recorded in very much the same way, at my Good Earth studios, although there was a growing disenchantment amongst the band. Ray Thomas, the flautist and third lead singer had only showed up for three days during the making of the last album; when he did he was intoxicated. Instead of his band mates offering their help on a song he'd written, they just told him to wait in the lounge on the days he did show up. Each of his visits began with, 'I want to do MY SONG!' He wouldn't accept that we were already working on another song. I didn't know how to handle this but I was told by the other members they had been there all too often and they didn't want to deal with Ray. Ray never showed up at all during the making of the second album.

I really liked the songs on *Sur La Mer*; they were in general better than those on the previous album. This album gave the Moodies a follow-up hit single to 'Your Wildest Dreams', 'I Know You're Out There Somewhere'. It was based on a teenage romance that Justin had with a local girl; their parents separated them when she got pregnant by him. The first song is about those days and the second song is kind of love song to her in the present day. In the video for IKYOTS (in Moodies fan jargon) Justin comes close to meeting his teenage sweetheart backstage at a Moody Blues concert.

Justin asked me to help him with a solo project. He was to record music for a BBC-TV sci-fi series, *Star Cops* – it was about policemen in outer space. We wrote some themes to run through the entire series, as well as a terrific theme song for the show called 'It's Not Easy' that we recorded at Good Earth studios. Justin then went on tour with the Moody Blues to promote *Sur La Mer*. When I moved to Chamberlayne Road I installed a home studio and that's where we recorded the incidental music. As the series progressed I had to come up with some original music and my 14-year-old son Morgan was an immense help playing bass and engineering.

Three years later, in 1991, I started work on my third and last Moody Blues album; it started on a bad note. We had a quarrel about payment of an invoice from my studio from the making of *Sur La Mer*. I understood that it was a 24-hour block booking and they insisted that they left at 7 p.m. each evening. But with all their equipment piled high and the board always set up for their sounds I couldn't possibly book time after 7 p.m. I can't remember how it was resolved. There was also a debate amongst the band as to whether they should use me as the next producer, although I was Justin's choice. They couldn't get an advance from their record company unless they started to record with a producer, so I was there under some sufferance. I was told that I'd only be needed for an initial seven songs and they would work with other producers. I didn't really blame them because I focused on Justin's songs on the previous albums because he was, in my opinion, the best writer. John Lodge would get almost as many songs recorded. In my opinion the other three, Graeme Edge, Ray Thomas and Patrick Moraz weren't writing songs up to the quality of Justin and John. There was a definite pecking order in the group and I was set up to make the decisive decision to record particular songs. This made me very unpopular with the other three.

Ironically, I was asked by Tom Hulett, the group's manager, to go to Ray Thomas's house and plead with him to sober up and come to the sessions. We sat in his sparsely furnished mansion and talked about family, life and, eventually, music. We sipped vodka neat in the three-hour meeting. I had never before had a chance to talk to Ray this intimately. When the time was right he pulled out a very wrinkled piece of paper from his shirt pocket and sang a rough melody to 'Never Blame The Rainbows For The Rain'; it was something he and Justin had started years ago but never finished. I promised him we'd get it recorded. He asked me to help write a countermelody in a quasi-Welsh style, known as *Penillion*; it's an intricate type of counterpoint. On the record you can hear the backing vocals intertwining with the lead voice and I have to thank my ex-wife Mary for my education in things Welsh. I'm very proud of the outcome. Ray also sang 'Celtic Sonant', which I also loved. I promised that we'd record it. Again, a Welsh choir was called for and Ray and I taught John and Justin how to approach the unique sound of a Welsh male voice choir.

Justin wrote the amazing, 'Say What You Mean'; a very long piece. We probably spent more time on this song than any other, with me programming much of the orchestral parts. This didn't bode well with Patrick Moraz and fuelled many an argument, which focused on Patrick feeling he wasn't being used properly and not getting respect. To add to the overall feeling of un-togetherness Graeme Edge was three weeks late for the start of the album because he was in Mexico on his yacht with his son having a vacation. We had started to work on 'Is This Heaven' on which the band wanted live drums; they asked me to book a session drummer, which infuriated Edge when he finally arrived. I was banished from the studio until the band had settled their differences with Edge, but when I was allowed back in I was chosen to be Mr Unpopular once again. Despite the arguments I think I did some of my best work for the band. At the beginning I suggested that they get Mike Pinder back in as a guest artist and their faces actually turned ashen at the suggestion. Even though Justin would wax lyrical about collaborating with Pinder in the past it seemed that Pinder did the unforgivable by leaving the group stranded in 1978, to go solo and live in California.

In 1988 after working on *Sur La Mer*, I went to record a young rock band. It was another with Celtic connections although this time it was Welsh. The Alarm had recorded one of their previous albums at Good Earth, but when we did *Change* we recorded in a brand new studio built in a loft in the East End docks, the Skylight Suite. There were no lifts so the equipment had to be raised to the top floor by a winch. It was a glorious summer and we were able to leave the huge loading doors on both sides of the studio open to enjoy the breeze coming off the Thames. The studio had an old Helios console, few were made and this one possibly came from Olympic studios in Barnes. It may even have been the one that was used to record the Rolling Stones, Jimi Hendrix, Joe Cocker and countless others. The band could really rock and I was particularly taken with the drummer, Nigel Twist. The guitarist, Dave Sharp, had a unique idea to record without overdubs. He split his guitar output to four Hi-Watt amps he'd bought from Pete Townshend. Each amp had a very distinct effect on it and the idea was to change the blend of amps on the mix for different sections of the song. The plan worked for almost all the songs. Just one or two had Sharp adding more guitar work. Eddie MacDonald was an excellent bass player. Mike Taylor added supportive keyboards to the group's sound, although he wasn't a permanent member.

We moved to Good Earth studios where the final vocal overdubs were recorded in the control room as Mike Peters belted into a handheld microphone with the music blasting. He hated headphones and I didn't care about leakage if it produced great vocals like that. The recording was only marred when Miles Copeland, the group's manager, visited the studio or phoned; he was less than constructive and would rant and rave to Mike that he should stick to safer subjects in his lyrics and stop writing about political themes, revolutions and the like.

I had a wonderful experience when we were invited to Cardiff by the BBC to record a live concert. In addition to the rock songs, I scored an arrangement for 'A New South Wales' for a male voice choir and orchestra, which the BBC graciously supplied and paid for. Part of the deal was that they let us have the master 24-track tape and we were able to embellish the live recording with overdubs and mix it in my studio. Being exposed to Welsh music by Mary, which included being taken to a rather ethereal *Eisteddfod*, helped me understand how to write for the choir.

In the mid 1980s I had visited New York to appear on a panel of record producers. After I had done my bit I was approached by a striking American-Asian girl who introduced herself as May, she looked so stunning I thought she was a model. She spoke to me as though we had met before but I couldn't place her and, not wanting to embarrass myself, went along with it. I was having dinner that night with a colleague and a female New York friend and so I invited May along and she accepted. I thought she had said her name was May Ling and despite having no recollection of her I kept up the pretence at dinner. As we talked she kept referring to 'John'; suddenly the penny dropped – it was May Pang, John Lennon's former girlfriend whom I had made a fool of myself in front of in Bowie's suite during the making of *Young Americans*. I'd even introduced her to my friends as May Ling; I wondered why she smiled – I had obviously made a fool of myself again. We had a couple more dates after that, but I went home to London a few days later and never kept up the contact.

In 1988 I went to lunch with four colleagues at the Groucho Club; it was diagonally just across the road from the studio. We were dining upstairs when I saw May and her friend Pamela Maythenyi emerge from the stairwell. May's eyes and mine locked instantly and she mouthed 'Tony' across the room. I got up and went to speak to her.

'I've lost you twice and I'm not about to lose you again. Will you please have dinner with me tonight?' said I, sheepishly.

'Well, you're pretty near the bottom of my list of people to see in London, added to which I'm busy tonight.'

'Tomorrow?' I asked.

I was asked to procure a date for Pamela and eventually asked a musician friend along for her on our subsequent date. Soon May and I dated constantly, this time for real. I really liked her easygoing, 'rock 'n' roll babe' attitude.

During May's trip to London she asked me to dinner with a friend of hers called Steve Saltzman; he ran a franchised radio show from London called Rock Over London, which is how they had met. Steve was married to a lovely young American girl called Tammy. I was May's date that night for a gourmet meal in a posh Chelsea restaurant, courtesy of the Saltzmans. Another guest was one of Steve's best friends, a vice-president at Continental Airlines. His name was Richard Havers. If you recognize his name it is because it is at the front of this book; he is my co-writer. Richard became a great friend, who aided and abetted our romance. Both May and I carried Continental 'upgrade' letters from Richard. When we arrived at check-in we'd show the letter and sometimes get an upgrade all the way to First Class, but always to Business Class. One check-in girl made the sarcastic comment to me, 'Oh, ANOTHER friend of Richard Havers.'

When we weren't visiting each other we were making long phone calls to each other. Thank God we were getting a break on airfares because the phone bills were astronomical. On one trip to New York I was May's date at a fancy-dress party. It was something like Tuxedos and Garter Belts ('suspender belts' in Britain). May looked ever so erotic in her corset and stockings. After the party, on the way up in the elevator to her ninth-floor apartment, our son Sebastian was conceived. It didn't take me very long; it was something I wanted to do all night – minus the conception, of course.

A month later I got a phone call in London from May, calling from a New York street phone box. I was amazed at the technology for the time. What was more amazing was her question, 'Do you like handing out cigars?' She then got serious and asked me if I wanted her to get an abortion, as she was definitely pregnant. I told her to give me 24 hours to make that decision. I hung up and turned to the singer I was working with, someone I had only just met, and said, 'I'm going to be a father.' I realized I had just made the decision. I called May back a little later and said I wanted her to have the baby. She asked, 'And what else?' And I asked her to marry me.

At Christmas time May came to London to spend it with Morgan and me. Richard Havers suggested that we have a real English Christmas at a beautiful country hotel, Chilston Park in Kent, owned and redecorated by his friends Martin and Judith Miller. It felt like the archetypal English Christmas of 100 years earlier; on Christmas Eve I slipped an engagement ring on May's finger.

I found us another house in Kensal Green in Haycroft Gardens, which I was able to buy; it was in a cul-de-sac with a genuine dairy at the end of the road. We married on 25 February 1989, and my son Morgan joined us there after we had moved in. My younger son, Sebastian, was born in London on 1 July.

Fortunately May didn't give up her New York rent-controlled apartment. In fact, she even flew to New York at a moment's notice because her name came up to the top of the list for a two-bedroom apartment for just a few hundred dollars more a month. At the time she was very pregnant and I thought she was mad to do this just so we could have a place to stay in New York; but her determination had a long-reaching effect on our lives.

Through May I had met the manager of a band called the Electric Angels during a trip to New York; I loved their kind of post-Glam music and image. The songs were great, especially the lyrics. Shane Mansfield (Tommy Riggins) was every inch a rock star front man. They came over to London to record their album with me. They have the distinction of being the very last band I recorded in Good Earth studios. Shane was very temperamental and when their A&R man, Toby Emmerich, arrived in London to hear the album, they had a big row about covering a Stevie Wonder song, 'Living For The City'. As it was already a hit song, Emmerich's logic was that it could be a hit again as a cover. In the end the band only used a couple of lines of it as an introduction to one of theirs. (A few years later Shane would punch Emmerich on the nose at a Sony Records Christmas party.) The album was mixed at Unique Studios in Time Square, New York.

The times were a-changing. In 1983 or thereabouts I had the ninth SSL console to be manufactured and I was charging up to £2,000 a day for a studio lockout, that is, a 24-hour booking. In 1989 there were almost 50 SSL consoles in the Greater London area alone, and Steve Budd, who was by this time my personal manager and studio manager, could only get a maximum of £500 per day. The writing was clearly on the wall; it was the end of my era. Young dance music producers were making entire records on

Akai 900 samplers and record companies loved this trend if only for financial reasons. Rock was dead; rather, record companies were attempting to murder it. I sold Good Earth for a healthy six-figure sum from a jingle company. I said goodbye to all the staff and the studio became Joe and Co.; the young chief engineer Paul Cartledge was kept on as their new studio manager. Steve Budd went on to greater things as a manager of today's top British record producers. Joe and Co. have since become a famous Soho establishment creating music for jingles, TV and films all over the world and Cartledge, now a composer, has remained a dear friend of mine over the years. As a sign of the times, Joe & Co have finished their 17-year residency at 59 Dean Street.

I put our house on the market and told Morgan that May and I were going to move to America. He arrived at the house on the day school ended complaining that he was tired of living with "women" (his mother Mary, his aunt Carol, his sister Jessica and, sometimes, visitor Betty Hopkin, his grandmother). I told Morgan he might think of moving back with his mother, but I held back tears of joy when he said he wanted to live in New York with me. Morgan already had dual citizenship.

May and I gave a lot of our furniture to friends because our New York apartment was much smaller. Before leaving I took one last walk around my lovely Haycroft Gardens garden. As I walked into the tiny greenhouse at the bottom of the garden I noticed a matchbox resting on a ledge. I opened it and there was a joint along with some matches; someone must've left it there after a party. I lit the joint and smoked it all; it was strong. I walked back into the house just as the limo arrived and May, Morgan, Sebastian and I rode to Heathrow. It was a surreal way to end twenty-two and a half years of living and working in England. That night we all slept in our New York apartment.

* * *

Almost from the minute we arrived in the city, and for many years after, I walked around like a gawking tourist. I had to relearn the geography, the best subway and bus routes, as well as the highways that led to the other four boroughs and Long Island, New Jersey, Rockland and Westchester Counties. Best of all it was possible to get in a car and drive to my parents' home in Walnutport, Pennsylvania.

The four of us lived in Ruppert Towers, a 25-storey building on 90th Street and 3rd Avenue on the upper east side of Manhattan for the next two years. The neighbourhood is called Yorkville and nicknamed Germantown because it was where many German immigrants first settled; James Cagney was Yorkville's most famous son. May's mother lived in a similar building on 91st Street. In 1991 we bought a three-bedroom house in New City, Rockland County, about 35 miles from NYC. Our daughter Lara was born on 6 June 1991. From right after she was born we had a long series of nannies to help May take care of the kids; they came from as far a-field as Iowa, Texas, Hungary, London and China – over the years we had about 25 in total.

We also kept the NYC apartment because May saw the rent control situation as a bargain, although we hardly spent anytime there until I made a practical decision to make it my home studio. It actually paid the rent because I did a lot of my mid-production work there, i.e. vocals, guitars, keyboards and percussion. Amongst the low budget projects I made there was a song with Luscious Jackson, 'Fantastic Fabulous' (featuring guest singer Debbie Harry), on their album *Electric Honey*. I recorded on an Apple computer with a program called Logic and inexpensive ADAT digital recorders. (Alanis Morrisette's *Jagged Little Pill* is perhaps the most successful ADAT recording.)

Not long after we moved back to New York May turned the radio dial to K-Rock, 92.3, and said, 'Listen to this, it's *The*

Howard Stern Show.' Fifteen minutes later I exclaimed, 'This guy is great!' This type of radio was light-years ahead of the puffed up British DJs I'd grown used to. If anyone, Kenny Everett was the closest Brit DJ to Howard Stern. One day, not long after this, May and I were sitting with a music publisher friend, John Titta, and we got on the subject of Howard Stern. He asked, 'Would you like to go on the show?'

Early the next morning we found ourselves in Stern's studio. I never expected Howard to look the way he did; since his voice reminded me of Groucho Marx I expected him to look like him too. Howard seemed unnaturally tall with long, curly, rock star hair. I was equally surprised to see that Robin Quivers was a beautiful African-American woman; her radio voice did not reveal that. May brought baby Sebastian to the show and during the interview he needed feeding. May opened her blouse and stuck Sebastian on her breast. Howard's joke writer, Jackie Martling, scribbled a quick note and put it on Howard's desk. 'Hey May, I can see that you have 'hot' and 'sour' tattooed over each nipple.' I collapsed. This was so funny, rude and racist. But Howard's own radio crew was made up of different ethnicities and they were brutal towards each other – his *schtick* was to make fun of racism.

'So Tony, what's Mary Hopkin doing these days?'

'Oh, she just cooks, bakes bread and shit like that.' I was chastised for using 'shit' and they had to hit a delay button. I didn't know the rules on this somewhat freewheeling show. I learned that Howard's show was carefully vetted everyday by the FCC (Federal Commission of Communications) for the slightest infraction of profanity. You either love him or loath him; I won't bother to defend him or my love of the show.

May and I, along with Angie Bowie, appeared on Howard's TV show; the theme being rock stars' wives. May was always talking to the media about her 18 months as John Lennon's girlfriend so she sort of qualified.

'Tony, has May ever called you "John" during sex?' asked Howard matter-of-factly.

'No, but she's called me "John" several times.'

'What does it feel like to know that May had felt John's "enormous power" during sex?' He was really yanking our cranks, feigning awe. By this time I had learned to euphemise: 'It did cross my mind that John Lennon and I shared the same love canal.' It got a laugh.

After a few years in New City, we felt we needed more room now that Lara was growing up. We found a beautiful five-bedroom house in Pomona, Rockland County, but it was necessary to give up the New York apartment to pay the high mortgage.

Since my twenties I had been having problems with my lower back, all too frequently putting it 'out'. I'd trusted chiropractors ever since one had cured me of bedwetting when I was eight years old. In my teens I had migraine headaches and another very gifted chiropractor not only cured them instantly but, as a side project, also turned me into an agnostic. In the 1980s I went down with full-blown sciatica and received treatment from an acupuncturist and osteopath. I accepted that I had a 'bad back', a situation that all my therapists confirmed. I had noticed that since I had started Tai Chi my back always felt great during my sessions, but I could never connect that feeling to everyday walking around. In 1991, when moving house from NYC to New City, I lifted a heavy box of CDs and felt a rip in my lower back; I was in agony and had to go to bed, but no amount of rest brought relief to the pain. May called a local chiropractor and made an appointment for the next day. It took almost 45 minutes to crawl from my bedroom to the car. I spent six slow months in recovery at the hands of the chiropractor and got progressively better, but something was gnawing at me. I didn't really believe I had a 'bad back', but felt I was doing something 'wrong' whenever my back went 'out'.

On a trip to London I was browsing around Foyles, the huge bookstore on Charing Cross Road. I bumped into a pile of books and one fell on my shoe. It was a book on the Alexander Technique; I'd heard about it but had written it off after my Tai Chi teacher gave it a bad rap. Leafing through the book I saw what I'd been thinking: back injuries are a result of not using the mechanics of the body correctly. I bought the book and finished it on the plane journey home. I mentioned to my masseuse, Rhonda Care, that I would love to learn the technique and she told me she studied singing with an Alexander Technique teacher. A few days later I took my first lesson with Martha Bernard in her home in Chelsea, New York City. Within five minutes I was beginning to have 'eureka' moments; it all made perfect sense. I could clearly see the mistakes I was making when I lifted heavy objects. I took a total of twenty lessons with Martha and by the sixth I had become evangelistic about 'the work' (as it was named by F.M. Alexander). I knew I wanted to become a teacher myself. When I told Martha her eyes rolled.

'Tony, my training was very hard and I'm now doing graduate training with a second teacher. Are you sure you want to put yourself through all that?'

I insisted I did and at another lesson she told me that there was a sudden vacancy at her teacher's school. Soon I was being interviewed by Thomas Lemens, head of the Institute For the Alexander Technique (IFAT) in Katona, New York. I passed his requirements and even took a lesson from him. As wonderful as Martha was, I could tell the difference; if this was a martial art then Lemens was a 'grandmaster'. I started school in September 1992. Normally at other schools 1,600 hours of training were required to get certification; Lemens' standard was much higher and expected 2,400 hours of training with him. And that's what

I did for four years. Tai Chi school in London prepared me for this new discipline. (I still worked as a record producer and would arrive at the studio by midday, ready for work. I also produced albums in other cities and had to make up lost training when I got back.)

For four years I awoke at 5:45 to arrive for an 8 a.m. start. We trained for three solid hours, no breaks. In the first year of training I wasn't permitted to do hands-on work until the last month or so, Thom and the senior students would work on me. In the fourth year I was not only working on my fellow students, I was also teaching volunteer members of the public who came in for lessons; we nicknamed them 'bodies'. Strictly speaking the Alexander Technique is not a therapy, it is an education, learning to apply the natural mechanics of the human body intelligently. Since I graduated in 1996 I have taught about 100 people to date, often giving lessons to singers I've since produced. I never wanted to become a full-time teacher, it was mostly something I had to do for myself – to avoid further injury to my back, and to complement my studies of Tai Chi. My back never went 'out' again; quite simply it's been life changing.

I worked again with Les Rita Mitsouko. We made a very interesting album, the most experimental yet, in Morocco; it came out as *Systeme D*. They dismantled their home studio in Paris and shipped it to Essouira, a small vacation town, and installed everything in a huge rented house with marble walls in every room. We were surrounded by the most incredible reverb situations. I would take a microphone and place it in a balcony, a floor up, or even in a room off the balcony. The drums sounded amazing when we added the distant microphones to the mix. We brought our families with us and my kids had a great time, although Lara was just one year old. Sebastian made friends with Moroccan kids even though they had trouble understanding each other's language.

The overriding feature of much of the '90s was working with bands that few people had heard of, although there were some notable exceptions. I co-produced four albums with a German underground artist, Phillip Boa. He had a loose-knit band consisting of his wife, Pia, and a bass player. Boa recorded the backing tracks in Germany and I would get involved after that; it was very adventurous stuff, borrowing some styles of Bowie. I also continued my French connection working on an album with Jerome Dahan; he sang in a whisper. I thought the songs were great and very atmospheric.

It was also in 1993 that I did an album with Louis Bertignac – a French rock legend and a former member of Telephone. In France he's loved by all and considered the greatest French rock guitarist, with a style inspired by Clapton, Beck and Hendrix. Louis wrote every song on this album with a lyricist friend, Olivier Lorsac, and we recorded the backing tracks with French drummer Manu Katché (who'd played with both Sting and Peter Gabriel) at Guilliame Tell Studios, Paris before moving the overdubbing operation to Louis's home studio in east Paris. Later we moved operations to NYC where we overdubbed some string players. An extra bonus was the backing vocals of Vanessa Paradis, who worked on a couple of songs with us. On a song called 'Oubliez Moi' we added the legendary Flo and Eddie to recreate some T.Rex warbling vocals; Richie Cannata (Billy Joel and the Beach Boys) played sax. My son Morgan played bass on the song 'Vanessa'. All in all *Elle Et Louis* turned out to be a very classy album.

I first met Marc Lavoine when Catherine Ringer did a duet with him at my studio in London. He was a young crooner with a huge female audience whose rather conventional pop ballad style couldn't have been further from the avant-garde rock genre that Les Rita Mitsouko created for themselves. During the Louis Bertignac album Lavoine and I met up again and he asked me to produce his next album. He was one of the most charming and gallant men I'd ever met. Even though his music was not exactly my taste, he had an aura of super hipness about him and that made me confidant that we could do alchemy.

I didn't at first realize what a big departure this was for Marc; it was the first time he was produced by anyone other than his co-writer, Fabrice Aboulker. His record label boss, Pierre-Alain Simon, kept a nervous eye on proceedings, perhaps because the band I put together was a mixture of French, English and American musicians. I used Richie Morales, a respected American jazz drummer, and Robin Smith, who was fluent in French, joined me as musical director and keyboard player. The rest of the band was from Paris, including the guitarist Sergio Leonardi and the bassist Roberto Briot, who are amongst the best musicians I've ever worked with. Adam Plack, a master of the didgeridoo (learned from spending years in the Outback), played and sang Australian aborigine 'totems'. Louis Bertignac played a great Dobro guitar on one song. My Alexander Technique teacher, Martha Bernard, sang some soaring operatic parts as well as pop backings with French-Italian singer Anna Rago. It all added up to one of the chic-est sounding albums I ever made. My schmaltzy side adores it. For some reason Marc's public missed Marc *le chanteur*, even though it wasn't very different from his normal style. *Faux Reveur* didn't do as well as his previous albums, sadly.

Just because artists have had careers that stretch back to the heyday of rock music does not mean they are not still able to produce interesting and vital music. One such artist I worked with in the '90s was Annie Haslam, who had been the lead singer with Renaissance – for me it was Art Rock revisited yet again. Annie and I met in the late 1980s when she asked me for Justin Hayward's number. She wanted him to give her a song to record on her next album, he duly obliged with the glorious 'The

Angels Cry'. Later she married an American and moved to Pennsylvania and we made contact again. Annie had been accumulating lyrics and called me about co-writing with her. She had never written songs before and told me that she was treated like the 'chick singer' while she was in Renaissance. We wrote a song the first day we met up. Soon we had enough material to record an album at my home studio in Ruppert Towers, Manhattan.

While we were writing Annie was diagnosed with breast cancer and began radiation therapy during the recording process. One day she came to the studio wearing a baseball cap. She went into another room to sing her vocal and came out without the hat. She was completely bald. I jumped at first, before we both started laughing. I loved Annie's spirit and hearty sense of humour. We used members of her live band to overdub special parts and her keyboardists, Rav Tesar and David Biglin, took my midi arrangements more than one step beyond. The title track *A Blessing in Disguise* was sung a cappella, with Annie singing the melody and me singing the rest. My neighbour, Jordan Rudess of Dream Theater, played incredible keyboard parts on some tracks.

At the other end of the spectrum was Johnny Andriani, a handsome Italian-American who oozes charisma and who should be a superstar but few people have heard of him. When I worked with him his latest incarnation was The Dwellers, a group of extremely good musicians from Westchester County in New York. Johnny wrote classic American radio rock hits and sang in a voice that was every bit as good as Springsteen's. But success has always eluded him. *Whatever Makes You Happy* was one of my favourite albums in the '90s.

To emphasize just how eclectic things were for me in the '90s I worked with John Squire, formerly of the Stone Roses. He had formed the Seahorses with a group of musicians from Yorkshire: vocalist Chris Helme, bassist Stuart Fletcher and drummer Andy

Watts. This band was kick ass and great to work with, although the drummer came under frequent fire from both John and myself. One day my son Sebastian, who was six years old at the time, overheard our conversation about the drums in the control room. He marched out to the studio, went up to drummer Andy and told him, 'You have to play more with the music.' Andy, a natural joker, was stunned by Sebastian's frankness and looked almost crushed. It was the last straw.

Squire was amazing to work with; his guitar was very easy to record as he was a brilliant player and he had some of the best guitars and amps I've ever worked with. Our A&R man was Tony Berg, a very accomplished and successful producer in his own right. I appreciated his feedback even if it took unusual and boundary-crossing forms. Once he was trying to explain how he heard a guitar lick in his head. Squire never seemed to get it exactly the way Berg heard it. Suddenly Berg grabbed the guitar out of his hands and played the lick. I don't think any of us heard the lick as we were shocked by his wresting the guitar from a guitar god. Another time Berg showed up to the studio with two programmers for MTV and they were asked to give their opinion of the guitar quotient of the singles. MTV, apparently, was only playing videos with a high level of rock guitar in the recording. Squire, a very sensitive individual, was very annoyed with Berg and the input from the programmers. It was fast becoming one of those, 'I love everything about you, but please change' situations.

During the recording we all stayed in The Oakwood, a residential area in North Hollywood, and drove to the beautiful Royaltone Studios to work – all except Squire who rode his bicycle. He had long buried his chemical demons, focusing instead on the music and keeping fit. The studio had two amazing rooms and we were in the soundstage studio, big enough to record 100 musicians for film scores. The place was managed by a six-foot-tall slightly eccentric Englishwoman, named Jane Scobie; she kept morale high with British food for the band. The studio also housed a huge hot tub and treatment rooms for massage, one of which Squire took as his personal rehearsal space to work on his solos over and over again. Andy Watts poured bubble bath in the hot tub and the suds rose to the ceiling, he then jumped in and ran around the studio naked, but only his eyes could be seen through the bubbles.

I had been told I would be working with an engineer of Tony Berg's choice; his name was Rob Jacobs, who did a lot of recording with The Eagles and solo with Don Henley. Jacobs was a very knowledgeable engineer who, like me, wanted to work with younger acts, so this album meant a lot to both of us. We had some conflicting views of how to record certain things but we worked through them. Jacobs was going through a phase where everything had to be recorded on vacuum tube mics and put through vacuum tube preamplifiers and compressors; that rendered the sound warm and fat – a little too much for my taste. But I was okay with it because it's common for the mastering engineer to brighten up the mixes at the last stage. Jacobs, however, mixed to analogue 2-track tape through vacuum tube compressors and took the tapes to a mastering engineer and asked him to fatten the mixes even more through more vacuum tube equipment. As Jacob was Tony Berg's choice I did my best to stay out of his way, but the results were too muddy to be acceptable – I phoned Berg and told him it sounded awful to me and he agreed. Fortunately we mixed simultaneously to DAT (digital audio tape) and sent both versions to mastering engineer Bob Ludwig in Portland, Maine. I asked Bob to decide what to master from and he said that the digital was much better. Making a record is teamwork, but as a producer the final responsibility for a recording is mine. Getting an expert's opinion helped me get my view accepted.

D-Generation, a hard rock group who were outrageous on stage, had been around for at least a decade before I made *Out Of The Darkness* with them in 1999. Lead singer Jesse Malin would climb all over the speaker bins and strip to almost nothing. I was told I had to see them live because that element was never successfully captured on record; I've heard this complaint many times. What A&R people fail to realize is with all the visual excitement and blasting sound, even a cement mixer can sound like a hit. D-Generation suffered from a lack of unified direction and terrible in-fighting. Maybe that disappeared on stage but that spirit never seemed to follow them into the studio. It was a good album, not a great one. Nevertheless it was a good experience working with them, as individually they were excellent musicians. Malin is a very well respected artist in NYC and he also is a part owner in a bar, Niagara, in the East Village. During the sessions we had a visit from Joey Ramone, and that was a real treat.

One day during a D-Generation session I had a call from May.

'David Bowie's just been on the phone and he asked me where your head was at. He's going to be phoning the studio in a couple of minutes.'

'Hi Tony, how are you?'

'I'm fine, you?'

The phone call was a nervous one for both of us. David was trying to do a lot of catching up in a short time.

'I'm so happy to hear your voice after fourteen years David.' My eyes welled up. I didn't realize how much I missed him until that moment. I'm not sure what the silence was really all about except that we never spoke after I told him I wasn't able to mix the sound for his Serious Moonlight Tour.

It was all water under the bridge anyway and we made a date for coffee.

chapter 13
full circle

May and I broke up in April 2000, having been in danger of doing
so since 1997. I slept on the couch in my home studio in the basement. In October 2000 I moved out of the Pomona house and
rented a drafty, wooden three-storey apartment in West Nyack,
Rockland County, NY. I chose to stay close to Pomona, which
was only 15 minutes by car, to be close to the kids. Ours was
a stormy marriage with confrontational, loud arguments that
frightened the kids. My fidelity weakened under such circumstances yet I learned much from the two years of therapy we had
undergone in an attempt to save the marriage. Number one, I
learned (finally) that I am not the marrying type. Music has been
my one, faithful mistress since I was a teenager. Also, I can't seem
to tolerate unhappiness for any length of time. I am a product of
the '60s, considering my hedonistic ways as not so much immoral,
but more amoral. That is not to say that I am a sociopath; I truly
regret the anguish I have caused – believe me, divorce proceedings
have been a just punishment. Second, through therapy I learned
that I never really knew the women I had married. I had an 'ideal
woman' in my head and I overlaid this ideal on three unsuspect-
ing women. My four children are truly great people who benefited
from both their parents. Through them I hope and believe that
I've learned how to be a better person.

*　　*　　*

David Bowie had begun working on a new album and had asked me to arrange several songs. David and Mark Plati, who had co-produced Bowie's *Earthling* and *Hours* albums, had co-produced the tracks, an interesting mixture of old and new Bowie songs. I was attending the Grammy Awards show in Los Angeles in February 2001 when David called me on my cell phone, 'Would you like to mix the album?'

The album, which was to be called *Toy*, revisited some of David's earliest songs, including some I had already produced in the 1960s ('Conversation Piece', 'Let Me Sleep Beside You'). It was a great idea to give those old songs a fresh reading in the twenty-first century. But there wasn't enough material, even though David had hundreds of his own compositions he could re-record, it was these particular songs he wanted to sing. He had started writing new songs and a different album was starting to emerge. For reasons that are not clear to me the album was never released as an entirety but almost every song has been used as a B-side or bonus track for singles released from the later albums. Most important of all was that we were working together again.

Some attempts to start an official studio album were postponed because we had conflicting schedules. But in April 2001 the time seemed right for both of us. I visited David at his work studio in NYC and we spent most of the day just listening to music; it ranged from the latest Beck album all the way back to Little Richard on vinyl. David and I had talked about him on the day we first met at David Platz's office thirty plus years earlier. We were looking for little creative tags to incorporate for the new album. I don't think anything really stuck that day, but it was such a nice reunion of talking up music and downing cups of strong coffee which David brewed every hour or so. I couldn't help thinking how great it was that we'd survived the indulgences of rock 'n' roll, we were alive and sober. That was important. Both of us were now long over our chemical romances. I had never seen my old friend look healthier and he remarked the same of me. We did manage to come up with some pointers for the album and only one musician was spoken about as a possible participant. His name was David Torn, a very surreal guitarist by David's description.

In June, David surprised me by saying he'd like to leave the city for a few days to come and stay at my house in West Nyack. I had told him that I had a little studio in the loft and we could work out a lot of things there, but I didn't expect that I would be playing host to David in my humble flat in my rickety house. My girlfriend joked that his limo would pull up in the driveway, he'd take one look at the place and say he'd forgotten something back in New York and leave immediately. When he arrived it was a glorious summer's day and the house and area must've looked okay because he took his bag and came inside. The house was recessed back in a lovely tree-lined road in a middle-class area. Maybe he could sense the good vibes in our peaceful home.

We eagerly set out to work in the studio loft and by the end of the first day the place was humming with no less than four recorded song ideas. I'm sure this was also some way of testing my Pro Tools and Logic chops as I cut up beats and sections of a song, made beat loops and pasted them in other places. We had never worked in this medium before and it was important that David felt that I knew what I was doing. Even though we were now working on a computer the way we worked was the same as it had always been. We'd speak in overlapping sentences, he'd show me something on guitar, I'd change it slightly with one or two notes, then he would change my changes . . . I loved this rapid fire creativity which I seldom experienced with other artists. That evening David wanted sushi and we went to one of my local favourites. The Japanese staff and other diners did not recognize him – why would David Bowie be in West Nyack?

The next day we took a trip to see Allaire studios, near Woodstock, in the Catskill Mountains. I had heard a lot about the place; prior to this at our first meeting with David Torn he confirmed that this was the best studio he'd ever worked in. Before we got on the road David realized that he'd forgotten his sunglasses back in NYC. It was a bright day and he needed sunglasses for his one eye that is permanently dilated (it makes the illusion of different coloured eyes). He asked me if I knew a place where he could get a 'nice' pair of sunglasses and I took him to my local optometrist. He was recognized there all right; they didn't make a fuss though they couldn't stop smiling at me. I merely introduced him as David. They knew I had produced his records so the vision of David Bowie in suburbia was not a complete shock. The resident eye doctor, a hard-core Bowie fan, was out to lunch when we were there, only to grimace in pain when he heard later of the unexpected visitor that he'd missed.

Allaire was an hour's drive from my house and the directions took us further and further into glorious mountain country to a location that you could never stumble upon by accident (unless you were an eagle). The elevation of the studio was apparent when I noticed that the oxygen was a bit thinner. We were too overwhelmed with the beauty of this place to take it all in; I took photos that I looked back at later in astonishment. Natalie Merchant was making an album there with T-Bone Burnett producing. She warmly invited us to listen to a few things and also to a lunch of tuna wraps. By then we were so eager to record there. Outside the studio was a giant outdoor veranda that overlooked the 25-mile long Shokan reservoir; we could see nearby hills and valleys of the Catskill Mountains area. For part of our visit we wandered unaccompanied and walked out on the veranda to see hawks soaring in the sky, while rabbits and deer scampered below us.

David had asked me to suggest musicians for the new album, most especially a drummer. I had been telling him about Matt Chamberlain, a great drummer I'd worked with on a project in LA; he had been the second drummer in Pearl Jam and was now a much sought after session musician. He was also right there in Allaire playing for Natalie Merchant; we booked both Matt and Allaire on the spot.

That night we worked a little, and went back to the sushi restaurant again. This time there were broad grins on the faces of the Japanese staff; someone had told them who David was. Thereafter I was always asked, 'Where is your friend?' followed by a wide grin. After dinner David said he had had enough recording for the day and wanted to rent a specific film, *A Requiem For A Dream*. He loved *Pi* by the same director, Darren Aronofsky, but we weren't prepared for the gruesome and graphic story of the spiral into hell of the four drug users in the film. Instead of 'chilling' we ended the evening on a chilling low. In the morning David said, 'This has been great. I've accomplished all I set out to do by coming up here. I've now got a clear picture of where I want to take the music.'

I burned a CD of the song ideas for him and he left in his limo in the afternoon.

The recording at Allaire was probably the best situation we could've had. David was not distracted by anyone in this isolation. We had a schedule that we followed daily. David would awake at the crack of dawn and write. After we exercised (Matt jogged, I did Tai Chi) Matt Chamberlain and I would meet him in the studio around 10:30 a.m. and we'd learn the songs of the day (usually two). I was the engineer but I had enormous help from the resident engineer, Brandon Mason. He was especially helpful as David had decided he wanted me to play bass. Everyday for two weeks we recorded in this fashion and we accumulated enough tracks for an album and B-sides. Because of the catering policy at Allaire dinnertime was always at 7 p.m. every night, which was nice – this clean living in the mountains gave us a ravenous appetite. As with all David's albums I've worked on, we had terrific backing tracks but no melodies or lyrics for most of them. After dinner David would usually spend the rest of the evening trying to write melodies and lyrics while Matt and I either watched a DVD or got to sleep early. This certainly wasn't a rock and roll life, by any stretch of the imagination.

Towards the end of our stay at Allaire tragedy struck on the morning of 11 September. David had the only television that worked. He phoned me as I was in the middle of Tai Chi and asked if I had any relatives or friends living in downtown New York. I said yes, my son Morgan, why? He said a plane had crashed into the World Trade Center and debris was falling into the streets. I ran right over to his house, just in time to see a second plane crash into the other twin tower. These were no tragic accidents; we slowly understood that New York was under attack. In a state of growing panic we both needed to phone our loved ones in NYC. David was just able to get through to his family in the city and found them to be safe. I couldn't get my son on the phone, only an announcement that all lines to NYC were busy. We watched the television screen in horror as the reporters tried to make sense of what was going on. In desperation I went online and looked for anyone I knew via my chat program. At about 11 a.m. I was able to IM Morgan, who was in an airport in Detroit. He was on a plane to LA when the towers were struck and his, like all other aircraft, had been instructed to land. Ironically the Internet was still working! I know this sounds strange under the circumstances, but we actually tried to record on that day, I guess to try and ignore the events that were unfolding. But we gave up after 45 minutes or so. Everyone at Allaire was simply stunned, too stunned to do anything except shake our heads in disbelief. When it grew dark we stepped out on the veranda and looked south; New York was 100 miles away, yet we could see a giant orange glow in the dark southern sky. The inferno of Ground Zero was visible for another five nights.

There was a ban on driving in and out of New York for a few days as the city was under martial law. But members of the string quartet we used on the album were all too willing to escape the city and come up to Allaire to work. We were able to temporarily turn away from the grief and play strings to the songs 'Afraid' and 'I Would Be Your Slave'. That night at dinner every musician had their own 9/11 story, and like members at a tribal meeting we all told our tales of sorrow.

All the lyrics to *Heathen* were written pre 9/11 but many fans have felt that they were written afterwards in response to those events. I felt that many of its songs are posed as questions to God. *Heathen* got rave reviews; most commented on the welcome musical reunion of David and me. But no one could have been happier than I was to be back working with my friend.

After the album was finished David decided to embark on a tour. He not only played all of *Heathen* on the first show at Roseland in New York, he also performed all of *Low*. He saw an affinity between the two albums. His touring band took a couple of months to learn the material from both musically challenging albums. When he was on tour David was so immersed I received perhaps three e-mails the whole time. This was a complete turnaround from seeing him every day in the studio so I became a member of Bowienet, David's Internet website, just to keep track of the tour.

As soon as David's long and gruelling tour was over he wanted to go back into the studio – he had written a new album. Instead of going back to Allaire, David chose to record the album *Reality* in New York. This time we used his regular touring band of Mike Garson (keyboards), Mark Plati (bass and guitars), Gerry Leonard (guitars), Sterling Campbell (drums), Gail Ann Dorsey (bass and backing vocals) and Catherine Russell (vocals). I also played many instruments, including bass, guitars, recorder (you can't keep a rock recorder player quiet for long!) and keyboards; I even sang backing vocals. We crammed into the small Studio B of Looking Glass Studios, owned by composer Philip Glass; most days it was crowded and felt like a kid's clubhouse.

Thanks to David, I'd met Glass a few years before; I had listened to his works for years and regarded him as one of the greatest composers of his time. David sang at Philip's annual charity concert for Tibet House, a cultural centre for Tibetans living in the USA – Philip is, like me, a Tibetan Buddhist. David asked me to play bass for him and to write a string quartet adaptation for some songs, 'Heroes' and 'Silly Boy Blue'. The concert was in February 2001. I have to admit this was one of the most exciting moments of my life, to play on the stage with David Bowie and have Philip Glass playing the piano, a part I had written for him. We were again asked back the following year and played two songs from the new album *Heathen*, performing 'Sunday' and 'I Would Be Your Slave'.

The atmosphere was completely different recording in New York. This album doesn't have the lofty scope of Allaire's mountain-top perspective; instead it has the angst of NYC. But it also has David's wit; he would play pranks on me from the BBC's show *The Office* since he'd become an ardent fan of Ricky Gervais. He'd dial my cell phone whilst he was in the same room as me and utter, 'Cock!' We had just seen the episode where Tim harrasses Gareth in the same manner.

When the album was finished David immediately went back on the road. The concerts were always sold out and the audiences were ecstatic to get David back so soon. I met up with David when he played Jones Beach in New York. I thought the show was fabulous but he later told me backstage that he didn't feel he'd connected with the audience. I was surprised to hear this and told him it didn't feel like that at all. For David the main problem was that the stage was separated from the audience by a water-filled moat. In the middle of our meeting Ronnie Spector was shown into his dressing room and we posed for a picture together; both David and I were big fans of hers – I had worked with her in the '90s on a tribute album for Otis Blackwell. After Ronnie had left David told me that he was tired. I could see that and I said I didn't blame him. From July 2001 to July 2004 David had been in the studio and on stage with hardly a break – and the man stays on stage for over two hours.

In July 2004 in Austria, David walked off the stage in the middle of the show and went directly to hospital with pains in his arms and neck. The band played on, wondering when he was returning to the stage. An angioplasty operation was performed immediately to unblock the arteries in his heart and that was the last time he appeared on stage for quite a while. Fortunately the operation was a complete success and David has since returned to both stage and studio, making cameo appearances singing with Arcade Fire in Central Park, TV On The Radio, Secret Machines and Kashmir. He's acted in the film *The Prestige* and the toe-curling comedy show *Extras*. I feel certain he's warming up for another solo album. I don't care if it's with me or another producer; like the rest of his fans I just want to hear more David Bowie albums in the future.

I probably would be dead or very ill if it weren't for Tai Chi Chuan. Having spent parts of my life abusing alcohol and drugs it was Tai Chi that stopped me from going overboard. I dropped drugs from my agenda completely in the 1980s and I stopped drinking on 26 December 1999. I had studied this martial art since the early '80s, and before that several styles of Karate and Wing Chun; it had become a part of my life. Grandmaster John Kells, who had taught me in London, had studied with a legendary master from Taiwan, Dr Chi Chiang-Tao, which meant I had really high standards for what I needed from a teacher. In 2003 I moaned to David Bowie that I couldn't find a Tai Chi teacher in NYC as good as John Kells. He told me that Lou Reed knew a teacher and I should speak to him. After several e-mail exchanges I was in a class being taught by the most awesome Tai Chi teacher I had ever met, Master Ren Guang-Yi. He is an expert in an almost mythical style of Tai Chi called the Chen Family Style, which was spoken about in the West but never actually seen in the '80s. It is the original style and resembles more what we associate with blatant Kung Fu, with leaps and quick movements!

Lou and I are both diabetics, Type II. We manage our blood sugar by diet and rigorous Tai Chi practice; we don't need to take insulin. I will continue this healthy life until the end of my days and I might actually get good at it. A music career and Tai Chi practice – does it get any better?

In 1995 May Pang recommended that I should join NARAS (the National Academy of Recording Arts and Sciences), the organization that owns and televises the annual Grammy Awards. She saw it was a career opportunity, as many industry insiders do, but I was very reluctant to join such an old-school organization. Throughout my career I was in the society of artists that mocked the Grammys. The familiar names of Tony Bennett or Barbra Streisand, with the producer of the year as Phil Ramone, who always won, seemed to be worlds away from the rock revolution that began in the late '60s. Not that I have anything against those wonderful artists, but added to the fact that Jethro Tull won the Grammy for Heavy Metal Band of the year and savvy rock aficionados would view the organization as 'Clueless' with a capital 'C'.

I was asked to join by the Executive Director of the New York Chapter, Jon Marcus, who told me that NARAS was painfully aware of the fact that they were perceived as old school and behind the times. They wanted to change all that with an internal campaign to recruit people like myself who made records with stars perceived as 'cool'. Within weeks of joining I was asked if I wanted to run for Governor on the local New York board, I said yes and was elected! My main motivation was still that the Grammys sucked, but if more like-minded people joined then we could change all that – a challenge I accepted.

I must say I found it disturbing after I joined the board, when I found many of the officers hadn't made a record since the 1960s but were still qualified to nominate and vote for Grammy entries and run for office. By the next board elections I ran for president of the board and won. I was the first president in recent history that wasn't an executive of a music corporation – I was a bass playing record producer. I was also re-elected for a second term. During my tenure I concentrated on the charitable acts of NARAS, mainly Grammy In The Schools. I wanted the kids to get great value and that our volunteer leadership had a satisfactory experience. I did my best to bring more awareness of rock and hip-hop to our board. I was elected to a national trusteeship and then I ran for vice-chair of the national board and also won. We met annually in Maui along with the professional and salaried staff of NARAS and created new policies and by-laws for the organization. I worked alongside fellow producers Nile Rodgers, Arif Mardin and Phil Ramone, who volunteered their time and advice unselfishly. As with many volunteer organizations I eventually found the commitment too much and have not run for office again since my vice-chairmanship came to an end, but I am still a card-carrying member of NARAS and I vote every year.

Since 2002 I've had a renaissance in my long career, partially due to the wisdom of my manager Joe D'Ambrosio. It took me a long time to realize that the phone doesn't ring by itself with a rock star on the other end asking me to produce their next record. (Well, that's what it was like in the '70s!) Times have changed and 'my people will speak to your people' is a commonly heard, and made fun of, sign of the times. I'm proud to say the Joe is 'my people'. A cardinal rule for choosing a manager is to have someone represent 'you' and, to all intents and purposes, that manager is 'you' at a business meeting. It's a well-known fact that most creative types do not represent themselves well in business dealings. Joe is simply the best manager I've ever had. He's a charming, handsome man who watches my back, brings in the work and wakes up earlier than anyone else in the music business – the secret to his successes.

I love Surround Sound, a technology that has become so popular since the 1990s, mainly as a medium for more realistic cinema sound. The concept is that more audio channels and speakers are used to create sounds coming from all directions, with a big subwoofer dedicated to very low frequencies. If you've seen action films like *Jurassic Park* in a Surround Sound cinema, you've heard dinosaurs screeching from behind you and their foot stomps shaking you in your seat. This technology was adapted to music with splendid results. There is more 'room' to hear all the different instruments, and especially the three-dimensional space they were recorded in.

Live recordings sound particularly great in Surround Sound. Carefully placing the audience audio tracks in the rear speakers gives you the complete depth and the illusion of sitting in the audience as you listen. In some instances you can hear people reacting just over your shoulder, making you want to turn your head to see who's there, and the subwoofer speaker recreates the low rumble of a kick drum and bass guitar that you 'feel' in concert. I have remixed *David Live*, *Stage*, *Ziggy Stardust Live* and *The Reality Tour* in Surround Sound, as well as studio albums *Heathen*, *Low* and *Young Americans*. Where Surround Sound succeeds over Quadraphonic Sound of the 1970s is that almost every modern movie has a Surround Sound audio track and you can also see your favourite movies at home sounding every bit as good as when you saw them in the cinema, especially if you're watching on a large flat panel screen.

It's Surround Sound that brought Marc Bolan and me back together, at least in the studio environment; I've remixed the T.Rex classic album *Electric Warrior*. Given that no one had thought of Surround Sound in the early '70s it's both fortunate and foresighted on the part of Denny Cordell that I was able to do this. Denny always told me to place a microphone or two in a corner of the room to catch the acoustics of a good studio; so since the beginning of my career I've always done just that. If the mics are recorded on separate tracks, then the room can be rebalanced at a later date, in this case after 35 years! Because most of *Electric Warrior* was recorded on 16-track I only had one track left to record the room mic. Thirty-five years later I was putting that room mic in the rear speakers and the band in the front speakers and suddenly you, the listener, are sitting in the studio with T.Rex in your lap and backing vocalists over your shoulder. The guitars wrap around you and the drums are reverberating from the wall behind you. The string players are sitting next to you on your left and right. You turn your head to hear the cello section sounding much clearer, something you never heard on your scratchy vinyl (I know, this is dangerous territory for the sentimentalists). You must treat yourself to this experience if you haven't already.

I was so grateful to be asked by Sanctuary Records to remix *Born To Boogie* too, both in stereo and Surround Sound. This was a great opportunity, especially in these times when little attempt is made to contact the original producer. After a long search the original analogue tapes were found in a bunker under Tottenham Court Road, London. This was part of an underground railroad that would take the Prime Minister and Royal Family to Heathrow airport in case of Nazi invasion. Now it is a storage facility for film companies to store film. Sanctuary found the analogue tapes and all the colour negative masters of *Born To Boogie* there. For me it was an exciting journey into the past. The negatives and tapes were in excellent shape and I was able to mix sound to the film running in my computer, something I wasn't able to do back in 1973. This time I could adjust the instrument levels appropriately when I could see the film at the same time. The Pro Tools programmer who worked with me, Mario McNulty, was able to remove the sonic 'trash' from Marc's vocal microphone when he wasn't singing, and also boost certain words that were inaudible in the original mix. It took about three weeks to do this properly. We don't often get second chances in life. With Surround Sound and a large TV screen you are sitting about 10 rows away from Marc – you are there!

Getting to work with David again and getting to grips with Surround Sound have been the dominant features of my working life in the last six years, but there have been other interesting projects along the way. Many of these have been with young and exciting artists with interesting things to say through their music, and equally interesting for me to work with. In many ways my work has been a reflection of what

I was doing in the late '60s and early '70s. I've been producing, arranging and even playing the odd bit of rock recorder.

I did some production and played bass on the Dandy Warhols' *Welcome To The Monkey House*; I've written string arrangements on Mercury Rev's *All Is Dream*; I worked with Paddy MacAloon and produced the Prefab Sprout album *The Gunman And Other Stories*. I went to Tokyo to record in the shadow of Mount Fuji with Yellow Monkey, Japan's Spiders From Mars and T.Rex combined. Dean Wareham and Britta Phillips, former members of Luna, recorded two albums with me. The music is both gentle and quirky, and the vocals are kind of whispered. I have made *L'Avventura* and *Back Numbers* with them.

I was thrilled to be asked to make an album with the Finn Brothers. Neil and Tim even made a special video Internet audition for me from New Zealand. Mario McNulty and I were amazed to be sitting in Looking Glass Studios in NYC watching this live transmission just for us. We made plans to record at Allaire studios and the sessions went incredibly well. After months of careful overdubs and writing string arrangements with Neil over the Internet, I conducted the strings and mixed the album in Chiswick, London at Power Station studios with the brothers present. While they said they were thrilled with the album, I was shocked when I heard that they were going to replace the drums and bass in LA with producer Mitch Froom, who had worked with Crowded House before. Eventually they replaced most things and the album came out in a very altered version of our original Allaire sessions. Ironically Froom used the drummer I had recommended in the first place, Matt Chamberlain. Some of my productions have surfaced as B-sides.

Hugh Cornwell (who was formerly in The Stranglers) and I hooked up in 2004 to make a third album together. I was supposed to do the whole of *Beyond Elysian Fields* but had to relinquish the start of the album to Danny Kadar in New Orleans because I was holding time for the Finn Brothers. I completed the album working at Looking Glass Studios, over-dubbing extra parts and playing a few instruments (you guessed it, rock recorder). Hugh, my former jogging partner in Brussels, is now free of The Stranglers' misconception that heroin is good for the voice and the album was a delightful experience. There are many people I look forward to working with again; Hugh is very much one of them.

Having worked in Copenhagen with The Strawbs and T.Rex it was great to be invited back to work with one of Denmark's national treasures. Kashmir had been together about a decade when I first met them in 2004. I did some pre-production with them in Copenhagen and went back to record them at Sun Studios there. Sun is about 500 yards from the old Rosenberg Studios where I had recorded *Telegram Sam* in 1973. The sessions were an incredible buzz in Sun. There was one song that was just crying out for David Bowie, 'The Cynic'. I asked the band if they would mind if I sent a rough mix to him and they were quite excited. We waited for days for David to send back an e-mail. When he said yes, the band whooped for joy and each of them had to read the e-mail to be convinced.

The band came to New York to mix the album at Studio B in Looking Glass. There was another track called 'No Balance Palace' (the title song) that had a spoken word section. I was asked to recite the little story in the style of Lou Reed. I said, wait a minute, Lou and I study Tai Chi with the same teacher and I could ask him to do it. Lou said yes. The band has the distinction of having the only other album with both Lou Reed and David Bowie on it since *Transformer*.

In September 2005 I was about to start on a new album in France when I got a call to meet with Merck Mercuriadis, the head of Sanctuary Records in NYC. He wanted me to consider producing the next Morrissey album, which was already in progress in Rome. Merck played two songs for me, which I instantly loved, although I told him the mixes were very murky. He agreed, but the beautiful thing was Morrissey's voice; he seemed to have found a new, more powerful voice inside him. This was an offer I couldn't refuse and I was able to postpone the other album I was due to start. Two days later I was on a plane to Rome.

I heard that when Merc told Morrissey that I wanted to work on the album he commented (jokingly, I hope), 'Is he still alive?' The album started with another producer, but very little work was kept except for the drum tracks that Matt Chamberlain had put down (yes, good old Matt again). I was greeted on the Sunday afternoon by Boz Boorer, Morrissey's long-time guitarist and musical director for the past 14 years, and taken to Forum Studios to listen to the works in progress. I had first met Boz in 1982 when he was with a delightful London-based Rockabilly band named the Polecats. We only made a single together, a cover version of Marc Bolan's 'Jeepster'. Rockabilly was one of my first influences so it was a fun project. We were reunited in April 2005, at the launch of the *Born To Boogie* DVD in London.

Every song of Morrissey's was a gem, in my opinion. Morrissey wanted me to hear the songs before we were to meet that night for pizza. When we met I told him that I loved the songs. He looked piercingly into my eyes and asked, 'But do you REALLY love them?' I assured him that I did.

Engineer Marco Martin and I worked for 45 days, taking maybe three days off. We worked on about 18 songs – 12 for the album, the rest would be B-sides. I was very amused when I heard the lyric, 'Visconti is me . . .' in the song 'You Have Killed Me'. Morrissey turned to me as the track was playing one day and asked, 'Have you ever heard another song with

full circle

your name in it?' Since then, whenever he sings the song in concert he's added 'Tony' in front of 'Visconti'. The song also mentions the director Paolo Pasolini and the 'Visconti' is in reference to director Luchino Visconti, not me. Moz, as he is affectionately called by those who work with him, makes his love of language no secret. In another song, 'The Youngest Was The Most Loved', he uses the term 'retrousse nose' and also asked me, 'Have you ever heard another song with the word "retroussé" in it?' With a hand over my heart I admitted I hadn't. Ironically neither had my computer's spell check.

My 45 days with Morrissey and his band have increased my admiration for his music and lyrics more than ever, especially after being part of what is now one of my favourite albums. I am a new, true-to-you Morrissey fan. Whilst I enjoyed his company both in the studio and socially, I am none the wiser to explain his uniqueness. He is not exactly aloof; but he seems to delight in giving oblique answers to direct questions, due in large part to his love of language. And it is fun, almost a pastime, trying to figure him out. Moz, like Bowie, is a rare breed in pop – a true gentleman.

One thing I've learned from working with Morrissey is that not stating the obvious is simply more fun. As open as I have been with my 'dirty laundry' I have washed it thoroughly and now I wear fresh clothes. I will borrow a leaf from Morrissey to admit, 'I am in love.' Since I was 16 years old I used to walk around picturesque Greenwich Village and I always wanted to live there. It is a vast area on the lower west side of Manhattan with Broadway as the east border and the Hudson River as the west. I used to play jazz bass in a coffee house on Christopher Street near Bleecker Street, not far from where I live now. I frequently pass the Café Wha? on MacDougal Street where Siegrid and I used to perform as *The Flying Viscontis*. 'The Village' was always associated with people in the arts, Hipsters,

Beatniks and the covert Gay world. It was exciting and always felt slightly dangerous to walk through the streets. I always wanted to live there and probably would have if I hadn't moved to London in 1967. It has since been gentrified. The few artistic types that remain are now wealthy, the gays are 'out' and wealthy, and thousands of young couples walk around with thousands of pedigree dogs and push thousands of baby strollers – but it is still a lovely place. I live in a building with a beautifully tiled roof garden, a mini park. I'm on the roof every morning to practise Tai Chi. I walk energetically to my studio and back everyday, 22 minutes each way. My teenage children adore the area. My son Morgan and his wife, Gynine, live very close in nearby Chelsea. My daughter Jessica is my only child that lives in the UK.

I received a CD from Kristeen Young in November 1999 called *Enemy*, and phoned her before the CD had finished playing. She was the most original singer/songwriter I had heard in a very long time. The music seemed part rock, part Bartok. She possessed a gutsy voice and could also sing in a bright soprano register. Her type of energy seemed more male than female, yet a beautiful feminine face stared back at me from the CD cover. We agreed to meet sometime soon in NYC, on her birthday unbeknownst to me. The first album I made for her, *Breasticles*, was really a collections of demos we had recorded with her band, which included her long-time partner 'Baby' Jeff White on drums. Both were from St Louis, Missouri. Without a record deal we had to make the demos sound better, sonically a patchy album. David Bowie was very taken with her and recorded a duet with her of her composition 'Saviour'. This was returning the favour of her singing back ups for him on *Heathen*. The second album we recorded together was *X (Ten)* and it had a more cohesive sound. Amazingly, Brian Molko of Placebo heard *Breasticles* and agreed to record a duet called 'No Other God' on *X*.

We were misled to believe that Kristeen needed a full-blown production with guitars up front for rock radio. But her live sound was very different. She was at her best when she only played keyboards and has Jeff White playing drums. We got feedback from her fans saying that's all they wanted to hear and we recorded *The Orphans* just that way.

Kristeen's latest fan is Morrissey. When I recorded *Ringleader Of The Tormentors* in Rome, I played a DVD of Kristeen and he saw it. I wanted to check it out on a PAL TV system and I played it in the studio thinking I was alone. When the DVD finished Morrissey was standing quietly behind me and asked who it was. He said he liked her music and the way she looked and dressed – Kristeen makes her own stage clothes. When *The Orphans* was finished I sent a copy to Morrissey. I never expected him to ask for Kristeen to open for him for three shows in Ireland, which led to her opening for almost every UK show in 2006.

Another joy has come full circle in my life. I resumed writing songs, a passion that never left me since I went off on a tangent to become a record producer back in 1967. I have collaborated with several NYC songwriters, namely Alex Forbes (who wrote 'Don't Rush Me' for Taylor Dayne) and Richard Barone, formerly of The Bongos, with whom I am completing an album of our compositions.

I still feel very strongly about whom I work with. I can't stand anything that's pretentious and shallow (unless it is a blatant send-up of pretension). I can't stand to sit in A&R meetings and be told that the group I'm about to work with has to sound 40 per cent Incubus, 40 per cent Coldplay and 20 per cent Keane. It makes me want to commit murder, or jump out of a window.

I have seen many changes in the culture of pop music and the recording industry. There are the obvious technical advances from the humble 4-track tape recorder to the 'studio in the box' digital storage method. The way we listen to music and what it means in our lives has also changed dramatically. Before the Sony Walkman, enjoying a brand new LP record for the first time was a ritual. It involved sliding the black vinyl out of its protective sleeve, carefully placing it on the deck and putting the tone arm down on the large black disc before hurrying back to your favourite piece of furniture. From there you had your very own private debut concert of the latest Beatles or Earth Wind and Fire recording. The artwork was large and detailed – are CD inlays artwork? The reading of the detailed sleeve notes and sometimes song lyrics were essential parts of the programme. You made sure you had something to munch on, a drink, a packet of smokes and maybe a companion or two to share this experience. It was impossible to walk down the road with your new album buzzing in your private headset. This was a concert, it was mandatory to sit there and listen. Your favourite artists knew this too. In the 1970s FM radio was the new 'short-wave' in America. There was no such thing as programming; DJs would just play what hit them in the moment – sometimes playing an entire side of an album whilst they shagged their girlfriend on the studio couch. 'Rotation' was something you did to your car's tyres.

Recently I was a speaker and one-on-one coach at a convention of songwriters. Before I spoke to the attendees I sat through a panel of six music business experts. The moderator started the discussion with the wonderfully outrageous question, 'Why does everything on the radio sound like shit these days?' The panel quickly recovered their composure and spent the next hour saying, basically, that's the way it is. Because of illegal downloading and kids spending their pocket money on video games they have to use strong marketing tactics and take no gamble on miscalculating the trends in music. It's become a formula and the situation is something we have to live with. The attendees were brutalized and deflated when this was over. The message was clear: the modern recording business is not looking for originality because it's too unpredictable and could be unprofitable.

'As future songwriters you will have to toe the line. Since kids aren't buying CDs write simple formulaic stuff for commercial radio, film soundtracks and commercials – that's it.'

Well, of course 'that's it' and that would be the message from executives who don't want to rock the boat and keep their high paying jobs with early retirement. It is this belief that has resulted in the worst record sales in the history of recorded music. I didn't agree with anything the panel said; I just had to wait until it was my turn.

'You've just listened to the wisdom of your six "wise" uncles. I'm the crazy uncle who's going to invite you up to my secret room in the attic and show you my anti-gravity machine – that really works.' This was my opening gambit. But my main message was to encourage them to spend time learning the skills and then write from the heart. The business doesn't have to be like this – originality and courage are what's missing today. Today's songwriters and musicians have the power to change it.

Corporate wisdom has narrowed down the selection of new music we can listen to – and it's pretty bland stuff: the lowest common denominator seems to get lower every year. When I was a little kid rock 'n' roll was only available a few hours a week on radio. AM radio has the peculiarity of having its signal bounce off low clouds and I could pick up southern gospel stations and country stations playing, to me, the most exotic music I'd ever heard when I was searching for more rock and roll. On a relative's short-wave radio I could pull in stations from Europe, the Middle East and Asia. I was starved for new music and there's little that's more exciting than making your own discoveries. Today the Internet is the new way to find what the big record companies think we don't need to hear. First Napster, then iTunes, then Pandora.com and their ilk have busted the music of the world wide open. An obscure unsigned singer from the north of England could get over a million 'hits' on her MySpace page and sell her music. Smart A&R are even looking for new artists this way – it saves them travelling to nightclubs or other cities. The Internet is our new short-wave radio! We just have to hope that the Internet escapes the control of corporate thinking because it would mean the end of culture – not only as we know it – the end of culture!

When I was a five-year-old living in Brooklyn my mother used to take me on the subway to Manhattan for singing lessons; since then I've travelled a whole lot further because of music. Philip Glass and I would often meet in the hallway of his studio and comment on how youthful each other looks. The last time I added, 'It's because the music business keeps us in a permanent state of immaturity.' I really believe this. Even now I slavishly listen to pop music and I'm still trying to 'make it' in that fickle marketplace. I still entertain fantasies of having my own hit album, of winning a battle against 12 adversaries – like they do in Kung Fu movies. I'm afraid I'm still a boy from Brooklyn.

While my profession can be hard, and not nearly as glamorous as many might imagine, it's given me a life that's been a great adventure; it's all been made possible through music – I still love it! I'd be the first to admit that being a studio workaholic has retarded my development as an adult – as my three divorces bear witness. I have finally come to understand that love and friendship are what's really important and should not be treated lightly – and sobriety is the best high.

* * *

Three thoughts. I first heard them while sitting behind a console in a studio – probably at some ungodly hour. They sum up my life.

'*Life's a gas.*' Marc Bolan
'*Life is a pigsty.*' Morrissey
'*We could be heroes.*' David Bowie

acknowledgements

Richard Havers, who kept me honest to the timeline and polished my grammar, Christine Havers, who kept typing when others would've stopped, Monica Chakraverty for her guidance, support and patience and Hugh Cornwell who introduced us, Joe D'Ambrosio a guiding light and a pillar of strength, Humphrey Price for his great suggestions, Kristeen Young who made many great suggestions and asked, 'Are you sure you want that in print?' and finally, the people of the United Kingdom who helped make my life a fantastic and unforgettable adventure.

And thank you most of all, Mom and Dad.

index

TV denotes Tony Visconti.